# FISHING
## *the*
# Finger Lakes

# FISHING
## *the*
# Finger Lakes

## J. MICHAEL KELLY

BURFORD BOOKS

Printed in the United States of America.

10  9  8  7  6  5  4  3  2  1

Library of Congress Cataloging-in-Publication Data
Kelly, J. Michael, 1949–
    Fishing the Finger Lakes / J. Michael Kelly.
        pages cm
    Includes index.
    ISBN 978-1-58080-172-0
    1. Fishing—New York (State)—Finger Lakes Region—Guidebooks.
2.  Finger Lakes Region (N.Y.)—Guidebooks.   I. Title.

    SH529.K46 2013
    799.109747'8—dc23

                                                            2013017271

*To Chickie, my true love now and forever.*

# ACKNOWLEDGMENTS

No writer of nonfiction publishes anything worth reading without some assistance, and I am no exception to the rule. I owe much to many. Glenn Sapir, peerless editor and great friend, thanks for bringing Peter Burford and me together. Peter, thanks for taking a chance on me.

Government biologists, fishing guides, and charter captains have always been a great help in my career, and the preparation of this book on fishing in the Finger Lakes is a prime example. Hats off to Frank and Melody Tennity, Jim Morgan and his first mate "Wolfie," Dick Withey, Randy Yager, Craig Nels, Chris Rockwell, Paul Lane, Ron Boyce, Mike Pikulinski, and Mike Jr. Kudos also to Dave Lemon, Emily Zollweg-Horan, Jim Everard, Jeff Robins, Dan Bishop, Web Pearsall, Linda Vera, Pete Austerman, Matt Sanderson, Brad Hammers, and grand DEC retirees Wayne Masters, Bill Abraham, and Les Wedge.

It feels right to thank those who came before me as authors on the subject of Finger Lakes fishing. I admire them all: my late buddy C. Scott Sampson, John Sander, the late Todd Swainbank, and the legendary Earl "Maverick" Holdren.

Finally, before this starts to read like an Oscars acceptance speech, I extend my gratitude to fishing buddies who have helped me get better acquainted with the Finger Lakes and nearby waters. Among them, thanks to Kid Corbett, Mike Brilbeck, Paul McNeilly, Rich Fallon, Gus Aull, Bruce Douglas, Spider Rybaak, Fred Neff, Jim Sollecito, Mark Gonzalez, Tom Scoda, Wayne Brewer, Wilfred "Bud" Eberlin, Mike DeTomaso, and my son, Sean.

# CONTENTS

# INTRODUCTION: HANDPRINTS OF THE GREAT SPIRIT

My late friend Dan Skinner, whose life was cut short by leukemia, loved to laugh, and did so often even in his last days. One hot summer afternoon, when he pedaled his bicycle over 7 miles of moderately steep local roads from Marcellus to Skaneateles, he took a break to gaze at Skaneateles Lake and let a southerly breeze cool his sweaty brow. He was watching a fishing boat trace a trolling route across the sun-splashed surface when a stranger approached.

"Excuse me, sir," the man said. "May I ask you a question?"

"Sure," said Dan, who knew a tourist when he saw one. "Go right ahead."

"Well," the man said, pointing south over the lake. "My wife and I were wondering, what do you call those mountains over there?"

"Mostly, we call them hills," said Dan, in that deadpan way of his.

He said the man seemed disappointed, but even in jest my friend was not one to lie. Although the Finger Lakes are incredibly beautiful and the collective result of a fascinating geological history, they are not shaded by any honest-to-goodness mountains. We who live in the region are quite satisfied with our many hills, however. Nor do we complain about the waterfalls, the scenic vistas, the wineries, or—least of all—the fishing, which is wonderful by just about any yardstick.

The 11 Finger Lakes, comprising (from east to west) Otisco, Skaneateles, Owasco, Cayuga, Seneca, Keuka, Canandaigua, Honeoye, Canadice, Hemlock, and Conesus, have diverse fisheries for more freshwater species than the average angler can identify by sight. Nine of the 11 Fingers—all except Honeoye and Conesus—have what biologists call "two-story fisheries," with warm- or cool-water species such as bass and walleyes dominating the shallower sections and cold-water-loving trout or salmon dominating the depths. These are not small fish, either. Several of the lakes, including Skaneateles and Seneca, occasionally reward lucky anglers with lake trout that weigh 15 pounds or more. Owasco Lake recently made headlines when one of its frequent fishers reeled in a brown trout weighing 20-something pounds, and Otisco Lake tiger muskies sometimes pull a spring-type scale to the 30-pound mark.

There are more mega-fish in the Finger Lakes, but instead of covering them all at once, I will sprinkle their stories through the rest of these pages.

If you think the Finger Lakes are gorgeous at ground level, you are right, but they are even more awesome from high above. Satellite images of Upstate New York make obvious the reason Native Americans said the Finger Lakes were the handprints of the Great Spirit. In the images transmitted from earth orbit, the lakes look like they were gouged in the land with long, bony fingers.

Actually, glaciers and waterfalls did that, over a span of millions of years, and profoundly benefited our modern fisheries in ways we can barely understand, even though the evidence of the glaciers' rough-hewn handiwork is plainly visible.

Before the region's great makeover, all of what we now know as New York was covered by a vast inland sea.

Then, about 10 million years ago, our part of the planet began a cool-down, presaging an ice age that began about 2 million years ago. If you think Central New York winters are bad these days, you can feel fortunate you missed the ice age. The neighborhood was covered with glaciers; in fact, so were lots of other neighborhoods. It's estimated the ice sheets at their peak extended over one-third of the globe.

The glaciers dug massive holes and scraped and pinched hills and other land formations together, coming and going. The going part didn't end until approximately 10,000 years ago. That's 100 centuries, a short time on the geological spectrum but an incomprehensibly long period for high-school kids to grasp.

Today we can see the glaciers' scars in the form of deep gorges, lakes with plunging shorelines, spectacular waterfalls, and geological features such as drumlins—cigar-shaped hills that were formed as glaciers pushed and deposited glacial "till"—an indiscriminate debris of rock, gravel, and boulders—in its wake.

In this book, you can read about the fishing in the Finger Lakes themselves, in their tributaries, and in other productive lakes and streams in the area. You will also have the opportunity to learn or review basic techniques and fine-tune strategies for catching trout, bass, and many more regionally abundant species—with fly, lure, and bait. Chapter topics range from fishing the region's famed rainbow runs to taking trout on open-water trolling gear. We even cover the hows and wheres of shore fishing, and for hard-water fans—ice fishing. It's a wide net we're casting, for the Finger Lakes region has something special for anyone who ever took up rod and reel.

I know you'll enjoy it.

—J. Michael Kelly

# FISHING
## *the*
# Finger Lakes

# CHAPTER 1

# Otisco Lake

**LOCATION:** Southern Onondaga County
**ELEVATION:** 788 feet
**SURFACE AREA:** 2,214 acres
**SHORELINE:** 13.4 miles
**MEAN DEPTH:** 34 feet
**MAXIMUM DEPTH:** 76 feet
**APPROXIMATE THERMOCLINE DEPTH:** 33 feet

For me, writing a book about fishing in the Finger Lakes region closes a circle. Back in 1970–71, when I was a senior in the Newhouse School of Journalism at Syracuse University, I penned a feature article for *Outdoor Life* at the behest of my magazine journalism professor, the late Dr. Andre Fontaine. He gave all the students in the class an assignment that could enhance or ruin their expressed desire to write for a living. Each of us was told to come up with an idea for a full-length article, write it, and sell it to a magazine. I don't recall how my classmates fared with their projects, but I earned an A on mine.

The high grade was satisfying, but an even sweeter reward arrived in my mailbox a few weeks before the end of the spring semester. The envelope with the embossed, raised lettering contained a complimentary note from *Outdoor Life* editor Chet Fish and a $400 check. The money was good, very good for those days, but the thought of how my young wife and I might spend it was temporarily shoved aside as I realized millions of magazine subscribers would soon be reading my prose and wondering, "Who is this kid?"

Their reaction was not at all what I expected.

"Otisco Lake Grab Bag" was the name of the article. It was about the rapidly changing ecology in one of the 11 lakes in the Finger Lakes chain. It recounted the establishment of alewives in the lake by persons unknown, and the Department of Environmental Conservation's subsequent decision to control the sardine-size baitfish by stocking thousands of hungry brown trout. The plan worked so well at first that my friends and I were soon catching 10 to 15 football-shaped browns a day, by simply

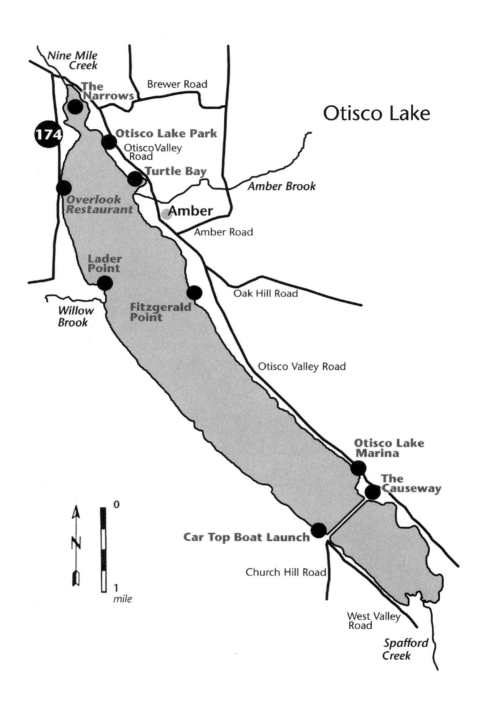

Nine Mile
Creek

Brewer Road

The
Narrows

Otisco Lake

**174**

Otisco Lake Park

Otisco Valley
Road

Turtle Bay

Amber Brook

Overlook
Restaurant

Amber

Amber Road

Lader
Point

Willow
Brook

Fitzgerald
Point

Oak Hill Road

Otisco Valley Road

Otisco Lake
Marina

The
Causeway

0

Car Top Boat Launch

N

Church Hill Road

1
mile

West Valley
Road

Spafford
Creek

trolling along the shore with flashy nickel spoons. We hammered 'em in 1969, the year before I took Dr. Fontaine's class, and smoked 'em really good in 1970, when I began working on the article. Heck, they bit pretty well in 1971, after I had accepted *Outdoor Life*'s purchase price.

Too bad the article didn't appear in the magazine until March 1973, a couple of weeks before the April 1 opening of the New York trout season.

## A LESSON LEARNED THE HARD WAY

Although I didn't realize it, alewife numbers in Otisco had recently declined, and the trout started to dwindle, too. The brownies left in the lake when the article ran weren't as fat as they used to be, and they were harder to catch. Oh well, I figured, most readers of "Otisco Lake Grab Bag" would understand.

They understood, all right. On April Fools' Day, 1973, the modern equivalent of the Spanish Armada descended on Otisco Lake, which covers a mere 2,214 surface acres and at that time had only one small, privately operated marina. Instead of forking over a $5 bill to embark from that cozy launch ramp, most of the hundreds of anglers who saw Otisco Lake for the first time that morning couldn't wait to dunk a line. They heaved their boats over highway guardrails or committed minor acts of vandalism by dragging vessels across wet, privately owned lawns. Few among the fishing hordes took home any trout at the end of the day, but visitors from half a dozen states wound up with boatloads of complaints about "Otisco Lake Grab Bag" and its young author. The locals were none too pleased, either, and they let me know it.

If there was any upside to the incident, other than my fat check, it would have been the things it taught me about the impact of a big story on a little lake or stream. Truth and perspective go hand in hand for outdoors writers. Ethical hook-and-bullet scribes do not exaggerate the quality of the fish or fisheries they encounter. They are acutely aware that the written or spoken word can weigh heavily on individual readers and fragile natural resources.

Now, that's the end of my pontificating, for since it had its day in the sun, Otisco Lake has been a great pleasure to fish; for me, anyway.

## TROUT FADING BUT OTHER FISH ON THE RISE

Its trout fishing certainly isn't what it used to be, but over the years Otisco has filled my idle hours with dark-of-the-moon walleyes, largemouth bass that will eat anything made of plastic, and smallmouths that respond to the sting of a hook with Olympian sprints and leaps. The lake is also home to some of the chunkiest bullheads I've ever seen, all sorts of small but scrappy panfish, humongous carp, and an increasing population of channel catfish. Its signature species, however, just might be the hybrid norlunge or "tiger muskies" that are stocked in the lake as 9- or 10-inch yearlings but every so often live long enough to weigh upward of 20 pounds and stretch more than 40 inches from stem to stern.

The easternmost body of water in the Finger Lakes, Otisco is the fourth smallest of the cluster, with only Canadice, Honeoye, and Hemlock taking up fewer surface acres. It has a maximum depth of 76 feet, but during most summers, Otisco's fishable zone is limited by low dissolved oxygen zones, about 30 feet under the surface.

"The main basin stratifies during the summer with the thermocline forming at around 30 to 40 feet down," said DEC fisheries technician Jim Everard, who oversees the lake's management. "Low dissolved oxygen levels occur below the thermocline by mid-August or so. During the late summer fish will be found mainly in the top 40 feet of water, in or above the thermocline."

Another unusual characteristic of Otisco Lake is its division into two distinct basins by an old roadbed, called the causeway. The structure, originally built for horse-drawn wagons, girdles the lake about a mile from its south end.

The author with a 39-inch, 14-pound tiger muskie from Nine Mile Creek via Otisco Lake.

## OLD ROAD PLAYS AN IMPORTANT ROLE

"Otisco can be thought of as two lakes," said Everard, "the deeper main basin, north of the causeway, and the smaller second basin south of the causeway, which has a maximum depth of 15 feet. The average depths are 34 feet for the north basin and 6 feet south of the causeway."

Besides the stark differences in their depths, one basin is relatively clear and the other quite muddy by any standard.

Otisco's major tributary, Spafford Creek, empties into the south end. On its way to the lake, it flows over a clay substrate. Any thunderstorm or heavy shower colors the creek, which in turn deepens the prevailing cocoa-brown tint of "the Pond." Thankfully, the causeway functions like a sediment trap, and keeps post-storm silt deposits from clouding the water to the north.

To get to the causeway, anglers need only turn west onto Sawmill Road, which is just south of the lake via Otisco Valley Road. After crossing Spafford Creek, take the next right, which is West Valley Road, and follow it to the west side of the causeway. Small cartop boats and canoes can be lifted over a guardrail and launched at this location, which is owned by the Onondaga County Water Authority, or OCWA. The authority manages Otisco as a major component of the county's drinking-water supply and distribution system.

A small opening in the middle of the causeway enables boaters to go back and forth between the deep northern basin and the shallow southern end, as they wish. The channel is also a favorite shore-casting spot, especially at night.

## FISHING PRESSURE IS A FACTOR

Ringed by camps along most of its 13.4 miles of shoreline and less than a half-hour drive from downtown Syracuse, Otisco Lake is fished hard, especially during the summer months, and it is churned up by all sorts of watercraft, from bass boats to Jet Skis to kayaks. Fishing pressure and recreational boat traffic are high, even by New York standards, but natural trends wreak more havoc with Otisco Lake in the long run. Zebra mussels are now common in the lake—indeed, they are present in every major watershed in the state—and their habit of filter feeding on drifting phytoplankton has cleared the water column considerably, enabled sunlight to penetrate deeper than ever, and promoted the growth of rooted plants. These changes in the local environment—echoed throughout the Finger Lakes region—have worried aquatic biologists for years but so far have had some positive effects.

For example, largemouth bass like to ambush prey in the nooks and tunnels of expanded weeds, while sight-feeding smallmouths can spot and chase more efficiently in waters clarified by millions of mussels. The crustacean condominiums formed as the prolific cluster on rocky areas of a lake bottom are food sources for freshwater shrimp and crayfish, which in turn are relished by yellow perch and other panfish.

Next to mussels and other potential foreign invaders—such as round gobies or ruffe, which have not yet found their way to it but could arrive there at any time—the most serious long-term worry facing Otisco Lake anglers is the agricultural runoff from the many dairy, beef, and crop farms that drain into the lake valley. Thanks to the stewardship of area farmers and the diligence of OCWA, the lake still teems with fish and is sufficiently clean to serve as a public drinking-water supply.

Most anglers who have fished it more than a couple of times will attest that Otisco Lake's mysteries seldom are easy to solve. The fluctuations in its food chain, with alewife populations soaring or crashing at unpredictable intervals, can put one or more game fish species in Fat City, but usually not for long. When alewives are abundant in the lake, angling can be maddeningly difficult for two reasons. First, Otisco's finned predators, including walleyes, smallmouth bass, brown trout, and tiger muskellunge, are stuffed with sardine-size alewives and therefore indifferent to other baits reeled through the neighborhood by fishermen. And as if that were not enough, the alewives that don't get eaten themselves can easily fill their bellies with the fry and fingerlings of other species, especially walleyes and yellow perch.

## HYBRIDS TOP THE HIT PARADE

Alewives are favorite snacks for tiger muskellunge, also called norlunge or even tigers by anglers. Norlunge are sterile hybrids created by the mating of purebred muskies with northern pike. Such pairings happen occasionally in nature but are accomplished on a production scale in fish hatcheries. Tiger muskies have been stocked in Otisco Lake for more than 30 years, initially in the hope that their voracious appetites would somehow curb the alewife problem. In truth, they have not made more than a small dent in the forage base, although they have become a popular target of many Otisco anglers. It seems tiger muskies do like alewives but also enjoy dining on shiners, suckers, perch, and just about any other bite-size fish, as well. Who could have foreseen such a startling development?

Because they are incapable of reproducing, tiger muskies are a fisheries manager's dream. If experimental stockings prove to be popular and

Craig Nels of Syracuse nets a tiger muskie in Otisco Lake.

consistent with established management goals, biologists need only place another order with the state hatchery system. On the other hand, if the tigers either don't take to their new home or prove to be detrimental to the fishery's other major components, the people in charge need only cancel future releases.

In Otisco, the minimum "keeper" size for tigers (as of October 1, 2012) is 36 inches, but catches of 10- to 20-pound norlunge (think 36 to 42 inches from stem to stern) have become fairly common, and the DEC is aware of several 30-pounders captured over the years. Some of the largest tigers have been pulled through the ice. A 27-pound, 5-ounce monster caught south of the Narrows in a winter fishing derby by Tom Boice of Syracuse was officially recognized as a world ice-fishing record.

"I don't think any of us [in the DEC] would be surprised at all if a new state-record tiger muskie were to come out of Otisco," said Everard. The extant record came from the Tioughnioga River and weighed 35½ pounds, he noted.

Besides the Narrows, which is within view of the north-end outlet dam, good ice-fishing spots for tiger muskies include the deeper water directly in front of the Overlook Restaurant (on Route 174, south of the Narrows), and the hump at the mouth of Turtle Bay, which is adjacent to the Onondaga County Park off Otisco Valley Road. Most tigers caught in Otisco Lake during the winter succumb to tip-ups baited with silver or golden shiners, the bigger the better.

## YEAR-ROUND TARGETS

From late spring deep into the autumn season, Otisco tigers can be caught throughout the lake—but some places definitely produce better than others. Patient shore casters who keep handy a heavy-duty spinning or bait-casting rod rigged with a 5- to 8-inch-long stickbait will often see tiger muskies rolling at the surface near the dam and around the opening in the causeway. Early morning, just before sunup, is the best time to hit these spots, but tigers are largely unpredictable and eat "whenever the hell they feel like it," a blunt-talking bank caster once reminded me.

In August, tiger muskies seem to go on a bit of a binge, but most of that action takes place well offshore, where muskie addicts can prospect at varied depths by running stickbaits and spoons on downriggers. In my experience, the summer bite is best at depths of 15 to 20 feet off Lader's Point on the west shore or the 1½-mile-long trolling run between Fitzgerald Point and the Otisco Lake Marina.

Craig Nels with another tiger muskie on Otisco Lake.

Tiger muskies cause many an angler's heart rate to rev up, but bass and walleyes are the most sought-after species in Otisco Lake. The bass, about evenly divided between smallmouths and largemouths, are distributed throughout the lake and keep anglers busy from late April through November. Naturally, I'm referring not only to the regular season—which runs from the third Saturday in June through November 30—but also to the catch-and-release activity permitted during the off season in the Finger Lakes. If the weather is conducive, Otisco Lake gets significant fishing pressure between seasons from bass devotees.

Since zebra and quagga mussels spread throughout the region, bass anglers have been forced to relearn the seasonal patterns in many Central and Western New York waters, and Otisco is no exception. Far from ruining fisheries, as biologists once feared, the prolific mussels have filter-fed so much phytoplankton from lakes that their water has become clearer than ever. For Otisco bass, the changes have been beneficial thus far.

Largemouths have thrived by lurking in the shadows of the underwater jungle that has sprouted along shorelines throughout the lake, ambushing any edibles that swim by. Smallmouth bass, in contrast, are primarily sight feeders. They like to roam around feeding areas, spot prey, and quickly chase it down. Increased water clarity helps them put on inches and pounds. Any of the rocky points in Otisco are reliable smallmouth producers, but if it has been a few years since you fished for bass in the lake, be aware that you may need to go deeper than you once did to be consistently successful.

## SEASONAL SUGGESTIONS FOR BASS

Otisco bass average about 1½ pounds, or about 13 to 14 inches, but if you don't get at least one 4-pounder in a morning or afternoon on the water, either you're doing something wrong or the lake is simply having a bad day.

For spring-season bucketmouths, I like to flip Senkos and other slow-sinking plastics around the fallen trees and other cover inside Turtle Bay or in the shadows adjacent to or just under shoreline docks, rafts, and moored boats around the Narrows or, less often, in the turbid south basin of the lake. It is merely good manners, of course, to steer clear of docks and other man-made structures when those platforms are occupied. Being a polite sportsman and steering clear of arguments will put you in good places over the long haul.

Bucketmouths in Otisco Lake don't vanish in the summer, but many of them try their darnedest to occupy two places at once. They like to hang out near bottom in 10 to 20 feet of water during the day, but they will often sneak into the weedy shallows around sunrise and sunset. There, they are on the lookout for frogs and other big gulps that can be imitated by an array of surface lures.

Smallmouths in Otisco Lake, as elsewhere, like water that's slightly cooler and deeper than largemouths favor. In the late-spring reproductive sweepstakes, bronzeback nests will often be within sight of a largemouth's spawning ground, and an angler with a reliable electric trolling motor can cast to both species all day long in late May and June by quietly gliding along the shoreline. By the time the regular season opens, however, small-mouths are usually scattered along the first drop-off or first weed line offshore from their spawning beds. To find them, work small crankbaits, spinnerbaits, or tube jigs around the structural edges I just mentioned. Later in the season, smallmouths will lurk in increasingly deeper water until, upon autumn's arrival, they tend to feed heavily before schooling up in flat-bottomed holes that will hide them and allow them to live on reserved stores of body fat until spring. In Otisco, these seasonal resting places can be found in the 30-foot depths north of the causeway and around the Syracuse water supply intake, midway between the Overlook Restaurant and the opposite shore.

## NIGHTTIME IS THE RIGHT TIME

I'm willing to concede that bass are New York's favorite sport fish, and that Otisco Lake is one of the better sites in the state to find largemouths and smallmouths sharing habitat. To me, though, walleyes are the top game fish in the lake. What other manner of beast could entice me, along with plenty of other anglers, to fish well after dark on one long, pitch-black evening after another?

Otisco walleyes are mostly stocked fish, obtained from the state hatchery at Oneida Lake whenever they're available, but many of them live to a ripe old age by dining regularly on alewives. In the spring, from the opening of walleye season on the first Saturday of May until mid- or late June, alewives unwittingly alert their mortal enemies by recklessly charging into near-shore waters to spawn. Most of the walleyes in the lake have already completed their own nuptial duties at this time, and they are regaining lost ounces by eating as many alewives as they can accommo-date in their swollen gullets.

The size of the baitfish that are available in a given year is important to walleye and angler alike. Some years, the alewives are mostly little fellows, averaging about 3 or 4 inches long. In that case, walleyes will consume more alewives than usual to gather their caloric requirements. Conversely, if the alewives that swarm the beaches this May happen to be robust-looking 5- to 7-inchers, your typical midsize walleye will be asking for a napkin and picking its teeth, figuratively speaking, after eating just one or two fish. This explains why Otisco night fishermen root for the little guys.

Alewives may show up along the shore at any hour of the night, but they seem to arrive earlier and stay longer when the moon is dark or at least obscured by clouds. Their presence is unmistakable, as males swarm in splashy circles, often in water less than ankle-deep. Every now and then, the alewives' vortex of passion is interrupted by a large swirl or even a slurping sound. Those are the noises made by a substantial walleye on the bite, or a larger bass, or an even bigger tiger muskie. Like the lottery commercial says, hey, you never know.

## EYES THAT GLOW IN THE DARK

One thing I do know, however, is that Otisco Lake walleyes run big. My personal best is a 27-inch brute. I caught it on a worm threaded on a floating jighead, while casting on the north side of the causeway. It

John Corbett with a nice walleye he caught night fishing on Otisco Lake.

was after midnight and inky black outdoors. Normally, you will work hard to hook even a single night-feeding Otisco walleye, but those you do manage to catch are likely to be of a nice average size. In recent years, my circle of friends has found the typical walleye in the lake to be a 22- or 23-incher, but a couple of our walleye crew members have smashed the 30-inch barrier. Walleyes in the low 30s usually pull the scale to 10 pounds or better.

Now, I don't want you to assume that you must stumble around in the darkness to catch Otisco walleyes. They can be gathered up by more conventional methods, too, such as trolling stickbaits or drifting with worm-and-spinner rigs. These venerable tactics can be very effective off Fitzgerald Point and Lader's Point, among other places. However, they aren't as much fun as seeing a pair of glow-in-the-dark eyeballs materialize in a foot of water just before you feel a tug on your lure and the rod suddenly begins to vibrate and hum.

And what about those big brown trout that inspired a budding outdoors writer to sell his first magazine article? They aren't what they used to be.

Starting October 1, 2012, the DEC approved a 12-inch minimum creel length for Otisco browns. That standard is 3 inches shorter than the

15-inch "keeper" size for browns in the other Finger Lakes. Occasionally, expert trollers will reel in a hook-jawed old brown that weighs 6 or 7 pounds, but reports turned in by participants in the state's angler diary program indicate that most Otisco trout are caught soon after stocking— or are never seen again. The two-year-old browns stocked in the lake by the Onondaga County fish hatchery in Elbridge usually are between 12 and 14 inches long on their release day.

The 12-inch minimum means those fish can be caught and eaten, if you so desire, instead of being put back to face other perils.

"We just realize there is limited potential for cold-water fish with the low dissolved oxygen levels and warm temperatures found in Otisco Lake," said Jim Everard. "Allowing anglers to keep 12-inch trout will make better use of the resource."

Otisco is easy to get to via US Route 20. Take that beautiful old highway east from Auburn or Skaneateles or west from LaFayette until you arrive at the intersection with Route 174 in the town of Marcellus. Turn south at the split intersection, not north. From there it's about 4 miles to the dam at the north end of the lake. Bear left onto Otisco Valley Road, which leads to the two private-but-accessible boat launches on the east shore.

# CHAPTER 2

# Skaneateles Lake

**LOCATION:** Southeast Cayuga, Southwest Onondaga,
  and Northwest Cortland Counties
**ELEVATION:** 863 feet
**SURFACE AREA:** 8,960 acres
**SHORELINE:** 32.8 miles
**MEAN DEPTH:** 145 feet
**MAXIMUM DEPTH:** 315 feet
**APPROXIMATE THERMOCLINE DEPTH:** 35 feet

Fishing for rainbow trout doesn't get much better than it is in Skaneateles Lake. I'm reminded of that not only when I walk its shores with rod in hand, but also when I slump before a television screen, gripping an ice-cold beer.

Now, I don't watch all that much TV these days, but when I do assume my couch potato posture, I usually alternate between the Outdoor Channel and the Sportsman Channel. The two stations are focused mainly on deer and turkey hunting, but they also carry a few shows that give their hosts plenty of opportunities to battle big trout in Montana, Alaska, Chile, and other bucket-list angling destinations.

I, too, daydream about angling adventures in far-off places, but at some point during the majority of those fishing shows I am reminded that the trout fishing in my own back-yard is pretty special.

Kid Corbett with a 24-inch Skaneateles Lake lake trout.

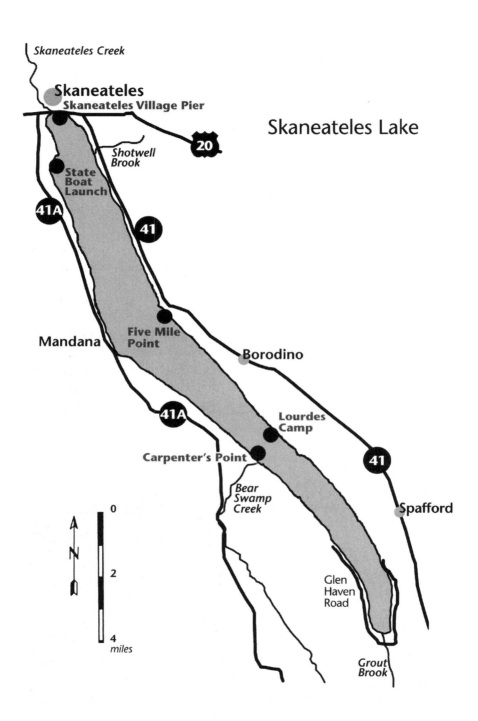

*Skaneateles Creek*

**Skaneateles**
**Skaneateles Village Pier**

Skaneateles Lake

*Shotwell*
*Brook*

**20**

**State**
**Boat**
**Launch**

**41A**

**41**

**Five Mile**
**Point**

**Mandana**

Borodino

**41A**

**Lourdes**
**Camp**

**Carpenter's Point**

**41**

*Bear*
*Swamp*
*Creek*

Spafford

0

N

2

Glen
Haven
Road

4
*miles*

*Grout*
*Brook*

Often, this revelation is triggered when the onscreen hero shoves a fat, glimmering rainbow trout forward so his cameraman and his advertisers can take a closer look. With the sound of rushing water in the background, the lucky angler stretches the truth, as well as his catch.

"That's a fish of a lifetime," he says. My response, as a viewer, ranges from several snorts to one or two guffaws.

"Heck," I scoff. "We catch them like that in Skaneateles Lake all the time."

## A WORLD-CLASS TROUT FISHERY

And we do, truly. This cold, clear lake stands out for its consistent production of big rainbows, whether it's being compared with its neighboring fishing holes in the Finger Lakes chain or the swift rivers of the Rocky Mountains. Skaneateles grows 20-inch leapers faster than your zucchini patch can sprout unwanted vegetables.

Give some credit for the lake and its silver-skinned residents to Mother Nature, sure, but let us also tip our caps to DEC fisheries managers, for stocking programs and regulations that make the most of limited resources.

Skaneateles Lake, which stretches across 8,960 surface acres in Onondaga, Cayuga and Cortland Counties, is one of the more scenic lakes in New York and probably boasts the purest water in the Finger Lakes chain. Residents of Skaneateles, the picturesque village that curls around

Kid Corbett of Syracuse shows off a typical Skaneateles lake trout.

the north end of the lake, are justifiably proud of their successful efforts to protect their favorite swimming and fishing hole from pollution and developmental pressures. A steep but otherwise first-rate state boat launch on the lake's west shore gives the public access to the fishery, and several shore-fishing venues are also popular with locals and visiting anglers.

With a maximum depth of 315 feet, Skaneateles is not quite roomy enough to support a legendary, tourism-boosting monster along the lines of Loch Ness's "Nessie" or Lake Champlain's "Champ." However, it is home to an addicting mix of cold- and cool-water fish species, including some king-size yellow perch and brown bullheads, loads of rock bass, gorgeous landlocked Atlantic salmon, and innumerable lake trout that are generally runts but occasionally grow to gargantuan length and weight.

The 20-pound lake trout that are boated at the rate of one every few years in Skaneateles certainly merit publication of a grip-and-grin photo on the local outdoors page and envious whistles at the boat launch, but the fact is very few anglers will ever connect with such a fish. Three- or 4-pound rainbows, on the other hand, are commonplace catches among those who target them, and rose-cheeked beauties up to 7 pounds or so are caught in the lake every year, according to data submitted by participants in the DEC angler-diary program.

## BREAD-AND-BUTTER 'BOWS

Jeff Robins, the Region 7 fisheries biologist who, as of late 2012, was coordinating the state's management programs for both Skaneateles and Owasco Lakes, has told me more than once that Skaneateles is in a class by itself, as far as he is concerned.

"Skaneateles Lake provides some of the best rainbow trout fishing in the state," he said. "There are undoubtedly a few small lakes and ponds that offer very good rainbow trout fishing, too, but most of the rainbows caught in them are small."

Nobody can get away with saying Skaneateles rainbows are on the small side.

The statistics generated by angler-diary research programs are often skewed by the knowledge and experience of individuals participating in the studies, and that certainly has been the case in Skaneateles Lake. In the early 1980s, total numbers of rainbows reported caught by diary keepers rose dramatically because of one person's intimate knowledge of the lake. Local guide Dick Withey, who recently moved to Florida, boosted Skaneateles Lake's reputation by including all catches by him and his clients in his DEC fishing journal. There was nothing wrong with that; in fact, it was perfectly proper. DEC diary keepers are supposed to enumerate all the trout they and their companions catch on each visit to the lakes fished. However, nobody fished more often or more effectively in Skaneateles Lake than Withey, and he and his sports swamped the Region 7 fisheries crew with diary data.

In 1981, for example, Withey et al. accounted for a near doubling of effort by diary keepers on the lake, to a then-record 1,018 "angler-trips" targeting trout or salmon. That same year, the number of anglers whose Skaneateles catches were submitted more than doubled, from 38 to 77. Not surprisingly, the total number of rainbows caught in the lake by diary program anglers shot upward, too, from a reported 759 in 1980 to 1,103 in '81. Catch rates, however, declined. It took program enrollees an average of three hours of effort to land a keeper-size salmonid—rainbow, laker, or salmon—in 1981. The year before that it took an average of 1.9 hours to catch one.

## A FISHING HOLE'S UPS AND DOWNS

Back then, Skaneateles Lake rainbows were abundant, but not as big as they are now. The 'bows creeled by diary program participants in 1980 and 1981 averaged 14.5 and 14.7 inches, respectively. In 2011, the Skaneateles rainbows kept for the pan by diary toters averaged an even 20 inches, which was an all-time record.

The lake's rainbow fishery is derived from a mix of wild and stocked trout. Most of the wild-strain trout are hatched in one of three spawning tributaries, Grout Brook, Bear Swamp Creek, or Shotwell Brook. These waterways draw significant rainbow runs between November and the ensuing April if their currents are flowing at an optimum rate for spawning. Angling opportunities in Shotwell Brook are extremely limited due to heavy posting and a lack of places for

Wayne Brewer of Seneca Falls admires his 20-inch Skaneateles Lake rainbow.

anglers to park along Route 41, which crosses the stream. On the opposite side of the lake, an impassable waterfall brings an abrupt halt to the
rainbow run in Bear Swamp Creek just a short distance from the stream's
mouth, at the privately owned Carpenter's Point.

These circumstances compel Skaneateles-area rainbow chasers to do
most of their spring fishing in Grout Brook, at the south end of the lake
in the town of Scott. Good old Grout happens to have superior habitat
for rainbow spawning, anyway, to the benefit of fish as well as fishermen.

On the map, you'll see that Grout Brook heads south for several miles,
then makes a rather sharp U-turn and hurries north to its rendezvous with
the lake. Although it averages only 10 to 15 feet wide, the brook has an
interesting mix of pools and riffles and a dependable run of rainbows,
which often outlasts those in other Finger Lakes tributaries. Grout Brook
is decorated with yellow-and-green PUBLIC FISHING signs immediately
downstream from upper Glenhaven Road in Scott for about a mile. You
will find intermittent public access along West Scott Road and lower Glen
Haven Road, but numerous NO TRESPASSING signs, too. Give wide berth to
them, for the sake of yourself and other anglers.

Most of the rainbows caught during the spring spawning run bite on
spawn sacs, but nightcrawlers or large garden worms work just as well. Fly
rodders take a Grout Brook fish now and then, although most of the stream
is so narrow and alder-lined that actual fly casting is almost impossible.

To put the spring fishing in Skaneateles Lake tributaries in perspective, most Grout Brook and Bear Swamp regulars consider a 20-inch
rainbow to be a very nice fish. Yet much larger trout can be had at times.
My personal best rainbow in Grout Brook was a 24-incher, but I know
other fellows who have landed spawners that stretched the tape to 27
inches and change.

## SIZE DOES MATTER TO SKANEATELES FISH

Most years, trolling accounts for a sizable majority of the rainbows (and
lakers and landlocked salmon) caught in the lake. One key to consistently
catching Skaneateles salmonids is the use of small lures. The lake has no
medium-size forage species to compare to the alewives or smelt found in
several other Finger Lakes, and anglers should be grateful for that, as any
attempt to introduce such prolific prey fish has the potential to cause an
ecological disaster. Instead of alewives or smelt, Skaneateles Lake fish dine
periodically on spot-tail shiners—which typically are less than 1½ inches
long—and the annual hatch of yellow perch, which can range from sparse
to thick until they're large enough to outswim predators.

"The absence of alewives or smelt in Skaneateles Lake eliminates an otherwise huge source of competition for food," DEC biologist Robins said. "Relatively few large predatory fish inhabit Skaneateles Lake, and thus, predatory pressure on rainbow trout is light. This combination of wild rainbows produced in the lake's tributaries and the annual stocking of rainbows results in a rainbow trout density that is higher than in many other lakes."

Consequently, anybody trolling for trout or salmon in the lake should rely, for the most part, on lures in the 1- to 2-inch range. Small flutter spoons, Needlefish, Mooselook Wobblers, Phoebes, and many other brand-name lures will catch rainbows when pulled at the right depth and speed. Streamer flies for the lake may be tied on 4X- or 6X-long hooks or constructed tandem-style, with the rear hook point facing up. Red-and-white and black-and-orange bucktails are dependable, but every Skaneateles Lake troller has his or her favorite pattern. Trust me, almost all of them are on the petite side, whether you're running your offerings near the surface or down deep.

Lake trout like this richly mottled specimen from Skaneateles Lake put up a good fight when hooked in the shallows on tiny jigs or streamer flies.

## BIG FISH AND BIG BAITS? NOT NECESSARILY

Even those whopper lakers that show up on a Skaneateles fisherman's stringer now and then are apt to be seduced by a miniature bait.

While trolling in the lake with his cousin and fellow Weedsport resident Tom Piascik in December 2011, Paul Tomaszewski connected with a huge fish. It was not one of the 2- to 4-pound rainbows that they were anticipating, but instead turned out to be the largest trout, by far, that either of the veteran anglers had ever boated.

The fish was a laker that stretched 40 inches on the tape and weighed in at 20 pounds, 8 ounces when plunked down on a certified scale.

The giant chased down a 2-inch Needlefish spoon, with a perch-painted finish, that was wobbling directly behind Piascik's boat motor, midway between a pair of Mickey Finn (red-and-yellow) bucktails connected to other rods. The lure was only a couple of feet down, in 14 feet of water, when the rod tip started bouncing and Piascik told his cousin Paulie to grab the rig and crank that fish into the boat. They were fishing near Five Mile Point, a traditional hot spot for autumn rainbows.

Interestingly, Piascik and Tomaszewski were trolling at a rate of 4 miles per hour, a speed that most lake trout anglers would consider awfully quick for the species. In Lake Ontario, for example, the rule of the road for most charter captains seeking lakers is 2 to 3 miles per hour. Luckily, fishing rules, like many other nuggets of conventional wisdom, are made to be broken.

Trout stocked in Skaneateles Lake are the offspring of wild Finger Lakes–strain rainbows netted at the Cayuga Lake Inlet and rainbows born and bred at the state's Bath trout hatchery. The wild–domestic crosses, as biologist Robins calls them, are released at Five Mile Point and at Lourdes Camp, a summer camp for kids that is owned and operated by the Roman Catholic Diocese of Syracuse. Happily, many of those "stockers" do not venture far from their release point and are inclined to visit their childhood hangouts during the autumn and winter months.

A fair share of the plus-size rainbows hauled out of Skaneateles Lake are hooked by shore fishermen, many of whom rely on a combination of cocktail marshmallows and angleworms for bait. The odd coupling of baits, which is explained in detail elsewhere in this book, comes into play sometime between Labor Day and Halloween, depending on water levels and temperatures. The colder and deeper the lake, the earlier the shore-fishing fraternity begins to cast for autumn rainbows at the Skaneateles village pier, the park adjacent to the Episcopal church in the village, and the gravel beach at Lourdes Camp.

Lourdes has been an "unofficial access" for Syracuse-, Cortland-, and Auburn-area shore casters for decades, and likely will remain so as long as fishermen and others who visit the place abide by a few commonsense rules. For example, there should be no littering, no loud or profane talk (which can be offensive to neighboring lakeshore residents), no consumption of alcoholic beverages, no driving on lawns, no building of fires, and no entering camp buildings without the approval of diocese officials.

The camp can be reached by taking US Route 20 to Skaneateles, then turning south onto Route 41. Take that road to the hamlet of Borodino, turn right onto Nunnery Road, and turn right again when you come to Richard Road. Drive with extra care on the steep, one-and-a-half-lane road, which dead-ends at the camp gate.

## TWO LEGENDARY MAYFLY HATCHES

Aside from the worm-and-marshmallow rig, shore casters on Skaneateles Lake rely on small jigs, which are better for lake trout than rainbows; minnows fished with a slip bobber; and, from mid-June to late July, big, high-floating dry flies. The flies should mimic two mayfly species that hatch in profusion in the lake early in the summer. First comes the brown drake, *Ephemerella simulans*, starting about June 20; next, around July 1, it's time for *Hexagenia rigida*, locally dubbed "the hex fly."

Ever punctual, the drake duns and spinners put on their show beginning from 30 minutes to an hour before sunset, and usually quit for the night just before dark. They're imitated with patterns tied on size 10 or 12 hooks and have speckled brown wings and light brown underbellies.

Paul McNeilly admires a smallmouth bass caught on a dry fly during the famed brown drake mayfly hatch on Skaneateles Lake.

Hexes are bigger, often matched with a size 8 hook, and sometimes don't appear in the water or fluttering overhead in mating swarms until the sun is just dropping below the horizon. Because the light is going fast by the time the big guys are emerging, the colors you are able to see quickly become more important than the hues detected by the fish targeting *H. rigida* duns and spinners. In the waning light, they see only a dark shape on the surface—and you are going to have a hard time watching for rises, too. I like to tie these "dark and gloomy night" floaters with thick, bushy calf-hair wings that stand tall in the impending darkness, but I might favor something a little lighter-colored if skies are cloudy. Here's how I decide: When the water is dark, I choose a light-colored wing. But it the water is light, a dark-winged fly is a better choice. Being able to see the fly and observe the trout's take is a huge advantage for a dry-fly fisher.

Permit me to backtrack a bit if I just left you with the notion that the big hatches in Skaneateles Lake are "trout-only" affairs. In truth, the banquet of bugs seems to attract every fish that swims. If you're restricted to shore, trout and landlocked salmon are probably out of reach; smallmouths roam closer to land, however, and my friends and I have caught many bronzebacks during drake and hex hatches, including a couple of 18-inchers. We've also hooked and landed rock bass, yellow perch, and even a couple of dandy bullheads on floaters.

## UP-AND-COMING SMALLMOUTH BASS

Of course all of these species can be caught on various baits and spinning lures, too.

Smallmouths, in particular, have grown in popularity among Skaneateles Lake aficionados. Up until the late 1990s, the lake was widely thought to have a "stunted" smallmouth fishery, and the DEC addressed the alleged problem by maintaining a special creel standard for it. In most other New York waters, the minimum creel length for smallmouth bass was 12 inches. Skaneateles was one of a handful of waters with a 10- inch minimum.

When DEC Region 7 biologists revisited the issue, they found that Skaneateles Lake's bass were not stunted but thriving on a more-than-adequate diet of crayfish, minnows, and mayflies. Since the short keeper size was abandoned in favor of the state-standard 12-inch minimum, many anglers have rediscovered the lake's potential for growing muscular, scrappy smallmouths. Although Skaneateles bass still average around 12 or 13 inches, 2-pounders are fairly routine nowadays. Further, if you hit the lake when the fishing is really hot—as happens to be the case in June or

The author with nice smallmouth from Skaneateles Lake.

October most years—you stand a pretty good chance of boating a 3½- or even a 4-pound smallmouth.

Tournament anglers pay little heed to the lake for two reasons. First, the state launch on the west shore off Route 41A can accommodate only two dozen or so bass boats on a typical Saturday or Sunday. To handle a larger field of competitors, arrangements will have to be made to embark from and return to private marinas, as well as the state ramp. Also, the lake's bass population consists almost entirely of smallmouths. Only a few largemouths share the weedy south end with perch, sunfish, and chain pickerel. The dearth of largemouths means competitive anglers vying in a hypothetical Skaneateles Lake tourney might well have a real shot at winning if they can reel in a final-day limit of five bass that average little more than 2 pounds each. Smallmouths that size are scrappy but not the stuff of dreams for would-be professional fishermen.

On the bright side, the modest amount of tournament action that takes place on Skaneateles Lake makes it an ideal location for the average angler who simply wants to catch lots of decent-size bass. Starting in mid-May and continuing through June, a fisherman who can drop a Pop-R or some other surface lure close to shaded docks and moored boats can hook one 10- to 14-inch smallmouth after another. Later in the summer, as smallmouths retreat to depths of 10 to 20 feet, drop-shotting works very well, and tube jigs hopped back to an anchored boat are also quite productive. In early October, bass may school near bottom in areas 40 to 50 feet deep, and tubes on jigheads weighing at least ¾ ounce are called for. Virtually the whole lake seems to give up big bass around Halloween, provided you fish at the right depth. Just keep moving until you locate good numbers of fish, then stick around until you figure out what they are taking. It's the same strategy Grandpa used—but electronic fishfinders have made it easier than ever to implement.

## PERCH PARADISE

Yellow perch are a major Skaneateles Lake angling attraction. While the jumbo jacks in Skaneateles may not be as large as those that school in Seneca and Keuka Lakes, they are of above average size and very abundant.

One afternoon in November 2011, I was shore-casting for rainbow trout. When I arrived, I noticed a parked boat trailer, and wondered what its owner was up to.

Just as I was getting ready to quit for the day, I heard a small boat in the distance heading in my direction. The vessel got louder until the boat and its two occupants came around the point just east of my casting spot. Then the operator cut the motor, and a few minutes later the 16-foot vessel was bobbing gently in knee-deep waves.

"How did you do?" I asked.

"Not bad," one of the anglers replied. "We have a pretty good mess of perch."

Actually, it was two "pretty good" messes of perch. Two large white buckets in the boat were each more than half full of paunchy jacks and egg-swollen hens. A large share of the fish were at least 12 inches long, to my eye, anyway, and at least half a dozen were in the 14-inch range.

"We're going to have a fish fry tonight," the older of the two anglers volunteered. "You're welcome to join us."

I had other plans that evening, but I gratefully accepted their follow-up offering of several 10- and 11-inchers for my supper.

Free perch are hard to turn down, but you can stuff your freezer on your own by fishing any of several well-known panfish hangouts on Skaneateles Lake. Tiny minnows often called "icicles" in tackle stores are the favorite bait, but if you prefer artificial enticements, try ⅟16-ounce to ⅛-ounce jigs tipped with mealworms, mousie grubs, or other wiggly larvae. Work on finding schools of perch in the 10- to 20-foot depths off the bluffs in the lake's southeast corner, the Syracuse municipal water supply intake pipe near the north shore, and the water just north of the

DEC boat launch on the west shore. There are many more likely spots, but these will get you started.

The main problem Skaneateles Lake perch seekers have in late autumn or early spring is not finding fish but discerning a place to launch a boat. State workers try to close the west-shore ramp before its entrance road becomes slick with ice, and they usually don't reopen the access until the last week in March or early in April. To complicate things even more, the floating docks at the site may be removed weeks before the gates are closed in the fall. Before you undertake a long drive to Skaneateles Lake, make sure the ramp is open and safe to use, by calling ahead to the DEC Region 7 office in Cortland, (607) 753-3095.

# CHAPTER 3

# Owasco Lake

**LOCATION:** Central Cayuga County
**ELEVATION:** 711 feet
**SURFACE AREA:** 6,665 acres
**SHORELINE:** 24.7 miles
**MEAN DEPTH:** 97 feet
**MAXIMUM DEPTH:** 180 feet
**APPROXIMATE THERMOCLINE DEPTH:** 37 feet

The 21-pound, 5-ounce brown trout that Auburn teenager Tom Klink hauled out of Owasco Lake in 1954 stood as the New York state record for an astonishing 25 years before a Keuka Lake brown took over the top rung. Since then, several Lake Ontario fish have worn the crown, and Klink's prize seems almost diminutive in comparison with the most recent record setter, a 33-pound, 2-ounce brown caught in Ontario's Mexico Bay in 1997. Even today, however, the Finger Lakes in general and Owasco Lake in particular are capable of growing some monster browns. Over the 2012 Memorial Day weekend, Moravia-area angler Gary Rule demonstrated the lake's continuing trophy potential by hooking and netting a brown that weighted 22 pounds, 8 ounces. The brown is widely thought to have been the biggest one ever caught in Owasco Lake, let alone the first one from the lake that was heavier than Klink's prize.

## WE STILL GROW THEM BIG

It was hardly a fluke, either, for Rule caught another Owasco brown in 2011 that weighed nearly 20 pounds.

Rule, who operates Reel Sportsman Fishing Adventures charter service, was on an afternoon boat ride with a few family members and friends when he connected with the big one. As *Syracuse Post-Standard* outdoors editor David Figura reported the story on his blog, the fish put up an admirable fight that lasted a total of about 45 minutes. The tug-of-war included three determined dives for the security of deep water, but Rule maintained the advantage throughout, despite being a bit under-gunned with his 8-pound-test fluorocarbon spinning line.

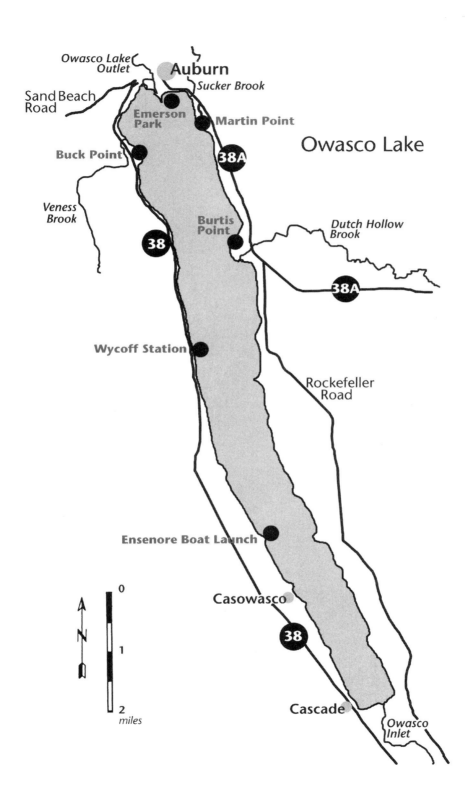

Owasco Lake Outlet

Auburn

Sucker Brook

Sand Beach Road

Emerson Park

Martin Point

Buck Point

38A

Owasco Lake

Veness Brook

Burtis Point

Dutch Hollow Brook

38

38A

Wycoff Station

Rockefeller Road

Ensenore Boat Launch

0

1

2

miles

Casowasco

38

Cascade

Owasco Inlet

His bait was a dead alewife (or mooneye), the same forage species favored by many fishermen throughout the Finger Lakes region. Mooneyes are available over the counter at many Central and Western New York bait-and-tackle stores and are easily obtained in the summer and autumn months. Many anglers say frozen, salted, or otherwise preserved alewives work as well as fresh, live specimens, but others insist that a lively minnow of any kind is better than a fat alewife that is dead or dying.

Readers, take your pick, but be aware that you must have a deft touch with rod, reel, and drag settings when you battle a 20-pound brown trout (or any other heavy fish) on 8-pound line!

Owasco Lake is known for its piscatorial smorgasbord—and its rewarding but difficult fishing. Remember that old line, "Would you rather be good or lucky?" On this body of water, many very good anglers have expressed a willingness to swap a little skill if they could only have a bit more luck in return. In addition to the occasional long-as-your-leg brown, the lake offers fine fishing for lake trout, bass, northern pike, and panfish, but none of its residents are pushovers. Whether you choose to target trophy salmonids with sophisticated trolling gear or go after blue-gills on their spring spawning nests with simple worm-and-bobber rigs, you can expect to earn whatever success you have. To compound the degree of difficulty, it seems that the food chain in Owasco Lake is always

Leon Archer with an Owasco lake trout.

in transition. If one or more key players in the natural drama thrive, you can be sure it will be at the expense of another species.

DEC experts and anglers alike have detected more lake trout but many fewer browns and rainbows in Owasco since the early 1990s. The trend is no coincidence, DEC Region 7 fisheries biologist Jeff Robins said. Lake trout have no compunctions about snacking on their relatives now and then, and in 2011, data collected from participants in the regional Finger Lakes angler-diary program confirmed that lakers are by far the dominant predators in the lake. The 13 diary keepers who logged their Owasco open-water catches for Robins in 2011 reported catching 133 legal-size (15 inches or better) lake trout. The other salmonids caught during the year by the data getters included four rainbows and a single brown! Clearly, something has been amiss in recent years, and Robins sums up the problem in three words:

## BEAVERS, WALLEYES, AND LAKERS

Not so long ago, I posed for photographs with an impossibly handsome example of rainbow trout manhood. Okay, it was quite a while back, although it scarcely seems possible that such a milestone in my fishing career actually occurred on April 17, 1982. Yet my angling diary is nonfiction, and the photo my late friend Dan Skinner shot that day

The author in 1982 with his largest Finger Lakes watershed rainbow trout.

cruelly affirms that I have changed quite a bit in the three decades since I caught my largest Finger Lakes watershed rainbow trout. That fish was 28¼ inches long and weighed 10 pounds, 6 ounces. In those days I was apt to keep such a trout, not knowing or reluctant to admit that its flesh would have the chewy consistency of rubber—and none of my neighbors really wanted to see it, anyway.

The hook-jawed brute I remember came from Hemlock Creek, a tributary of Owasco Lake Inlet, which happens to be the main stream feeding Owasco Lake. I'll bet the large majority of gallons of water that flow into the lake—which covers 6,665 surface acres and has a maximum depth of 180 feet—pass through the inlet first, and that substantial flow beckons to the lake's rainbow trout at spawning time.

Back then the inlet and its spidery tributaries drew substantial runs, and when the trout season opened, the April Fool was just as likely to be the fish as the fisherman. Hemlock Creek, which contributes its flow volume to Owasco Inlet in the Cayuga County village of Locke, was a personal favorite early-season spot, but the big pools of the inlet were great, too. Come to think of it, other Owasco tributaries such as Dresserville (Mill) Creek and Dutch Hollow Brook were also fine April streams.

The rainbow fishing was extraordinary, but in the late 1980s and '90s, something awful happened.

"It's those damned beavers," said Robins. "There's just no doubt."

Never one to mince words when this topic comes up, the DEC biologist is adamant that the Owasco trout fishery, in both the lake and its tributaries, was plunged into mediocrity by an industrious adversary. The enemy of trout lovers everywhere, in Robins's view, has sharp, buck teeth, an annoying tail that slaps the water loudly when trouble is looming or just for the heck of it, and, worst of all, a knack for weaving mud and sticks into dams that transform turn cold, running water into stagnant puddles.

## THE OWASCO BEAVER WARS

In the mid-1990s, when Robins started getting complaints about beaver activity on some of the streams entrusted to his care, he and Wayne Masters, a Cortland DEC office colleague, assembled the required paperwork, grabbed a couple of rakes on their way out the office door, and breached more than two dozen beaver dams on a single stream, Dutch Hollow Brook. As time and other duties allowed, Robins went after dams in different parts of the watershed, with a vengeance. He disrupted beaver colonies from Peruville to Moravia, and eventually added dams and lodges along streams in Cortland County to his hit list. In most cases, he collaborated with licensed nuisance trappers, because a beaver dam opened and abandoned is a beaver dam rebuilt and reoccupied. That's just the way beavers are.

Left unchecked, beavers are fascinating to observe, but their handiwork eventually is more than trout can tolerate. The dams block the flows of swift streams and strip tree cover from banks, reducing shade, raising water temperatures, and lowering dissolved oxygen levels. When dams inevitably break due to flooding or their own crushing weight, the eruption of backed-up water licks the stream bottom clean, but who knows where the tons of silt will wind up? Frequently, the mud piled high by beavers smothers aquatic insects, trout eggs, and even trout themselves.

Robins is convinced beavers deserve much of the blame for Owasco Lake's diminished rainbow run, and probably for reduced numbers of resident and lake-run brown trout, too. The browns that swim up Owasco tributaries have the same rites of propagation as the 'bows, with one important difference. Instead of running the creeks in the spring, the browns are autumn egg layers.

With more dam removal campaigns and constant vigilance regarding "nature's engineers," the numbers of rainbows and browns in Owasco Lake will increase over time, Robins assured me.

Landowners could play a key role.

"First and foremost, they can help by allowing trappers on their property to remove the beavers," Robins said. "Unless all beavers are removed from a problem area, the problem will not go away."

If DEC staff can't tackle a particular beaver dam or colony for some reason, they can almost always refer a landowner to a nuisance trapper, Robins said.

## UPSETTING THE APPLE CART

All those who've ever picked up a spinning rod see themselves as fisheries managers, just as all the fans who review NFL line scores while eating at the diner on Monday morning think they know more about the game than their favorite team's coach. In the case of football, that's why volatile team owners are so quick to give their guy his walking papers. As for fishing, the real pros are painfully aware that catching them isn't nearly as hard as raising them or protecting their habitat. Well-meaning projects carried out on a certain stream or lake may work out but often as not turn out to be failures, and real fisheries managers, like real coaches, are prone to being second-guessed.

The plan hatched by Auburn schoolteacher Chet Crosby in the 1990s to bring walleyes back to Owasco Lake was not entirely ill conceived; in fact, proponents could argue that it worked. Where once there were no walleyes, now there are some, and a few are of exceptional size. Stocking of fingerlings lasted 10 years, from 1996 to 2005. Crosby's Owasco Lake Anglers Association raised the little 'eyes in privately owned ponds for the first five years, and the DEC hatchery system carried the ball for the next five.

Although stocking has come to an end for now, and quite possibly for good, you can still catch a walleye or two in the lake on a given day, if you happen to be heading for the right spot at the right time. However, the state is adamant that it is no longer stocking the lake with walleyes, and private fish-rearing groups also appear to have lost interest.

To Robins and his colleagues in the DEC Cortland field office, that shift in the cosmos is cause for a collective sigh of relief. Walleyes had previously been absent from Owasco Lake for 40 years at least, and they will be among the missing again because they did not get along with their neighbors. They were fun to catch (and eat) but they gobbled down lots of trout—mostly rainbows but some browns, as well—before they ever felt the sting of a hook themselves. Or so goes the prevailing thread on the subject. In actuality, there are times when fisheries managers, like the rest of us, have to guess the answer to a riddle, instead of waiting for a definitive answer. The DEC's educated guess in this case is that voracious walleyes were at least partly to blame for the ongoing decline in Owasco Lake's rainbow trout population, and walleyes likely had an unexpected impact on brown trout numbers, too.

If the debate about walleyes versus rainbows was put to a vote, the trout would win, said DEC Region 7 natural resources supervisor Dan Bishop. In September 2012, he reported that a survey on the subject was in the works. The plan (still under way as of this writing) calls for distributing a questionnaire to hundreds of anglers living in the eastern Finger Lakes region. If the response indicates overwhelming support among Owasco Lake–area sportsmen for policies benefiting trout, fisheries managers will focus their efforts on the cold-water species. Conversely, strong support for walleyes among the survey participants will likely compel the DEC to reevaluate its plan for managing the lake.

## WALLEYES OR TROUT: CHOOSE ONE

No mere tree hugger or bureaucrat, Bishop was the regional fisheries manager before be was promoted to the natural resources post. He is widely admired within the DEC for his research on Lake Ontario and the Finger Lakes, and his opinion carries some weight in Albany. As far as Owasco Lake is concerned, Bishop concurs with Robins and other fisheries staffers who have decided that Owasco Lake—although 12 miles long and having a mean depth of 97 feet—simply isn't big enough to accommodate rainbows, browns, and walleyes.

"It is now clear that we cannot manage the lake for both walleyes and the trout species," said Bishop. "If we could, we would."

The good news is that Robins, Bishop, et al., have detected some encouraging trends among Owasco Lake trout since walleye stocking ended.

Lake trout, the undisputed rulers of Owasco's deeper environs, will never be swept aside in favor of other game fish, but the state has cut back stocking quotas for lakers in order to give rainbow and brown trout a jump start and also take some pressure off forage species. In 2005 and again in 2009, lake trout slated for stocking in Owasco were diverted to Lake Ontario, instead. As of 2010, Owasco no longer received any share of the state's yearling lakers. These measures undoubtedly accounted for a steady decline in Owasco's lake trout population between 2009 and 2012. Nor does it seem coincidental that alewives and smelt, the two most abundant baitfish in the lake, are more plentiful than they were a few years ago. Alewives, in particular, have rebounded to levels not recorded by DEC netting crews since the 1980s.

Boats cluster over a school of lake trout in Owasco Lake.

Walleyes, though not likely to be stocked again in Owasco Lake in the near future, are still fairly common, and Robins said some of the older ones have matured into 10-pounders. Anglers who yearn for consistently good catches of the species must focus their efforts around known walleye haunts, such as Burtis Point and Martin Point, both on the lake's northeast shoreline; and Buck Point, which is opposite Martin Point on the west shore. According to Robins, survey results and angler scuttlebutt confirm that most walleye fishing in the lake takes place in the northern third, roughly between Emerson Park in Auburn and Wyckoff Station on the west shore.

## PARK PIER IS PRIME FOR PERCH AND PIKE

The pier at Emerson Park is a favorite spot for a variety of species depending on the time of year but is locally known for providing fair to good action for walleyes after dark, both spring and fall. Walleye lovers everywhere know the drill. Success hinges mainly on getting there before sundown and hurling skinny stickbaits into the darkness until you have landed your limit (three of 18 inches or better in Owasco) or are so bone-weary you just have to go home and get some sleep.

Interestingly, small watercraft with all the required nighttime warning and navigation lamps are frequently spotted off the pier, too. The trollers and shore-bound anglers are essentially doing the same things. Both rely on lures that mimic local prey species in shape and action, if not necessarily in color. I have yet to see any real, live fish that's silver on the belly and fluorescent yellow on top, let alone one wearing the current best-selling "clown" color pattern of red, green, and silver. Like most fishermen, I am willing to try anything that works, and clown-finish lures and silver and hot yellow both have caught me some very nice fish elsewhere, so why not Owasco Lake?

In search of walleyes, trollers and bank experts both strive to vary their speed of presentation and retrieve, until they stumble onto the pace that works best on the chosen evening. Boater and shore caster alike focus on finding schools of bait as much as locating the walleyes themselves. This strategy, at first glance, might appear to give boaters an edge, but even with modern sonar gear it can be difficult or impossible to track alewives and other forage species that are hugging the shoreline or roaming at random through 4- to 10-foot-deep water. In contrast, anglers who are willing to plug away at beaches, points, or other structures that consistently attract schools of bait after dark often do quite well. Lighted piers like the one in Emerson Park draw baitfish and predators alike, and therefore are reliable locations for after-dark anglers to ply their trade.

Tom Piascik of Weedsport used to frequent the pier in late autumn, but his visits fell off as walleye stocking came to an end. Occasionally someone still catches a walleye or two from the pier, but the action is not even close to what it used to be. Owasco appears to be one of many lakes in which walleye fry and fingerlings are imperiled by panfish (yellow perch), game fish (bass, trout, and other walleyes), and even forage species (alewives). As a result, the walleye sport fishery probably wouldn't last unless it were bolstered by regular stockings of fingerlings—and preferably advanced, larger-than-usual fingerlings.

## DON'T BE IN THE DARK ABOUT NIGHT FISHING

Emerson Park is still productive on dark nights in May through early June and again from mid-October through November, but the fish most often caught there are northern pike, lake trout, and perch, not necessarily in that order.

Lake trout bite fairly well at night, especially during the late October through November period when the deep-water species moves close to shore for its annual spawning duties. The autumn action is signaled by the appearance of large schools of lakers, swimming close to bottom in 70 or 80 feet of water, off Buck, Burtis, and Martin Points. At first, these groups of game fish seem to be flitting this way and that, like the flocks of migratory sparrows that are also feeling restless at this time of the year. Then, as the schools settle down and begin to feed one last time before spawning, vertical jigging with a ¾-ounce or 1-ounce white jig or Kastmaster spoon can be extremely effective.

Along with the north-end points listed just above, lake trout fans should do some wading at Ensenore, a town-of-Scipio-maintained boat launch that's on the west side of the lake, about 7 miles north of Moravia, via Route 38 and Ensenore Road. It's a small spot, but casting with Little Cleos and similar spoons can be worthwhile through Christmas, weather permitting. Assuming that a typical Central New York winter is in the works, ice fishing for lake trout is usually good at Ensenore over 80 to 100 feet of water. The locals use vertical jigs and lift them about 2 to 3 feet before letting them flutter back to the bottom. Some like to dress their jigs with a minnow, while other fishermen prefer their jigs unadorned with any sort of meat. Then again, a plain alewife (also known as a sawbelly or mooneye locally) is hard to top, whether it is dead or alive on your hook.

Northern pike are an overlooked component of the after-dark fishing in Owasco Lake. Since the walleye population began to dwindle, catches of multiple northerns have become fairly common at the Emerson Park pier, Piascik said. Although giants of the species are more apt to be found in the dense weed beds at the south end of the lake, pike measuring from 26 to 30 inches can be expected at the north end by patient anglers. Long, skinny stickbaits, such as Husky Jerks and magnum floating or suspending Rapalas, will draw bigger fish now and then. Good color schemes, besides the clown lures I touted a while back, include the universally popular fire tiger and black and silver variations. In addition to stickbaits, large spinnerbaits with round or willow-leaf blades will take cruising pike after dark. Another extremely effective lure for northerns in spring or fall is a bucktail jig, tied on a size 2 or 1/0 hook and weighing from ¾ to 1 full ounce. It should be black or brown in color, and as a final touch, a large white or yellow curly-tail grub is attached to the hook bend. What this strange critter looks like, I am not sure; but to pike it must resemble something good to eat!

Of course, northerns being the ambush-feeding, quick-swimming, voracious predators that they are, no artificial will work any better after dark than a big, lively shiner hung on a hook below a quill-type slip bobber. Just don't forget your quarry's sharp teeth. A wire leader is a big help, at the very least, and probably an essential component of the rig used by most knowledgeable pike fishermen.

## SOME SUMMER STRATEGIES

When their spring spawning activity wanes, Owasco pike are inclined to tuck into weed beds for the summer. They especially like those that sprout along deep-sloping points and other natural ambush locations. Anecdotal evidence should always be received with some reservations, but most veteran Owasco fishermen share a belief that the vast majority of northerns caught from their lake come out of the south end—and most of those in the Cascade area—either through the ice or by casting in the Owasco Inlet during the first week or two after the May season opener. However, any weedy habitat in the lake is worth a thorough try, and the requirements are well met off any of the north-end points.

One unsung facet of the Owasco Lake fishery is its excellent smallmouth bass population. Bronzebacks in Owasco and throughout the Finger Lakes chain have benefited from the proliferation of zebra mussels since the recent turn of the century. The mussels are filter feeders that remove large quantities of plankton from the water column. As a result, the water is notably clearer and sunlight penetrates to greater depths. This means smallmouths and other sight-feeding fish can spot their prey at greater distances than before, and expend fewer calories in the capture process. Of course, pike, largemouth bass, and other ambush feeders have also fared well, because the increased sunlight down below triggers more weed growth and thereby creates more hiding places.

A few years ago, during a meeting of the New York State Outdoor Writers Association in Auburn, I had the pleasure of sharing a boat with local bass tournament competitor Randy Yager. We connected with several dandy smallmouths, in the 3- to 3½-pound range, by dragging tube jigs slowly across the bottom, in mid-lake and about ¼ mile due south of the Emerson Park pier. Yager, who has since moved to Florida, concentrated on making precision passes along the length of a city water-intake pipe. As I recall, we did best in about 15 or 20 feet of water. That trip was in mid-October—a good time to target bass, which are moving toward deep, flat wintering areas and feeding heavily as they go.

Along with tube jigs, hefty swimbaits with flat tails and a good vibrating motion are deadly on staging bronzebacks. In the spring and summer, when smallmouths are coming off their spawning nests and resuming their restless, roaming ways, experienced bass fishermen use lures that cover lots of water via long casts and quick retrieves, such as deep-diving crankbaits and spinnerbaits.

Smallmouths of 14 to 15 inches are about average size in Owasco Lake, and I believe one of 20 inches and close to 5 pounds would be almost anybody's personal best in this beautiful fishing hole. This impression

Randy Yager battles a smallmouth bass in Owasco Lake.

comes from interviewing Owasco experts like Yager and George Fiorielle of Moravia, and tagging along on DEC netting surveys. The bass are there, for sure.

## SOMETHING FOR THE FRYING PAN

Since cable and satellite TV blossomed and hunting and fishing shows began to air 24/7, we have become more fixated than ever on trophy-size fish, fowl, and beast—yet many anglers remain deeply loyal to bluegills, perch, and other species that are destined to be somebody's dinner. That's certainly true in Owasco Lake, where panfish are abundant and, as elsewhere, more admired for their flavor than for their fight.

Some of the most remarkable fish being caught in the Finger Lakes these days are platter-size pumpkinseeds. Not as coveted as yellow perch, perhaps, and definitely not as well known, these pretty scrappers sometimes measure 10 or 11 inches long in Owasco Lake. Such specimens weigh close to a pound, and anglers who know how to wield a fillet knife can make a meal of four or five sunnies like that.

The most admirable quality of jumbo pumpkinseeds is their ability to turn grown men and women into little kids. Once you locate a bay or weed line that shelters a good number of sizable sunnies, catching them does not require much guile. Cascade is one of many likely spots in Owasco Lake. When you get within casting range, just serve your sunnies an inch-long piece of nightcrawler on a hook, and keep the bait off bottom with the help of a small bobber. The target fish will home in on the offering as soon as it splashes down, and kids of all ages will enjoy what comes next.

## SUCKER PATTIES, ANYONE?

Along with sunnies, Owasco Lake has fishable populations of bluegills, yellow perch, bullheads, rock bass, chain pickerel, carp, and white suckers. Of these, bullheads are frequently caught off numerous tributaries in the spring, and perch in the 8- to 11-inch range can be trusted to show up at each of the north-end points (Martin, Burtis, and Buck) at that species's spawning time in April and again in October, as various small forage species school close to shore.

One natural phenomenon that draws a small but enthusiastic cadre of anglers is the annual sucker run. I have seen schools of several hundred white suckers below the village-of-Locke stretch of Owasco Inlet, when I was after trout. Most were between 16 and 24 inches long and put up a heck of a fight when they bit on worms or salmon egg sacs. Contrary to the habits of some folks, these fish should not be tossed up the streambank for the raccoons to eat. When my kids were young, I occasionally kept a few white suckers. To avoid problems with their pitchfork-shaped bones, I simply filleted and skinned my suckers as I would any large fish, and then ran them through a grinder two or three times. The zesty patties I made from sucker flesh were more appreciated than trout amandine at my house.

The city of Auburn's main interior road, Genesee Street, is intersected by Route 38, which runs south along Owasco Lake's west shore; and also by Route 38A, which parallels part of the east shore for several miles before taking a hill-country swing west. The road veers southeast again in time for it to meet 38 in the village of Moravia.

# CHAPTER 4

# Cayuga Lake

**LOCATION:** Seneca, Tompkins, and Cayuga Counties
**ELEVATION:** 382 feet
**SURFACE AREA:** 42,956 acres
**SHORELINE:** 84.8 miles
**MEAN DEPTH:** 181 feet
**MAXIMUM DEPTH:** 435 feet
**APPROXIMATE THERMOCLINE DEPTH:** 70 feet

Most of the Finger Lakes are home to an interesting variety of fish, but Cayuga Lake's diversity is dazzling. Virtually every species present in Cayuga thrives, for this big body of water has habitat and elbow room for all of its residents. It is a classic two-story lake, with shallows ruled by northern pike, pickerel, panfish, and largemouth bass and deep water that's cold enough, year-round, to sustain robust fisheries for Atlantic salmon and lake, rainbow, and brown trout. Smallmouth bass feed greedily in the transitional zones, which are a little too cold and deep for largemouths but slightly warm for trout.

With a maximum depth of 435 feet and a mean depth of 181 feet, Cayuga Lake is the second largest body of water in the Finger Lakes chain. Among the Fingers, only Seneca Lake is deeper and covers more acreage. How big are these two fishing holes? Geographic terminology doesn't tell the whole story, so consider the Big Two in terms of human mortality. Each holds so much water, end-to-end and top-to-bottom, that the most precise (or obsessive-compulsive) angler would require several lifetimes to systematically pull a trolling lure through every cubic inch of the lake. Therefore, if you ever bump into fishing guides, tackle shop owners, or marina operators who claim to have fished every patch of water in Cayuga Lake or Seneca Lake, you can say no, they haven't, and they never will.

## DIARY PROGRAM TELLS THE STORY

The broad spectrum of Cayuga Lake's fishing is most easily seen by browsing through the data turned in by the volunteers who take part in the DEC's Region 7 Finger Lakes angler-diary program. Because the

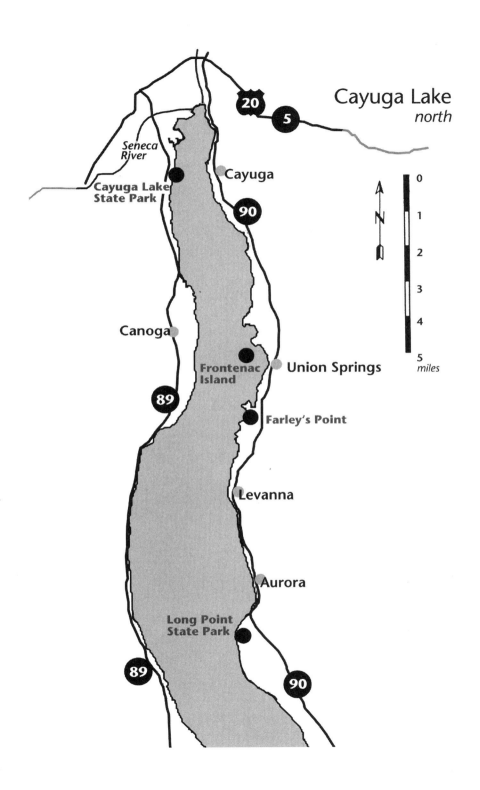

Cayuga Lake
*north*

20
5

Seneca River
Cayuga Lake State Park

Cayuga

90

Canoga

Frontenac Island
Union Springs

89

Farley's Point

Levanna

Aurora

Long Point State Park

89

90

0
1
2
3
4
5
*miles*

N

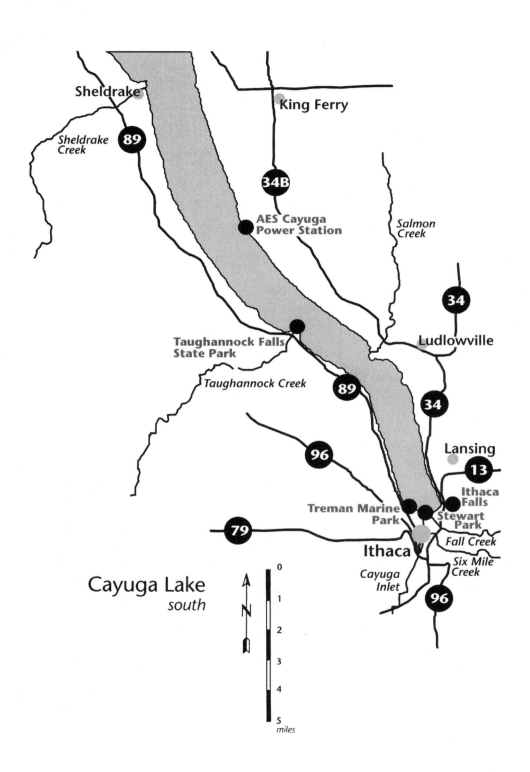

Sheldrake

Sheldrake
Creek

**89**

King Ferry

**34B**

AES Cayuga
Power Station

Salmon
Creek

**34**

Taughannock Falls
State Park

Ludlowville

Taughannock Creek

**89**

**34**

**96**

Lansing

**13**

Treman Marine
Park

Ithaca
Falls

Stewart
Park

**79**

Ithaca

Fall Creek

Six Mile
Creek

Cayuga Lake
*south*

N

0

1

2

3

4

5

*miles*

Cayuga
Inlet

**96**

information is collected annually, the data collated by senior aquatic biologist Emily Zollweg-Horan amounts to a snapshot in time and doesn't, by itself, predict any long-term trend.

Nevertheless, the catch totals and daily catch rates shown in the report definitely portray a lake in good health. The 2011 Cayuga diaries were turned in by dedicated fishermen who each filled in one or more of three types of logbooks—open-water trout and salmon fishing, tributary fishing for trout and salmon, and open-water fishing for warm-water species.

A total of 47 program participants filed open-water trout and salmon reports during the year, while 10 anglers turned in warm-water diaries and 11 sent in tributary data.

Among them, the open-water trout and salmon specialists reported catching 1,663 salmonids that were legal or big enough to creel according to state regulations. That added up to an average of 1.8 keeper fish per outing. They caught trout or salmon at an overall rate of 2.7 hours per fish and caught at least one legal fish on 83 percent of their Cayuga trips. The Cayuga salmonid total included 1,373 legal lake trout, of which 611 were actually creeled. The biggest reported laker was 36 inches long.

Lakers accounted for 83 percent of the diary program's total 2011 salmonid catch, well over the 65 percent share the DEC is shooting for, but diary keepers also logged in 38 legal rainbow trout, 71 legal browns, and 181 legal landlocked (Atlantic) salmon, Zollweg-Horan reported. Among those fish, the largest rainbow was a 30-incher. The biggest brown was another 30-inch fish, and the longest Atlantic checked in by the diary jotters was a

Kid Corbett fly casting for trout and salmon at the scenic Ithaca Falls on Fall Creek.

27-incher. The fact that the average landlock noted in the diaries was 20.9 inches long surely cemented Cayuga Lake's reputation as one of the best places in the United States to catch trophy-size Atlantics. Specimens weighing 6 to 8 pounds are not out of the ordinary in Cayuga Lake or its tributaries, which receive a modest run of spawning Atlantics each fall. In most years, that migration takes place about the first or second week of November. However, it's not rare to see sleek Atlantics holding in the tail-out of the Ithaca Falls pool on Fall Creek, or in the old trestle pool in the Cayuga Inlet three or four weeks earlier than that. Fish, like people, are individuals.

## TRIBUTARIES ARE PRODUCTIVE FOR TROUT, SALMON

Stream fishermen do quite well in Cayuga Lake feeder creeks, although something as unpredictable as an early snowmelt, or a rainstorm that lasts a day longer than the weather prognosticator has calculated, may have a profound effect on the catch.

In 2011, the cadre of tributary anglers who filed diary data for Zollweg-Horan caught 55 trout or salmon, a mere 5 reportable fish per participant. Their combined catch consisted of 37 landlocks, 14 rainbow trout, and 4 browns that made or stretched past the legal keeper mark on the tape. At the time, the minimum creel lengths in the tribs were 15 inches for trout and 18 inches for salmon, but the diary program tributary anglers were a conservation-minded lot. They actually creeled just 16 of the legal trout they caught: 8 rainbows, 7 landlocks, and 1 brown trout. The largest fish caught were a 27-inch rainbow, a 24½-inch brown, and a 26-inch land-lock. I suspect most folks would be impressed by those numbers.

Aside from net samplings carried out by DEC biologists and techni-cians, angler diaries are the primary tools that biologists use to monitor the quality of fishing for warm-water species in the Finger Lakes. In 2011, the fishermen who took a few minutes to fill in a few diary-page blank spaces at the end of each trip on Cayuga Lake had a hot time on the water. They reeled in 245 legal northern pike, chain pickerel, and largemouth or smallmouth bass. That total included 117 legal largemouths, including one 20½-inch specimen; 39 legal smallmouths including an 18-incher; 53 keeper-size pike, one of which was 32 inches long; and 36 pickerel, topped by a 23½-inch "chain."

## IF YOU WANT IT, THIS LAKE PROBABLY HAS IT

"Cayuga Lake is a diverse and many-layered fishery, with some fantastic opportunities for anglers of many interests, all year round," said Zollweg-Horan, who seems to have a gift for understatement.

Three-fourths of the diary program participants' open-water trips on the lake, for both cold-water and warm-water species, met the biologist's definition of a "successful" day of fishing. That yardstick is simply the capture of one or more legal fish per outing. Tributary anglers who maintain diaries for the DEC don't do quite as well as some open-water friends, but their recent 40 percent success rate isn't half bad, especially when you take into account the hurdles that must be cleared or circumvented by stream fishermen in quest of spring rainbows or autumn-spawning salmon. Aside from the inevitable early-season issues of crowded water and poor behavior by some inconsiderate anglers, tributary experts must attract strikes from fish, spring and fall, that are so intently focused on the propagation of the species, they scarcely have the time to grab a quick meal. Seasonably cold temperatures don't boost the angler's chances of tying into a silvery rainbow, either.

Before you get the idea that fishing in Finger Lakes tributaries is overwhelmingly difficult, let's all of us take a few deep breaths and relax. I'll discuss effective baits and techniques for spawning rainbows in a separate chapter. Meanwhile, please be reassured by the fact that tributary fishermen have improved their catch rates in many streams over the years. Those diary program anglers who turned in Cayuga Lake data for 2011 caught an average of one legal trout or salmon for every 4.3 hours of fishing. That was the fourth best catch rate in the last 10 years for Cayuga tributary fishermen, but did not come close to the all-time best catch rate for the venue, which was one salmonid every 1.6 hours.

## REMEDIES FOR RAINBOWS

Where catch rates have fallen off lately, stricter regulations and pumped-up stocking programs should have a positive impact on the quality of our sport. The tributaries of Cayuga Lake have had their share of environmental setbacks in recent decades, including a train derailment in 1997 that resulted in a substantial kill of juvenile rainbow trout in the upper and middle reaches of Cayuga Inlet. However, the watershed is in good shape, overall, and fishermen can reasonably anticipate some rewarding spring-season fishing in the near term for rainbows in Fall Creek in the city of Ithaca; in Cayuga Inlet from its mouth upstream to Danby; and in Salmon Creek below the falls at Ludlowville.

To give Cayuga's rainbow trout population a boost in the near term, fisheries managers decided to stock an additional 5,000 yearling rainbows in Cayuga Inlet and Enfield Creek for several years beginning in 2012.

John "Kid" Corbett casts for salmon and trout in Ithaca's Fall Creek, with icy spray all around him.

In the long run, Zollweg-Horan said, she and her colleagues "are working toward a more diverse salmonid fishery, with lake trout being less dominant than they are now, and more brown trout, rainbow trout, and landlocked salmon recruiting to the fishery for both the open-water and tributary anglers.

"These tweaks may take time to be noticeable to fishermen, but that's the direction of our efforts," she added.

Meanwhile, boating anglers will find that Cayuga Lake supports fair numbers of rainbow and brown trout, and provides some of the best lake trout and landlocked salmon action in the world, starting with ice-out in the spring and continuing at least through November. The browns and rainbows run up to 10 pounds or so and can be hooked most readily on conventional trolling rigs, including downriggers, three-way swivel setups, planer boards, and Dipsy Divers. When they're near the surface or hugging the shoreline, both trout species are susceptible to Maine-style streamers and bucktails fished with sinking-tip fly lines or on long, ultralight "noodle" rods. These stratagems will be discussed fully in another chapter.

Lake trout action usually picks up steam starting about April Fools' Day along the west shore between Canoga and Sheldrake, and also around Levanna, which is north of Aurora on the east side of the lake. At this time, lakers averaging about 4 pounds or so will follow alewives or smelt into the shallows at night. Occasionally, they get so close to shore that fishermen in hip boots can get in on the fun, by casting and retrieving spoons (Krocodiles and Little Cleos, for example) or Rapala-type stick-baits in black-and-silver or blue-and-silver patterns. Gravel-bottomed areas are most deserving of attention because that's where the baitfish do most of their spawning. Naturally, permission to fish on private strips of the shoreline must be obtained from the owner. Trespassers make things tougher on the rest of us. With that caveat, after-dark casting is worth a try almost anywhere in the lake during the first several weeks of spring.

## SPRING IS TIME TO SPREAD OUT

Deep-water fishing is very good in the spring, too. The same schools of bait that draw lakers near shore at night retreat into the depths when the sun starts to climb each morning. If you see a bunch of crescents on your sonar screen close to the bottom in 40 to 100 feet of water, you're prob-ably looking at lakers that have alewives or, less likely these days, smelt in view. Downrigging with Sutton 44s, Northern Kings, Michigan Stingers, Evil Eyes, Needlefish, Alpena Diamonds, and similar spoons will pick up some of these fish, and drifting with live or dead mooneyes close to the bottom should work, too.

Summer fishing for lakers in Cayuga Lake is pretty much like it is everywhere else in the chain. Deep trolling with downriggers is the standard approach, and normally it is very effective. However, during the period when the lake stratifies, June through mid- or late September, schools of lake trout will suspend in or just below the thermocline, which will be about 70 feet down in 90 feet of water. As in the spring, the fish are in diligent pursuit of bait, but they will not go far out of their preferred temperature range of 46 to 50 degrees Fahrenheit once the lake strati-fies. Trollers should be looking for areas where sizable schools of bait and favorable temperatures for lake trout are in close proximity.

## STRATEGIES AND TACTICS FOR AUTUMN

In late September and October, Cayuga lakers move into spawning grounds in 60 to 100 feet of water, and lay their eggs on gravel-bottomed points, most in the southwest quadrant of the lake. As individual trout finish their reproductive duties, they often stay near shore for a few days or weeks to fill up their tanks. Anglers who target these fish with spawn sacs presented on slip-sinker rigs have a good chance of hooking a 10-pounder.

Winter fishing for lake trout can also be quite productive, but most of the fish will spend the cold months in mid-lake, off Levanna. Anchoring and fishing with dead alewives or smelt or slowly bottom-bouncing with white jigs should get you a couple of fish, but most Cayuga anglers put their deep-water gear away until spring. If they fish much at all over the winter, they will focus their efforts on shore casting in open water or on taking warm-water species through the ice.

Among Cayuga Lake's most appreciated features are its excellent bank-fishing opportunities. Folks who don't own a boat big enough to safely navigate Cayuga on a gusty day, and don't have the nerve to ask private landowners to grant permission to fish, can always try a couple of public-welcome locations.

The best of these are Taughannock Falls State Park, which wraps around the mouth and lower channel of Taughannock Creek on the west shore of the lake via Route 89, and the AES Cayuga coal-fired electrical power station that is across the lake and a mile or 2 to the north on the Milliken Station Road.

The park is a great place to cast spoons or, better yet, to fish a live shiner or mooneye over a steep drop-off with the aid of a slip bobber. In September and October, it's one of the better spots in the lake, by far, to connect with pre-spawn lake trout or landlocked salmon. The latter stage along the drop-off at the end of Taughannock Creek and then swim upstream to spawn below the impassable waterfall, which is a short walk from the road.

## GET THEM WHILE THEY'RE COLD

At various times, but especially in the early winter, rainbow and brown trout are caught regularly along the edges of the park. Although the park entrance is not normally staffed from October through March, anglers should come prepared to pay a modest daily-use fee, just in case New York State adds new access fees to generate some badly needed revenues for its park system.

Fishermen do not need waders or hip boots to reach the productive water at the mouth of the creek nor that found at the point on the park's south end, but they do need a long-handled net to have a prayer of landing any big fish they hook along the park retaining wall.

Many Taughannock regulars like the park best after dark, and use battery-powered bobbers to catch the attention of cruising fish and improve their odds of noticing a strike in the darkness.

AES Cayuga, however, should be fished with caution, and then only during daylight hours, due to the strong currents created when the plant is operating and discharging warm wastewater through its generators. Anglers who slip and fall or who wade too close to the discharge currents face a very real chance of drowning. When prudence is exercised, brown trout and salmon, as well as the occasional smallmouth bass or northern pike, will bite readily on anything that resembles the baitfish hanging out in the power plant's foaming currents. Spoons, spinners, glittery streamer flies, and live bait all work at various times.

## SOME OVERLOOKED FISHING IN THE PARK SETTING

AES Cayuga is accessible year-round, but shore casters who try their luck in the winter must beware of ice buildup along the path that leads from the parking area to the fishable shore.

One overlooked shore-fishing spot for Cayuga Lake anglers to try is the estuary and boat channel adjacent to Stewart Park, at the southern tip of the lake in Ithaca. It's good in the spring for panfish and rainbow trout, the latter as they hurry through the estuary and on to the DEC-operated fish passageway just upstream. The area in and around the Allan H. Treman Marine Park, on the west side of the channel off Route 89, is very good for carp fishing in spring and summer. Carp are underrated fish that are admired in Europe but disdained as bottom-feeding trash in much of the United States. While I much prefer trout, walleyes, and other traditional game fish, I have done just enough fishing for carp to know that they deserve more respect than they get on this side of the Atlantic.

Carp will take night-crawlers that are lightly hooked and presented to them on a line threaded through a slip sinker, but they bite much better on fragrant doughballs, or "boilies" as carp tournament anglers call them. You can try your own recipes for dough-balls, pick a few tried-and-true flavor combinations on carp-related websites, or buy a supply from one of the major fishing supply catalogs. Of all the Finger Lakes, Cayuga likely has the most carp, and therefore the greatest potential to milk

Mike Pikulinski of Syracuse with a nice largemouth bass from Cayuga Lake.

some dollars from competitive carp angling if it turns out to be the next Big Thing after pro bass fishing loses some of its luster.

The current Big Thing in fishing, of course, won't soon fade from fame. Tournament bass fishing just seems to be more popular with each passing year, and Cayuga Lake is a proving ground for would-be pros from throughout the Northeast. From mid-June into October, the lake is host to a constant parade of bass boats. Virtually every weekend brings at least one and usually several cast-for-cast events to public and private marinas. These contests range from local club fish-offs, to regional events that serve as qualifiers for more lucrative tournaments to be held in the South over the winter, to big-money invitationals sponsored by the Bass Anglers Sportsman Society.

## THE IMPACT OF BASS TOURNAMENTS

Obviously the participants enjoy themselves or they wouldn't keep coming back for more, but whenever a big tournament comes and goes, you can always find a local angler with a grievance to air. Most of the complaints are minor in nature or based on a misunderstanding of what actually takes place during typical tournaments, but one gripe is reasonable. That is, all that commotion can sometimes make it harder for local bass fishermen to get any fish! Aside from the obviously intense fishing pressure aimed at Cayuga Lake during a big tournament, participants cart limits of nice bass in livewells from who knows where to temporary weigh stations set up at state parks and private marinas. Most, though not all, of those fish are put into boats and scattered about the lake at day's end, and recuperate that night far from the places they used to call home.

On the other hand, attending a few tournaments as a spectator (or even competitor) is a great way to learn more about bass, and there is plenty of value to be gleaned from Cayuga. More than the other Finger Lakes, Cayuga is very evenly divided between largemouths and small-mouths, and mixed bags of the two species are common at its tournament weigh-ins. Often, contestants who know the lake well strive to catch a limit of five smallmouths of any size during their first couple of hours on the water. When that goal is achieved, they rev up the outboard and head for the dense weed bed or other cover, which might hide a lunker large-mouth or two. When they find a largemouth of decent proportions, they will put that one in the livewell and simultaneously "cull" or release the lightweight bronzeback. Hopefully, the heaviest largemouth of the day is the "kicker fish" that will enable the wily anglers to land on the tournament leader board.

## WHEN YOU WANT TO GAIN WEIGHT

The sector of Cayuga Like most apt to yield a kicker or two is the north end, from the cove off Farley's Point and the Union Springs boat launch ramp to the railroad bridge that spans the lake between the village of Cayuga and the Cayuga Lake Wildlife Management Area. Its structure, including thick weeds everywhere, hanging tree limbs along the railroad bridge, and the weeds around tiny Frontenac Island, off Union Springs, simply reeks of largemouths. One fine May afternoon long, long ago, my friend Bill Lang of Marcellus, now deceased, joined me in an expedition in search of sunfish and black crappies. We were exploring the sun-warmed rip-rap along the railroad span, and were on our way to filling a bucket with fillets when Bill's rod bent over double. Instead of another fat bluegill, he was fast to a largemouth of considerable girth. Our pocket De-Liar scale pegged that old-timer at 23 inches long and 6½ pounds, and I know Bill never forgot it.

To get to Cayuga Lake from the north, I go west on Route 20 from Skaneateles through Auburn. If I am planning to drive down the east shore, I turn left (south) at Route 90 and take that road to King Ferry. There I can turn right onto Route 34B all the way to Cayuga Heights and on into Ithaca. If my idea is to go to Taughannock Falls State Park or elsewhere on the west side of the lake, I simply continue past that turn onto Route 90, going by the Seneca River and the Montezuma National Wildlife Refuge main entrance, and take my next left onto Route 89. That road goes all the way to Ithaca.

# CHAPTER 5

# Seneca Lake

**LOCATION:** Seneca, Schuyler, Yates, and Ontario Counties
**ELEVATION:** 445 feet
**SURFACE AREA:** 43,343 acres
**SHORELINE:** 75.4 miles
**MEAN DEPTH:** 291 feet
**MAXIMUM DEPTH:** 618 feet
**APPROXIMATE THERMOCLINE DEPTH:** 88 feet

Seneca Lake has been the home of the National Lake Trout Derby since 1964, and the Memorial Day weekend event always attracts enough contestants and spectators to make Geneva-area business owners very, very happy. That's because Seneca lakers are abundant, edible, and often weigh more than 10 pounds when entered in the derby. In this lake, *Salvelinus namaycush* is the top dog, and there is virtually no doubt about it.

And yet, if anyone were to conduct a scientific poll on the subject and take bets on the outcome, I'd wager even money that the most coveted fish that swims in Seneca Lake isn't the lake trout, but something lakers—and most people who fish for lakers—really like to eat.

For what could be finer than to meet you at the diner for a platter of fresh, quick-fried fillets of yellow perch?

I can't recall ever meeting fishermen who grimaced or shook their heads or used any other negative gesture when confronted with an opportunity to wrap their gums around a few fat perch. Perch are simply too tasty to turn down, and most people who eat perch are so satisfied by the experience that they rate them one of the most delectable fish in the world, if not the greatest eating fish of them all.

If that last claim should be challenged in court—as most important issues are, these days, sadly enough—I hereby volunteer to take part in a blind taste test at the time and place of the plaintiff's choosing. I swear that I will keep an open mind and consume all samples of perch and any challenger fish that are not laughed out of the jury chamber before their representative fillets are placed upon a fork.

May the best flesh win, I say!

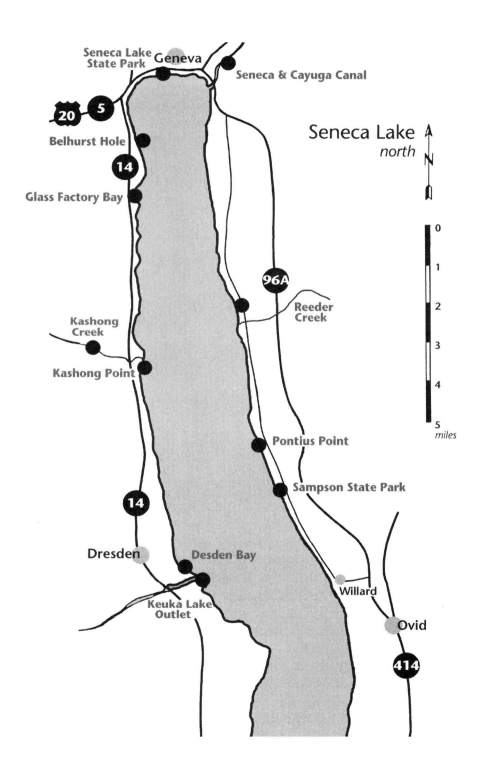

Seneca Lake State Park

Geneva

Seneca & Cayuga Canal

20  5

Belhurst Hole

14

Glass Factory Bay

Seneca Lake
north
N

Kashong Creek

Kashong Point

96A

Reeder Creek

Pontius Point

Sampson State Park

0
1
2
3
4
5
miles

14

Dresden

Desden Bay

Keuka Lake Outlet

Willard

Ovid

414

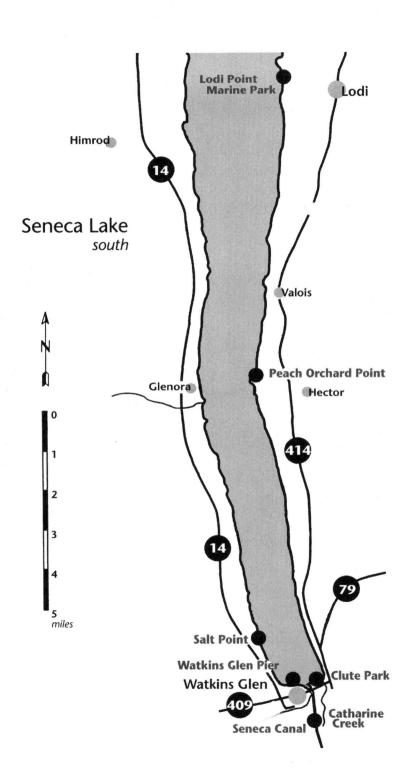

Seneca Lake
*south*

Lodi Point
Marine Park

Lodi

Himrod

14

Valois

Peach Orchard Point

Glenora

Hector

414

14

79

Salt Point

Watkins Glen Pier

Clute Park

Watkins Glen

409

Catharine
Creek

Seneca Canal

N

0
1
2
3
4
5
miles

And when the advocates of yellow perch emerge triumphant from the courtroom, as seems inevitable, I will invite all present to reconvene at Clute Park in Watkins Glen, at the south end of Seneca Lake. In that picturesque setting, we will prepare about four or five perch for each attendee. Don't worry about there being enough to go around, because Seneca Lake quite likely holds bigger perch, and possibly more perch, than any other lake in the United States.

The pier at Watkins Glen is popular with fishermen and tourists alike.

## JUMBO THE ELEPHANT PERCH

How big are Seneca perch? They're so big that the whoppers among them are dubbed "elephant perch," or just "elephants" for short, by resident sportsmen. Fourteen inches isn't long enough to qualify for pachyderm status, and 15 inches is borderline. If you want to make the guys' jaws hit the dock back at the marina, you'll need to have at least a couple of perch that nudge the 16- or 17-inch marks on a yardstick.

The bar for elephants is set so high, for shore fishermen especially, that anglers who work hard to collect a mess of 10- or 12-inch eaters that are just right for filleting as "Poor Man's Lobster" are apt to grumble or whine about all the pesky "grass perch" they have been running into. Some of the old-timers still in the perch game are just plain spoiled, in my opinion.

On one occasion, I watched in horror as a fisherman at the Watkins Glen pier, disgusted by the shortage of what he called "decent perch," tipped his bucket to dump half a dozen barely swimming 11- to 12-inchers he had caught in a full afternoon of fishing. Too much trouble to clean, he barked. Having none to show for my half day at the dock, I didn't bother to remind him that if you keep several "decent" perch on Thursday, then catch several more on Saturday, you're only a couple of fillets shy of a satisfying supper for you and yours.

Ron Boyce of Rochester, who orchestrated a series of "Perch Masters" fishing tournaments a couple of years ago, unhesitatingly picks Seneca and Keuka Lakes as New York's best perch waters, but he opines that Seneca isn't nearly as good as it used to be. In the not-so-distant past, before complaints about greedy commercial fishermen led to the imposition of daily limits for panfish, a skilled angler could easily fill a medium-capacity trash can with perch large enough to fillet, including a couple of genuine elephants.

During more recent seasons, experts have had to work hard to collect a 50-perch limit. Boyce said Seneca has remained the lake of choice for broad-shouldered jacks but does not produce the large numbers of perch it once did. If Boyce wants to bring home a limit of perch to feed visiting friends or relatives these days, he usually heads for Keuka Lake rather than Seneca. Whether this trend of fewer but bigger perch lasts much longer in Seneca Lake or is disrupted by unexpected changes in the lake's ecosystem, only time can tell.

Another view of the Watkins Glen pier.

Two things that set Seneca Lake apart from the rest of the Finger Lakes and most other fishing holes, as well, are its sheer size and depth. Totaling more than 43,000 surface acres, and plunging to a maximum depth of 618 feet, Seneca has ample room to grow big fish. The whole lake has oxygen levels suited to fish survival, and its perch—along with its trout, landlocked salmon, bass, pike, and assorted panfish—have more room to run and hide when they are fleeing hungry predators or just taking an exploratory swim.

## NO ICE CAN BE NICE

Another plus, from the vantage of the fish at least, is that this lake never comes close to freezing over. In extremely cold years, ice thick enough to walk on may form inside the marina at Sampson State Park or in part of Dresden Bay or some other locale that happens to be ideally situated for ice development during a freakish weather pattern, but that's the extent of it. This means, among other things, that anybody who wants to go after a few nice Seneca perch in the winter will have to bring along a boat or locate schools within casting distance of shore.

DEC research in the early 1990s confirmed that perch in Seneca Lake have approximately normal growth rates. They don't morph into elephants because of any secret diet, either.

"The reason they get so big is they live so long," retired Region 8 fisheries boss Carl Widmer once told me. According to his data, Seneca Lake perch grow about 3 inches in their first year of life, another 3 inches in their second year, 2 more inches the third year, and roughly an inch more every year after that. Add the numbers and you will see that a 15- or 16-incher from the Dresden cove or some other Seneca Lake hot spot is about 10 years old.

You can probably guess why so many Seneca perch are graybeards. Given the immensity of their living room, it figures that they are harder to find than your average perch in smaller, shallower lakes at any time of the year, even with the assistance of the most precise sonar fish locators. More important, the complete absence of ice-fishing pressure means a great percentage of the perch going into a Seneca Lake winter will be around to spawn and, by the way, grow another inch or more in the warm months ahead.

## PERCH-FISHING FANATICS

The flip side to that situation, of course, is that the absence of ice encourages a few fanatics to spend hundreds of dollars on heavy-duty winter clothing and thousands more on boats and motors. If you want to be part of Seneca Lake's winter wild bunch, just remember that the rewards are many but calamity is only a well-timed whitecap away. Obey state law and wear an approved life jacket when you're looking for a winter perch mother lode. Make sure your boat has every possible safety feature on board. Watch your rod tip, yes, but keep an eye on the sky, too. Precisely because it is ice-free, Seneca Lake's winter days are punctuated by sudden and powerful gusts and choppy seas. Take no chances, not even for a perch big enough to sprout tusks. You can always try for that one again when the water warms up.

Catching Seneca perch is mainly a matter of finding them, and that hunt is not always easy. However, zeroing in on a school of big ones is accomplished most readily during the March–April spawning run.

The easiest way to get in on the action is to scan the water for anchored or drifting boats. They probably won't be more than a couple of hundred yards offshore, in depths of 10 to 20 feet, because that's where most perch stage at spawning time. I wouldn't recommend squeezing your way into the middle of a perch-fishing flotilla. Instead, try to pick a few fish off the edges, meanwhile noting the spots where the bite seems to be most consistent. The next time you fish the area, try to beat the other guys to that spot.

Another way to find areas that are currently producing perch is to visit one of the lakeside bait-and-tackle shops and ask for some tips. Try Roy's Marina (also known as "Japp's") in Dresden, on the west side of the lake, (315) 789-3094. It's about 8 miles south of Geneva on Route 14. Another good source of Seneca Lake fishing information is Seneca Marine Bait & Tackle, on Route 414 in Watkins Glen. The phone number there is (607) 535-6690.

## HOW TO JOIN THE GANG

Some spots on the lake are proven perch producers and can be fished with some confidence year after year during the spring egg laying. These include, following a map clockwise from the north end, Glass Factory Bay in Geneva, especially around the hotel pier; and Pontius Point, which is off East Lake Road about 2 miles north of Sampson State Park. Also good in March and April are the Watkins Glen pier area and the water off Clute Park at the south end of the lake, the aforementioned Dresden Bay; and Kashong Point, about 4 miles south of Geneva off Route 14.

No matter where you fish for Seneca Lake's yellow perch, load up on $\frac{1}{32}$- to $\frac{1}{4}$-ounce jigs, as well as your favorite perch minnows. When local stores have them in stock, don't forget to buy several dozen cranefly larvae, which are commonly called "oakleaf grubs" in the Finger Lakes. These tough-skinned creatures are much loved by perch and other panfish, as well. The amazing thing about them is their appeal to fish even when they have virtually been chewed to shreds. You can often catch three or four perch on a single grub, and I think it's safe to say these are the "secret baits" of veteran Seneca Lake perch fishermen—although the secret has been out for many years.

Perch can be found at or near the spots just listed and in many other locations in Seneca Lake in spring, fall, and winter, but their schools seem to disperse in the summer and become difficult to catch in any numbers from about the Fourth of July until late September.

Lake trout aren't so seasonal. They eat at every opportunity and thrive all year in Seneca, which has steep contours, cold water temperatures, and high dissolved oxygen levels throughout. Most important, thanks to their strong numbers and average size, they are at the top of the food chain in a lake that also harbors numerous rainbow and brown trout, land-locked salmon, bass, and northern pike. Anglers fish for them diligently, despite their reputation for being a little on the sluggish side when they're connected to a fishhook. That reputation is unwarranted, in my experience. Whether a lake trout fights hard or not depends on how deep it is swimming when it encounters a lure, how it is fought by the angler at the opposite end of the connection, water temperatures, and other factors.

## LAKE TROUT ARE THE BREAD AND BUTTER OF SENECA

I'll just leave it to you to form their own opinions about the attributes of lake trout—or any other fish, for that matter.

"Lake trout are still the bread and butter fish for most Seneca Lake anglers," said Brad Hammers, the Region 8 biologist who oversees the management of the lake. "Angler-diary program results show that typically 85 percent or more of the trout caught in Seneca are lakers."

Lake trout have always been popular among Seneca Lake anglers but the possibility of hooking one that's worth $5,000 makes them even more coveted.

A group of Geneva-area organizers has staged the National Lake Trout Derby over the Memorial Day weekend since 1964. In the 1990s, rules were changed to award the five-grand first-place money to the captor of the tourney's biggest salmonid—whether lake, brown, or rainbow trout, or landlocked salmon—but lakers took the big money in all but 4 of the first 48 derbies.

The derby draws an average of about 1,500 contestants annually, according to event coordinator Colin Morehouse of Geneva, and the winning fish is almost always bigger than 10 pounds. The record holder was caught in 1969 by Lyle Hardgrave of Geneva. It weighed 17 pounds, 13 ounces and was indeed a lake trout.

With catches of double-digit lakers a daily possibility for anglers who are skilled, lucky, or both, why shouldn't lake trout be the fish of dreams in Seneca Lake?

Lake trout succumb to a diverse array of lures and tactics in Seneca, from vertical jigging and dead-bait fishing in the winter to trolling in the thermocline with downriggers or Seth Green rigs in the summer and bait flipping from anchored boats or shore during the autumn spawning session.

I well remember my introduction to Seneca Lake's autumn fishing. It was about 20 years ago, before the public-access fishing pier in Glass Factory Bay was rebuilt. It was early November, and the old pier was crowded with a dozen or so anglers. All were trying for lake trout, which were circling the shallows within easy casting distance of the crumbling pier. Everyone there except for me fished with spawn sacs, which were lobbed into the 5-feet-deep water and then left in place to be noticed by passing fish.

## EGGS ARE NOT THE ONLY LAKER TAKERS

All I had was a medium-action spinning outfit, and a small assortment of ultralight lures that I normally used for brown and brook trout in Syracuse-area streams. I was very happy to catch three nice lakers that afternoon, two on copper-finish Phoebes and one on a Dardevle red-and-white spoon. My trio of trout weighed 3 to 5 pounds, which the other pier fishers said was just about average for the lakeshore.

The new pier doesn't attract lake trout as regularly as the old one did, but it and the rest of Glass Factory Bay remain good places to look for lakers on a fall feeding spree. If you don't mind spectators, the scenic Watkins Glen municipal pier and the adjacent marina and breakwall attract spawning lakers, too. Sampson State Park, located off Route 96A about 7 miles south of Geneva, is a third spot that is likely to have some near-shore lake trout activity in the autumn. At Sampson, where the lake bottom consists mainly of cobble and long casts are the rule, I'd recommend the use of a slip-sinker rig or a three-way swivel, to minimize tackle loss and keep your bait in the water as much as possible. Alternatively, if you are positive about the depth you are fishing, you might try a slip-bobber setup as a means of keeping your bait just above that hook-eating cobble.

Another excellent place to look for pre-spawn, spawning, and post-spawn lake trout is the water around Peach Orchard Point, where the DEC used to collect most of the ripe hen lakers needed by state hatcheries, before Cayuga Lake got the egg supply assignment. Peach Orchard Point is in Hector, about 6 miles from Watkins Glen, off Route 414. One more spot worth trying in the fall is Lodi Point State Marine Park, about 14 miles south of Geneva on Route 414. Some locals do quite well there by casting just after dark or just prior to daybreak.

As the modest fishing story I recounted above suggests, spawn sacs are widely used for Seneca lakers, but spinners and spoons will also produce nice fish. So will the same old, reliable stickbaits that every knowledgeable Finger Lakes trolling captain keeps in a safe place. There are many reasons why Rapala and their competitors sell millions of their lures annually, and their appeal to lake trout is one of them. As long as you can hurl them far enough into Seneca Lake's notorious west winds, they'll catch you some fish.

## NO ICE, BUT PLENTY OF PLACES TO FISH

Over the winter, fishing pressure in Seneca Lake is quite limited, as many warm-weather regulars with a weak spot for hard-water sport temporarily shift their weekend loyalties to lakes that freeze over. Yet you can find some very productive fishing, not only for perch but for game fish, as well.

Anglers with seaworthy, space-heater-equipped vessels can play with 4- to 10-pound lake trout all winter long by trolling in the famous Bellhurst Hole, which is located in mid-lake off the Bellhurst Castle resort in Geneva. This narrow trench is a cinch to find if you have a working sonar unit. In the hole, the lake depth quickly drops from 40 to 130 feet. It is a major wintering area for lake trout, as well as alewives. That concentration of prey and predator guarantees good fishing, albeit in very cold weather, throughout the winter months. Deep-water jigging and dead-bait fishing are both efficient at this time. White hair jigs with or without plastic curly tails affixed to the hook bend are dependable, but these lures must stay close to the bottom to draw strikes consistently. Dead alewives, also known as sawbellies in this part of the Finger Lakes region, should be jigged along the bottom or fished on floating jigheads about 2 feet from a bell- or egg-shaped sinker.

Once spring has sprung, which is right around the first week of April, Seneca Lake trout activity heats up quickly, and lake trout become very catchable off points and creeks with substantial runoff plumes. A not-so-secret example of the latter lake trout attractor is the small creek just north of Sampson State Park, which used to be a navy training base. It's referred to as "Officers Club Creek" by local anglers and it holds lake trout within casting distance of shore from April into June, or until the lake begins to turn over and near-land water temperatures rise into the mid-50s. Incidentally, the Sampson breakwalls also provide excellent fishing for spring lake trout.

## SPRING FLING AT THE BREAKWALL

April and May usually see anglers lined up around the Watkins Glen pier and other structure at the south end of the lake. They are in search of lake trout, primarily—but the fishing for brown trout and landlocked salmon can be even better at this time.

Provided that the breakwall is not chained off for safety reasons, as it may be on occasion, anglers who gingerly make their way along the rip-rap have a good shot at a 5-pound salmon or a 10-pound trout. The methodology couldn't be much less complicated. Simply heave a Little Cleo or Krocodile as far out in the lake as your strength, skill, and equipment will allow. Retrieve at a fast but staccato pace for best results. If the breakwall is closed and the pier itself doesn't look promising when you visit, spend an hour or two at nearby Clute Park. There you may hook lake trout or perhaps a big, hungry rainbow, fresh from spawning in world-famous Catharine Creek.

The "Seneca Canal," immediately east of the park, essentially is the dredged mouth of the creek, which attracts between 500 and 1,000 anglers on April 1, the first day of New York's general trout season. After the first weekend of the season, the crowds nearly vanish, and the few patient or stubborn anglers who drop by in the next several weeks have the creek and the canal virtually to themselves. The rainbow fishing is surprisingly good in late April, and some large fish are still around in mid-May.

Other Seneca Lake tributaries that attract spawning 'bows include Keuka Lake Outlet, which enters the lake at Dresden; Kashong Creek on the west shore; and Reeder Creek on the east side of the lake. These, and other small streams with rainbow runs, are privately owned for the most part, and anglers should ask for permission before trespassing on any water not open to public fishing.

More information on the rainbow run is included in a separate chapter. When you read it, be aware that the same race of rainbows that makes tributary fishing so thrilling can be caught from shore in the fall and also in or just above the lake's thermocline—about 80 feet down in mid-lake—all summer long.

## COLD SEASON IS THE HARBINGER OF BIG SALMON

The hottest fishing in Seneca Lake since the new century made its debut has come courtesy of the landlocked salmon that school up in the south end of the lake from late autumn through the following April or May. In the winter of 2011–12, when the salmon phenomenon appeared to peak, it was not unusual for a pair of fishermen trolling with small spoons or streamer flies to be rewarded with 40 or 50 hookups in a single morning or afternoon. The fishing was best in the area off Salt Point, which is approximately 1 mile up the west shore, via Route 14, from Watkins Glen. Most of the salmon were shorter than the 18-inch minimum creel length, but there were enough 20- to 26-inch beauties to excite anyone seeking a wall mount.

As great as the cold-water angling happens to be in Seneca Lake, there are many anglers who fish it strictly for warm-water species. Permit me to sum up the traveling fisherman's prospects for Seneca Lake's panfish (aside from perch, about which see above), northern pike, and bass, in that order.

Regarding panfish, whenever folks ask me where they can get a few truly large pumpkinseed sunfish or bluegills, my first thought is of a sunnie I caught in the weeds off Dresden perhaps 15 years ago. It was the size of a pie plate, not counting its tail. I should have weighed it because it must have been a pound and a half, but at the time I didn't know I was holding the largest sunfish of my fishing career.

You can catch sunfish that big at the marina in the state park in Geneva, or along the park shoreline, too, if you get there in early April. When they're that big, they like small minnows, as well as their traditional snack food, an inch-long piece of a nightcrawler. Put either tidbit on a small jig for best results.

If bullheads are your personal favorite breakfast fish, pick out a good spot on the bank of the south-end canal or explore the water offshore from the mouth of Kashong Creek in mid-April. Keuka Outlet is good, too, and fishing with the usual nightcrawler rig in the tributary's lowermost reaches gives you an outside chance to top off your stringer of bullheads with a couple of late-running rainbows.

Bass fishing is good in Seneca Lake even though the habitat is limited by the extreme depth and limited weed beds. The lake's littoral zone (or shallow-water habitat) amounts to just 13 percent of its surface acreage, according to a 1980 DEC report. Although smallmouth bass are found on or near all of the larger points and most shoals and humps in less than 50 feet of water, largemouths are primarily weed-oriented because of their tendency to ambush their dinner. Because weed cover is most widespread at the north end and also at Dresden Bay, that's where most serious bass fishermen begin their quest for a five-fish limit.

On average, Seneca largemouths weigh about 1 to 2 pounds, but the lake holds enough 3- and 4-pounders to keep things interesting during local tournaments. Smallmouths of 1½ to 3 pounds are the norm. Bass of this size are just right for eating, and keeping a couple now and then won't damage the resource. If you intend to keep any bass during a summer outing, consider buying a couple dozen softshell crayfish, also known as butter crabs. They are a fantastic bait, not only for bass but for yellow perch as well. Fishing one or two softshells on one rod and a small Senko or other favorite soft plastic lure is a productive way to explore an unfamiliar spot on those frustrating days when your old haunts seem to be running out of bass.

Captain Jim Morgan at the helm as he guides on Seneca Lake.

## PIKE DESERVE RESPECT, TOO

On Seneca Lake—and most others with good bass populations—smallmouths become hard to catch between mid-July and Labor Day. One way to improve your catch in the dog days is to set your fishing-day alarm clock ahead. Showing up early, perhaps half an hour before sunrise, will give you first crack at the shallows and mid-depths, where the smallmouths are hanging out and looking for a quick bite before the day's heaviest boat traffic churns the water to a froth. Cast and retrieve small but highly visible crankbaits at a quick, herky-jerky pace. You should have some nice fish on before the sun warms the water.

The Rodney Dangerfield of Seneca Lake's cast of characters is the northern pike, which is an overlooked but impressive component of the fishery. Brad Hammers, the DEC biologist entrusted with Seneca's well-being, described the pike fishing as "high quality," and it truly is. Twenty-pound northerns have been caught in the lake, although specimens of 4 to 8 pounds are the norm and anything heavier than 10 pounds would have to be considered prime taxidermy material.

Some of the changes wrought in the Finger Lakes and elsewhere by invasive plant and animal species have turned out to be good deals for pike. For example, the zebra and quagga mussels that have advanced rapidly through most of the eastern United States in the last 20 years or so have eaten uncountable amounts of plankton and other tiny organisms. As a result, the water in mussel-occupied lakes is much clearer than it used to be. The greater clarity means sunlight penetrates deeper in the water column than it used to, and the extra sun leads to heavier weed growth and expanding habitat for pike and other denizens of the underwater jungle.

You can take advantage of all this by fishing for Seneca northerns along weed edges for most of the open season. Focus on the shallow side of the weeds when pike season opens in early May for a couple of weeks, then work the deep weed lines through the summer and all the way into late autumn. From Christmas until the season closes on March 15, fish shore structures, such as the empty boat docks in the marinas at Watkins Glen and Sampson State Park, with minnow-and-bobber rigs, spoons, or stickbaits with lots of built-in wobble action. Color-wise, fire tiger is hard to beat.

One last tip for pike fishermen: If you are targeting marinas and see anglers catching plenty of perch or other panfish, you can be pretty sure there aren't many pike in the neighborhood. But if the panfish action suddenly stalls, stare into the water with your polarized-lens sunglasses and look hard for the lean, tubular forms hiding under the docks and moored boats. Show those lurking pike something that looks good to eat and hang on to your rod.

Seneca Lake stretches south from US Routes 5 and 20 in Geneva. Its south end is in the Schuyler County village of Watkins Glen. You can get from Geneva to the Glen, or vice versa, by following Routes 96A and 414 on the east side of the lake or taking Route 14 along the west shore.

## NATIONAL LAKE TROUT DERBY

One of the longest-running sponsored fishing contests in the eastern United States is the National Lake Trout Derby, which has been held on Seneca Lake in Geneva, New York, every Memorial Day weekend since 1964.

The three-day event has drawn as many as 2,815 entries, but in recent years an average of about 1,500 fishermen have participated. Aside from the thrills that come with catching some very nice trout, the chief incentive for entrants is the grand prize of $5,000 in cash. It goes to the angler who reels in the contest's heaviest salmonid—which may be a lake, rainbow, or brown trout, or even a landlocked Atlantic salmon.

Non-lakers have been eligible for the grand prize since the 1990s, but to date 44 of 48 big winners of the event have been lake trout. Brown trout have won the top prize four times.

The all-time largest grand prize winner was a 17-pound, 13-ounce beauty caught by Lyle Hardgrave of Geneva in 1969.

Far from a small-town, parochial contest, the annual derby has had entries from 26 states and provinces. It is organized by an eclectic group of businesses, clubs, and community organizations under the promotional umbrella of Finger Lakes Sports-O-Rama, Inc., which divides and distributes any proceeds that remain after the fishing winners have received their share.

For entrance requirements and other information about the derby, contact Sports-O-Rama at P.O. Box 586, Geneva, NY 14456; or visit the derby website, www.laketroutderby.org.

# CHAPTER 6

# Keuka Lake

**LOCATION:** Northeast Steuben and Southern Yates Counties
**ELEVATION:** 715 feet
**SURFACE AREA:** 11,370 acres
**SHORELINE:** 58.4 miles
**MEAN DEPTH:** 101 feet
**MAXIMUM DEPTH:** 186 feet
**APPROXIMATE THERMOCLINE DEPTH:** 33 feet

Any kid who grew up in New York and had to memorize the bodies of water in the Finger Lakes chain can remember his earth science or geography teacher rummaging through a desk drawer and pulling out a tuning fork with the obligatory "Ta-da!"

"You know this is a tuning fork, right? Now what's the name of the lake that looks like a tuning fork when viewed from an airplane flying overhead?" the teacher would ask.

And inevitably, the classmate who waved her hand most frantically would be called upon to give the answer.

"It's *Cayuga* Lake," the excited student would declare.

"*Wrong*," the teacher would answer back, with an audible groan and a glance at the wall clock. "It's *Keuka*, with a *K*, not *Cayuga* with a *C*." Then the whole class would have to do the litany of lakes all over again, most likely in alphabetical order.

"*Canadice*," we kids would proclaim. "*C-A-N-A-D-I-C-E*." (If anybody in your family ever played backgammon, "Can-of-dice" was a snap.)

## THE TUNING FORK LAKE REVEALED

Keuka Lake, the one that's spelled with a *K* up front and shaped like a tuning fork, may not be the easiest Finger Lake to remember, but it surely is among the hardest ones to forget. It is gorgeous to look at and a pleasure to fish. Most of the people who frequently put their boats on Keuka's shimmering surface develop a proprietary interest in it and truly enjoy showing the lake off to friends who haven't been acquainted with

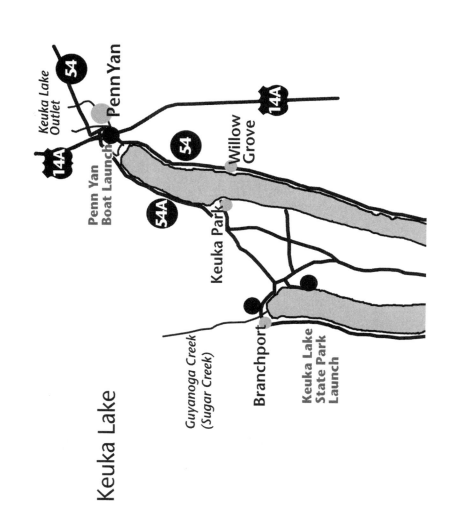

Keuka Lake

Keuka Lake Outlet

Penn Yan

Penn Yan Boat Launch

54

14A

14A

54

Willow Grove

54A

Keuka Park

Guyanoga Creek (Sugar Creek)

Branchport

Keuka Lake State Park Launch

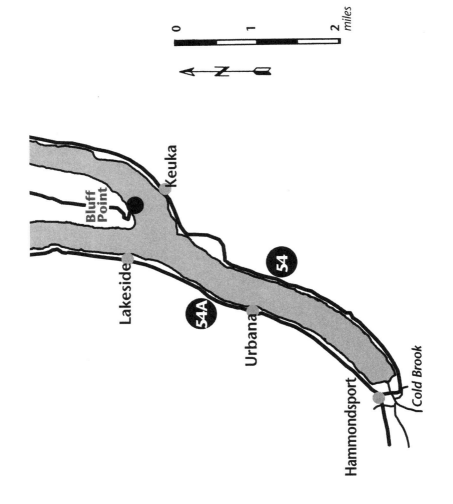

Bluff
Point

Keuka

Lakeside

54A

Urbana

54

Hammondsport

Cold Brook

0

1

2
*miles*

N

Ron Boyce with a nice Keuka Lake chain pickerel.

it as yet. Ron Boyce is one of those proud folks. When the Rochester resident set us afloat at the Keuka Lake State Park marina, he waited quietly for five minutes while we drank in the scenery.

"Beautiful, isn't it?" he asked, and I smiled and nodded vigorously rather than attempt to be heard over the chugging outboard motor and the 2-foot waves slapping against the launching ramp's side walls.

And then we were off, and heading south from the park near Branchport on a hunt for jumbo perch and smallmouth bass. Big perch and even bigger bass, Boyce explained, if things worked according to plan.

This was our first time fishing together, and it came to be after several years of phone tag, emails, and postponements. Things happened when one of you had a teenage athlete at home and the other was taking care of the grandkids and working feverishly on a new book. It's just how the world works, that's all. So when this half-day event we'd been talking about forever finally fell into place there were no regrets, only smiles and handshakes and anticipation of catching some nice fish.

I bet Brad Hammers would have enjoyed the ride and the fishing, too. We'd have to keep him in mind for the encore. He's the DEC Region 8 biologist who gave me the stack of pre-trip briefing papers that got me so pumped up about the lake.

Keuka (with a *K*, remember?), Hammers said during an email interview, "is a deep and steep-sided lake with a drainage basin encompassing 187 square miles."

## LOOKS CAN FOOL YOU
The lake has two high-quality tributaries—Cold Brook (also known as Keuka Lake Outlet) at its south end in Hammondsport and Guyanoga (or

Sugar) Creek at the tip of the northwest arm, in Branchport. In the past, both of those streams have had very fishable runs of spawning rainbow trout in the spring and some very large brown trout in the fall, but in recent years anglers have complained about poor catches. Hammers and his colleagues hope to reverse that trend as tighter regulations and revamped stocking plans are implemented in Region 8 tributaries.

Meanwhile, Keuka Lake itself has a thriving population of naturally reproducing lake trout and a modest, hatchery-supported landlocked salmon fishery to keep cold-water anglers happy. It also offers fishermen great opportunities to stock their freezers with perch and other panfish, and is also home to largemouth bass, chain pickerel, and some of the biggest bronzebacks in the Empire State.

Size apparently makes a difference to Keuka Lake anglers, as 40 percent of all angler-hours spent on the lake are focused on bass, and, according to both Hammers and Boyce, the bulk of that effort is aimed at sizable smallmouths.

Before we dig deeper into Keuka bass, however, you might wish to hear more of what the DEC has to say about the lake's cold-water species.

"The self-sustaining lake trout population appears to be supporting an excellent fishery for lake trout anglers," Hammers told me.

Angler-diary program participants reported that their combined catch rate for salmonids peaked at 0.83 per hour in 2004. That's the same as reeling in an average of one legal-size trout or salmon every 1.2 hours. Since then, Keuka log keepers have had three years with average catch rates of 1.3 hours between fish and two more with 1.7 hours between them. That strikes me as being good fishing on a consistent basis—which is pretty much what most anglers desire from their sport.

The trout fishing in the lake might be getting a bit monotonous, however, since lakers now account for approximately 90 percent of the total salmonid catch. Keuka's rainbow and brown trout used to be bigger slices of the pie than that. Rainbows, especially, have been part of Keuka's cold-water picture since 1897, when, according to DEC records, approximately 30,000 rainbow trout fingerlings from California were stocked in Cold Brook by personnel from the Rome State Fish Hatchery. Progeny from that stocking apparently reproduced successfully, and often enough thereafter to establish a Keuka Lake strain of wholly "wild" rainbows. The rainbow fishing in Keuka was very good for decades, but since the mid-1990s, angler complaints about poor catch rates have become increasingly common. In 2003 and again in 2007, diary program participants did not creel even one rainbow. They did, however, manage to reel in 731 lake trout for the frying pan in 2003, and Keuka angler logbooks listed 443 lakers that were kept in 2007.

## WHAT ARE WE MISSING?

Clearly something was out of whack, and Hammers and other DEC Region 8 staff suspected it had to do with poor recruitment. In fisheries management parlance, *recruitment* is a term for the passage of fish into adulthood, as in "recruitment of fish from the 1992 hatch of walleyes in Big Lake appears to have been very good."

When Hammers and crew did an electrofishing survey in Cold Brook in August 2011, they estimated the average density of young-of-the-year rainbows in the stream at 3,077 per acre. That was the 11th lowest YOY density out of 14 samplings ever conducted in Cold Brook, Hammers reported.

Yearling rainbows were also relatively scarce in the 2011 study. DEC workers turned up an estimated average of 313 per acre. That's about one-third the average yearling population density observed in Cold Brook over the years.

One positive number that stood out in the 2011 research was what Hammers described as "very high" yearling densities (greater than 10,000 per acre) recorded in the upper reaches of the brook.

All in all, however, the electrofishing data appeared to lend credence to angler complaints about dwindling numbers of rainbows in the lake and its major tributary, as well. Since similar concerns had been voiced by fishermen about other regional fisheries, including Hemlock Lake, the DEC held open discussions and formal meetings about proposed means of dealing with the problem. These gatherings led to the state agencies' decision to reduce creel limits and also to stock trout in some fisheries that had been wild-trout waters in the past.

## TIGHTER CREEL LIMITS SHOULD HELP

The rules changes include a reduction in the number of rainbows that anglers may creel when fishing the Region 8 Finger Lakes populated by trout (Seneca, Keuka, Canandaigua, Hemlock, and Canadice ) and their tributaries. Previously, anglers fishing the affected lakes had been allowed any combination of five trout or salmon, except that no more than three lakers or three landlocks were permitted. Now the lake limit remains at five trout or salmon in combination, but the creeled quintet can't include more than one rainbow trout or three landlocks. The other change is that a person fishing in the affected lakes may now keep a five-fish limit made up entirely of lake trout, if desired. Tributaries of the Region 8 Finger Lakes, meanwhile, now have a three-trout-and-salmon limit that includes no more than a single rainbow per day.

Creeling some of those "extra" lake trout and removing them from the scene (and to a freezer) would be a pleasure for most Keuka Lake anglers, whether they favor more rainbows, browns, and salmon or not. By most accounts, catching lakers in Keuka is challenging at some times but almost easy on other occasions. The forage base seems solid, if not overabundant. Alewives have larded Keuka fish for more than a century, while the lake's once-abundant rainbow smelt "have almost totally collapsed," according to Hammers's assessment of data from netting expeditions. The point is, lures that are alewife-size, 3 to 7 inches, and sort of round in shape work very well in Keuka Lake.

Early action for lakers begins at about the same time remnant rainbow runs are trickling through Cold Brook and Sugar Creek: early April. The fish are mostly on or near bottom at that time, with major concentrations of lakers at the south end and also in the water just off Keuka Lake State Park, where Boyce and I launched. The usual downrigging tactics produce plenty of trout at these locations, but many old-timers will attest that fishing after dark, using live bait and an intense lantern beam to lure schools of alewives to your boat, is even better.

After pigging out on alewives for a few weeks, most of the lakers will migrate toward Bluff Point, the area where the two "prongs" of the tuning fork come together.

From mid-June, when the Keuka thermocline is well established, until local lakers start spawning (usually about November 1), most hookups will happen in water that registers between 45 and 55 degrees. You are apt to find such temperatures 40 to 70 feet down. After spawning, look for schools to be hugging bottom, and go after them with dead alewives or use the various permutations of white jigs that have become standard-issue togue takers throughout the Finger Lakes.

## REINFORCEMENTS ARE ON THE WAY

Although Keuka Lake has been known for its totally "wild" rainbow fishing, a new trout-stocking project means wild fish will have to make room at the chow line in the near future. Already, state hatcheries supplied about 4,000 rainbow fingerlings in 2010 and 5,000 more in 2011; and three more stockings are expected to take place in the next few years. All of these rainbow releases will be carried out at locations in Cold Brook, rather than in Keuka Lake itself.

Anglers, whether diary keepers or not, have been asked to help the state monitor its trout-stocking experiment by dutifully notifying their DEC regional fisheries office whenever they capture a fin-clipped trout in the lake or one of its tributaries.

Along with rainbows, brown trout and landlocked salmon seem to have struggled in Keuka in recent fishing seasons, and state fisheries mavens are trying to trigger a turnaround with those species, too. Brown trout were extremely hard to find in 2011—only five were reported caught in the lake by angler-diary program participants. Landlocks were few and far between, too. Only three salmon—averaging 21 inches in length—were creeled by diary keepers.

Because state hatcheries can raise only limited numbers of trout and salmon for distribution in New York lakes and streams, DEC biologists are reluctant to stock fish that are more likely to be eaten by predators than caught by anglers. If research in Keuka Lake shows lake trout are waxing fat by eating stockers as fast as they are dropped off the hatchery truck, somebody in Albany with a sharp pencil will decide it's time to cut losses by diverting the next scheduled delivery to another fishing hole.

## TRIBUTARY BROWNS CAN SAVE YOUR DAY

With all the controversy about maintaining the Cold Brook rainbow run, some fishermen might lose track of the other fish that live in that beautiful little stream. As state electrofishers wade up the brook on their annual, pre-trout-season excursion, dozens of anglers tag along. I was among the spectators at one such survey, perhaps in 2002 or 2003. Unfortunately I neglected to make an entry about it in my own angler diary, so I'm not sure of the year, but I do remember how the state workers kept turning up stream-bred brown trout.

As I recall, the typical trout collected that morning at Hammondsport was a brown of 12 to 14 inches, too small for an angler to creel. The minimum keeper size for trout in western Finger Lakes tributaries was 15 inches, and we did see a couple that stretched out to 16 or 17 inches. These are fish that should be treated with kid gloves, since few can legally be creeled. You don't want to release a dying brown trout if you can help it, do you? I'd recommend pinching down the barbs on any hook you use at Cold Brook, to avoid injury to the small ones.

As for rainbows, I don't think we saw more than three or four lake-run fish that day. The biggest rainbow captured during the survey might have weighed 3 pounds, and that's with two full skeins of her own developing eggs in her bulging belly. Where did all the other rainbows go?

Hammers said Cold Brook has had its share of problems with beaver colonization, too, and suggests that this might be a factor in the lower-than-desirable recruitment. If so, his colleagues across the state might have some no-quarter-given advice to keep the "cold" in Cold Brook.

Watching fish thrash at the surface when the electrofisher's wand sent a numbing current through the icy water made me think of the gigantic brown trout that reputedly were caught in this very same brook in the 1960s and '70s. They weighed 10, 15, even 20 pounds or better, as I recall, and they won monthly or annual prizes in the since-defunct Genesee Fishing Contest. A couple of them were even recognized as state record setters, until a string of Lake Ontario browns shoved their Finger Lakes cousins out of contention for that crown for decades to come and maybe forever. Nowadays, DEC officials wink knowingly and suggest that most, if not all, of the monster browns linked to Hemlock Lake and Cold Brook were probably brood stock "escapees" from the state's Bath Fish Hatchery, which perches alongside the brook just a few miles above Hammondsport.

I hope these tales of hatchery happenings were carved from a big wedge of baloney, and I'd also like to think there still are a few waters in New York where a guy in hip boots has even a one-in-a-million chance to catch a 20-pound trout.

## WARM- AND COOL-WATER SPECIES

But that's enough about Keuka Lake's salmonids. Its pickerel, smallmouth bass, and perch could do with some compliments, too.

When we made our first stop after a quick sprint down the lake from the state park marina, Ron Boyce gave me a choice. Did I want to work on a mess of perch with some ultralight tackle, or would I rather toss some heavy jigs as far as I could and then bounce them back through an underwater neighborhood populated by some humongous smallmouth bass? Seeing that his heart was set on the latter, I gladly reached for the perch rod.

It was early November, one of my favorite times of the year, and I would have enjoyed myself even if we didn't catch anything. We caught plenty, as it turned out, and the fact that we had to work for them just made our three-hour outing that much sweeter. The tally, most of it recorded in 15- to 20-foot depths in the Branchport arm of the lake, included about two dozen perch in the 9½- to 12½-inch range, plus a dandy pickerel and a 2-pound smallmouth. Then just as we were thinking it was getting a little late, a fish to remember joined in on the fun.

Ron Boyce with a Keuka Lake smallmouth.

"Now, that's what I was expecting," said Boyce as he set the hook, hard; and the fish pulled back, harder. It came out of the water, nose-dived back into it, and then began to trace stubborn circles somewhere down below. Boyce's rod had some backbone to it, and the fight was over in three or four minutes. But we sure got our money's worth.

"That has to be a 5-pounder," I said between shots with my digital camera. The smallmouth had to be all of 20 inches, too.

"Pretty close, anyway," said Boyce. "Maybe a little over 4½. I hoped we might get into a few like this one but I guess that's how it goes."

Judging by the grins in the photos, I don't think the day disappointed him much at all. Me, neither. I cleaned and ate most of the perch that evening, and frankly I'm at a loss to find the right words. Plain old "delicious" will have to do, I guess.

Boyce, a regular competitor in regional bass tournaments as well as the Perch Masters events he pioneered, believes Keuka Lake now offers the best combination of perch and smallmouth action to be found anywhere in the Finger Lakes. I am stingy with hyperbole because its use invariably triggers a frustrating argument. Selecting the "best" of anything is ultimately a matter of opinion, which is why a veteran newspaper editor I know routinely excises the word whenever he finds it in a story, and replaces it with "better." I'm not sure Keuka is the best of the Finger Lakes for catching heavy smallmouths or lots of perch, but anyone who hesitates to exaggerate about their favorite fishing spot has insecurity issues. The "best" remedy for such an ailment, and many others, too, is to go fishing as early and as often as you can.

Keuka Lake is about a half-hour drive from Geneva, which straddles US Routes 5 and 20 at the north end of Seneca Lake. To find Keuka, turn south onto Routes 14A and 245 just west of the Geneva city limits. When 14A and 245 go their separate ways, follow 14A to Penn Yan, at the north end of Keuka. From there, follow signs to Route 54A, which takes you to Branchport and the west shore of the lake; or take Route 54 along the east shore to Hammondsport and Cold Brook.

Besides the state park launch that this chapter described, anglers can put in at the Guyanoga Creek site; at the Route 54A bridge at Branchport, which is a gravel ramp launch with limited parking; or at the village of Penn Yan's launch, which has a hard ramp surface and parking for up to 120 cars with trailers.

# CHAPTER 7

# Canandaigua Lake

**LOCATION:** Ontario and Yates Counties
**ELEVATION:** 688 feet
**SURFACE AREA:** 10,558 acres
**SHORELINE:** 35.9 miles
**MEAN DEPTH:** 129 feet
**MAXIMUM DEPTH:** 278 feet
**APPROXIMATE THERMOCLINE DEPTH:** 49 feet

Every year in late March, a few days before the April 1 start of the state trout season, the Department of Environmental Conservation's fisheries management crew drives south from the Region 8 office at Avon and heads into the heart of New York's wine country.

At around 9 in the morning, the gang will come down the long straightaway on Route 245 and pull up near the bridge that spans Naples Creek. Come rain or shine, at least 200 or 300 people will be waiting when the dark green pickups and sport-utility vehicles with the DEC "air, land and water" insignia finally come to a halt.

The crowd, buoyed by the presence of at least one local television camera crew, surges forward and surrounds the newly arrived state workers before they can shuck their shoes and pull on their chest waders. You really can feel the excitement. Some of the folks in the audience are so anxious to begin the morning's festivities that a first-time spectator might reasonably wonder if the crowd is on the verge of becoming a mob.

But the worrywarts soon relax, for most of the onlookers are fishermen playing hooky from work or junior-high-school students on a field trip. This is the annual field survey of Naples Creek, the major spawning ground for Canandaigua Lake's rainbow trout. If the DEC's experts have timed things correctly—and they almost always do—the folks watching the show from the streambanks will get to see some of the biggest and prettiest trout in the Finger Lakes, up close and personal.

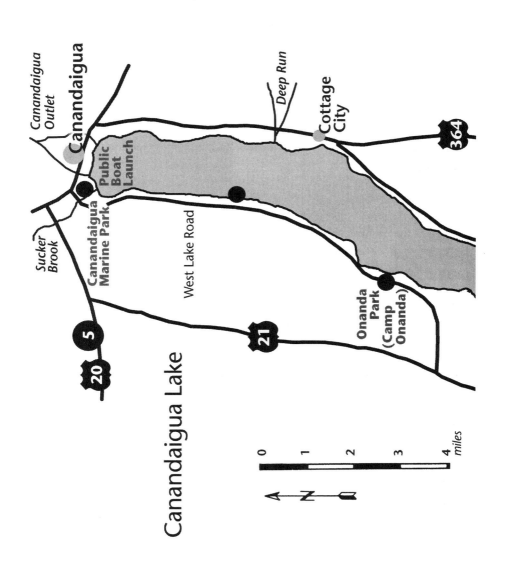

Canandaigua Lake

Canandaigua

Canandaigua Outlet

Canandaigua

Public Boat Launch

Sucker Brook

Canandaigua Marine Park

West Lake Road

Deep Run

Cottage City

364

5

20

21

Onanda Park (Camp Onanda)

0
1
2
3
4
miles

N

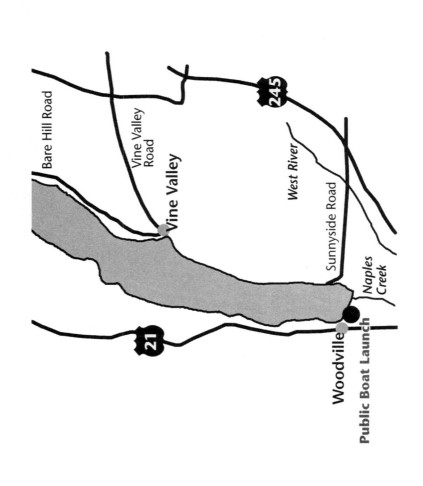

Electrofishing by the DEC at Naples Creek.

Welcome to the annual pre-trout-season electrofishing expedition to Naples Creek. Although the event has limited scientific value, it is a public relations coup for the DEC employees, who thoroughly enjoy a day outdoors that otherwise would be dedicated to answering the phone, staff meetings, and paperwork.

## THEY HAVE WAITED ALL WINTER

"The spring electrofishing surveys are sort of like our spring awakening," said Brad Hammers, the DEC biologist who usually leads the Naples Creek surveys. "We typically have been in the office, working on reports and so on, and these surveys are our first field days after a long winter, so it is fun to get out. Plus, it is always nice to handle some big, beautiful rainbows."

While the crowd watches from the streambank, the state crew uses gas-powered backpacks to sends jolts of direct current into the creek via insulated cables and long-handled metal rods. Stunned fish begin to roll and flop weakly at the surface, and wader-clad technicians hurry to scoop them up in widemouthed nets before they can recover. The captured trout, some of them weighing upward of 8 pounds, are held in a partly sunken,

DEC biologist Peter Austerman holds a 13-pound rainbow trout captured by electro-fishing in Naples Creek on March 21. State workers weigh and take samples from the fish in front of a crowd before returning them to Junction Pool in the village of Naples.

mesh-sided pen while a designated section of the creek is sampled in the same way. Finally, the fish are measured, weighed, held aloft for snapshots, and perhaps even petted by a couple of shy children. One by one, the fish are set free, and the anglers watching the process keep their fingers crossed in the hope some of those gorgeous rainbows will still be there when trout season finally opens.

If you attend these trout-fishing pep rallies a few times, you will learn how to take advantage of your presence. You will scout the creek, observing the size, location, and condition of the fish sampled. With enough experience, you will be able to prepare a game plan for catching a couple of those trout a few days hence.

For example, if the electrofishers find that most of the rainbows they see are dark in color and have dropped most of their eggs, you can assume the peak of the spawning run is either past or at hand. Conversely, when the creek sampling is full of fat-looking, silvery rainbows and most of the fish captured by the state workers were found in the lower reaches of the creek, the run is just getting started and opening day should be quite productive.

Many Finger Lakes tributaries have sizable rainbow spawning runs, but the Naples Creek event is particularly rich in tradition, matched only by the one in Catharine Creek for numbers of fish and popularity among anglers.

## A GREAT STREAM AND A GREAT LAKE

The run in Naples is special in great measure because the lake it flows into is special. Canandaigua Lake is a rich environment in which little rainbows can grow up to be big rainbows. Although some anglers may be skeptical of the findings, DEC officials have reams of data on catch rates, trout growth rates, and other barometers of a fishery's health to suggest that rainbows born in Naples Creek or one of its high-quality tributaries are off to a great start. Their prospects after they have smolted and left the creek to live in the lake are also promising. Not all trout are so lucky; the rainbow populations in several Finger Lakes (Keuka, Hemlock, and Owasco) have dwindled to the point that some concerned anglers have urged the adoption of lower creel limits and other restrictive measures to reverse the decline.

However, the Finger Lakes are not practicably managed as 11 individual entities; otherwise, anglers really would require the assistance of one of those legendary "Philadelphia lawyer" types to explain the regulations, lake by lake. To keep things simple, Region 8 biologists agreed to apply a new, one-rainbow-per-day limit to all of the Finger Lakes and tributaries under their purview—whether individual lakes and streams actually needed it or not. This explains why, as of October 2012, anglers may not creel more than one rainbow a day from Canandaigua Lake or Naples Creek at a time when they, unlike several other lakes in the chain, appear to have robust rainbow populations.

You might say Canandaigua Lake anglers took one for the team. It will be interesting to take a fresh look at the situation a few years from now. It would not surprise me to see Naples Creek stuffed with spawning trout as a direct result of the new, one-a-day rainbow creel limit.

A Naples Creek rainbow trout.

While we wait, we might as well grab a fishing rod. Canandaigua Lake is a true two-story lake, with a variety of salmonids in its deeper sectors and plenty of warm- and cool-temperature-loving species in shallow- and mid-depth habitats.

Pete Austerman oversees Canandaigua's management. The DEC biologist told me it has "some of the better rainbow trout fishing in the Finger Lakes," in case there was any remaining doubt.

"A few other things come to my mind when I think about Canandaigua Lake," Austerman told me. "[Such as] large chain pickerel on the south end, 8-pound-plus brown trout caught by trolling near shore in early spring, and how a few lake trout over 15 pounds seem to be caught every year. Largemouth bass fishing can be very good in the weed beds at the south and north ends of the lake, too."

Canandaigua Lake also has some excellent smallmouth fishing—more about that in a little bit—and a regular smorgasbord of panfish, featuring some dandy yellow perch, bluegills, pumpkinseeds, rock bass, black crappies, and bullheads.

So where do we begin our look at this superb, well-balanced fishery? Let's start at the bottom, where those lake trout lurk much of the time, then work our way back to the shallows, where bass and panfish can keep your rod tip pumping all day long.

## ICE-OUT STARTS THE BALL ROLLING

In mid-March or thereabouts, whatever ice formed at the north and south ends of Canandaigua Lake and on any of the small bays in between, such as those at Vine Valley and Gooding Point (off Cottage City), will melt. So will the ice clogging dozens of small streams all around the lake, and the combined turbidity of all these events will muddy the shorelines, attract schools of alewives and smelt, and trigger a feeding spree by lakers that weigh 4 pounds on average but occasionally are three or four times that size.

The most popular method of catching those early-season lake trout is casting with live or frozen alewives or smelt and simply waiting for something to pick them up. Slip-sinker rigs are essential because they allow line to slide through the weights unimpeded when a fish takes the bait. If you are marking plenty of fish on your sonar screen but not catching any, substitute a white-painted floating jighead for your usual bait hook; this will lift your minnow a foot or so off the lake bottom so hungry fish are more apt to notice it.

These bottom-fishing tactics work well through April, May, and early June. They can be extra effective after dark, in depths of 40 to 60 feet. At night, many anglers who target lake trout augment their legally required running lights with a large camp lantern. The lamplight draws baitfish near, and voracious lakers will be close behind them.

Shore fishing for lakers can be quite productive on Canandaigua from ice-out until May or later, but unfortunately public access for that purpose is pretty limited. Austerman mentioned Camp Onanda, a state-owned but town-operated park that's about 6½ miles south of Canandaigua on West Lake Road, as one location where shore casters can hurl their baits and lures beyond a fairly deep drop-off.

## SUMMER LAKERS ARE DEEP-WATER DENIZENS

In late June, July, and August, downriggers are necessary for consistent lake trout action. Austerman said Canandaigua Lake's depth—a maximum of 278 feet and a mean of 129 feet—causes its thermocline zone to form by early summer. Lake trout tend to school in or just below the thermocline, which is usually about 50 feet beneath the surface until a strong wind temporarily smears the neat horizontal pattern trolling techies like to visualize. Browns and rainbows like somewhat warmer temperatures than lakers prefer and therefore tend to school higher in the water column. Modern sonar equipment is very useful for spotting groups of fish and hazarding a reasonable guess as to their identity. Having located a cluster of probable lake trout, summer trollers need only pick a favorite spoon or stickbait, then settle into that day's perfect boat speed. Try 2.3 to 2.7 knots, but don't hold me to it! Some lakers are quicker and more aggressive than others, after all.

Brown trout, stocked in Canandaigua Lake at the rate of about 8,000 yearlings in the spring, sometimes do their hatchery caretakers proud by attaining weights of 7 or 8 pounds before they are caught. Most of the big ones the DEC is aware of were taken close to shore in April or early May by anglers flat-lining or using side planers to steer their stickbaits into water no more than 5 or 10 feet deep. Black-and-silver or blue-and-silver lure patterns that mimic alewives and smelt are reliable in the spring and worth a try at other seasons of the year, too, as long as they're presented at a depth where trout will see them.

## BASS FISHING TO TREASURE

And that brings us to Canandaigua's warm-water fishery, which in my mind is underrated. What other conclusion could I reach after catching my two career-best smallmouth bass during my maiden voyage on the lake?

Chris Rockwell catching smallmouth
bass in Canandaigua Lake.

Chris Rockwell of Naples, an up-and-coming tournament angler when he invited me to try the pre-season, catch-and-release bass fishing on his local lake, said I was in for a treat, and he wasn't exaggerating.

After launching at the marine park in Canandaigua, we hurried down the east shore about 2 miles and rigged up with unweighted Zoom Flukes and medium-light spinning tackle. I was surprised by the buoyancy of the minnow-mimicking lure, but Rockwell urged me to let it do its own thing.

"You want it to just wiggle a little bit or retrieve it with short jerks," he explained. Then a brown-colored fish suddenly appeared behind the bait. It swam close, but disappointed me by dropping down and out of sight.

"Did I do something wrong?" I asked.

"No, sometimes they want it still and other times they respond aggressively if you give it a couple of quick yanks," he said.

The same fish that followed my white fluke on the first cast clobbered it an inch beneath the surface on the next presentation. I had a solid hookset, and a few minutes later a big smallmouth was flopping in Rockwell's net. My host didn't have a scale on board but did have a measuring tape glued on a gunwale.

"That's a 20-incher," he said. I informed him he had just netted and released the longest smallmouth I had ever caught. We were both pretty pleased, and felt even better when I caught that fish's twin about half an hour later.

## HIGH-END FISHING IN A RITZY NEIGHBORHOOD

That morning we boated 40 or so bass, including a single largemouth. Rockwell outfished me two to one, easily, but I would have taken the lunker prize—twice. White and pink flukes seemed equally effective on the bass, which appeared to be selecting or guarding nest sites around boat docks, clusters of boulders, and other cover within 30 or 40 yards of the heavily developed shore. I learned later that Canandaigua Lake's east shore is one of the most ritzy and desirable neighborhoods in West Central New York. That's no wonder, either, considering the beauty and fertility of the lake itself.

Austerman said my spring outing with Rockwell was not unusual, given the time of year and the area we fished. Shallow-water spots for spawning are coveted but hard to find in much of the lake, and Rockwell had graciously shared one of the prime areas with me.

"The smallmouths can be a little more difficult later in the season as the fish move deeper and become harder to locate," the biologist said. "They will often suspend over deeper water then, and anglers will need to use good electronics and spend some time to locate them."

What could be better than 4-pound smallmouths? Many bass fanatics would say 5-pounds-and-change largemouths, and many tournaments at Canandaigua have been won by such fish. You can catch largemouths of 2 to 3 pounds routinely in the weedy north- and south-end weed beds, but be forewarned: If you fling spinnerbaits or spoons at the south end, and happen to be using a line that's too fine or slightly frayed, you are bound to be a bite-off victim. The perpetrator will be one of the 22- to 26-inch pickerel that roam the lake's thickest weed beds. If you like pickerel patties, try using a shiner and bobber with a thin wire leader.

The panfish that live in or near the weeds throughout Canandaigua Lake are mostly of a respectable size and can be caught in a predictable sequence—bullheads and crappies in early April followed by perch and rock bass—as they approach shoreline cover to feed and spawn. The municipal pier at the north end of the lake is a productive spot for panfish in general, but is especially good for perch.

Canandaigua Lake's north end is bordered by Routes 5 and 20 in the city of Canandaigua. To get to the city from the state thruway, follow the signs south from the Manchester exit.

Public boating access to Canandaigua Lake's great fishing ranges from the tiny cartop ramp at the West River fishing access on Route 245 between Middlesex and Naples to the large, first-class-all-the-way Canandaigua Lake State Marine Park on Routes 5 and 20, which can handle up to 110 cars and trailers. Expect to pay a modest fee for use of the latter, which is operated by the state Office of Parks, Recreation and Historic Preservation.

The other public launch sites on Canandaigua Lake is the Woodville launch, run by the DEC. It's about 3 miles north of Naples on Route 21 and has room for 86 cars and trailers.

# CHAPTER 8

# Honeoye Lake

**LOCATION:** Western Ontario County
**ELEVATION:** 804 feet
**SURFACE AREA:** 1,772 acres
**SHORELINE:** 10.8 miles
**MEAN DEPTH:** 16 feet
**MAXIMUM DEPTH:** 31 feet
**APPROXIMATE THERMOCLINE DEPTH:** None (the lake is too shallow
   for it to turn over)

Honeoye Lake is so full of largemouth bass that anglers new to its weedy waters have a good chance of catching one on their first cast, no matter where that cast is aimed or what lure is on the line. You can cast inshore, offshore, toward cover, or away from it; with something that floats, or with something that sinks. Odds are better than even that a bass will see that bait of yours and wrap its lips around it.

And no, I have not violated my own principles about exaggerating the quality of fish or fishing in small bodies of water. Although Honeoye Lake, covering 1,772 surface acres and bottoming out at 31 feet off the east shore directly across the lake from California Point, is relatively small, it is big enough to take a lot of fishing pressure. In fact, if you launch a boat on the lake after a lazy breakfast and haven't hooked 20 or more bucket-mouths by the time you have to order the local diner's blue-plate special for supper, either you've had a very slow day or you just aren't much of a bass fisherman. Honeoye is that good.

DEC Region 8 biologist Pete Austerman, who oversees the management of Honeoye Lake, marvels at its productivity.

"I think it is one of the best places in the state to take someone who wants to catch a lot of largemouth bass," he said. "They may not always catch a 5-pounder, but they will be able to catch good numbers of quality bass."

## QUANTITY AND QUALITY, BOTH

In New York, biologists consider an electrofishing catch rate of 20 adult bass per hour to be a high one, Austerman said. The DEC's most recent

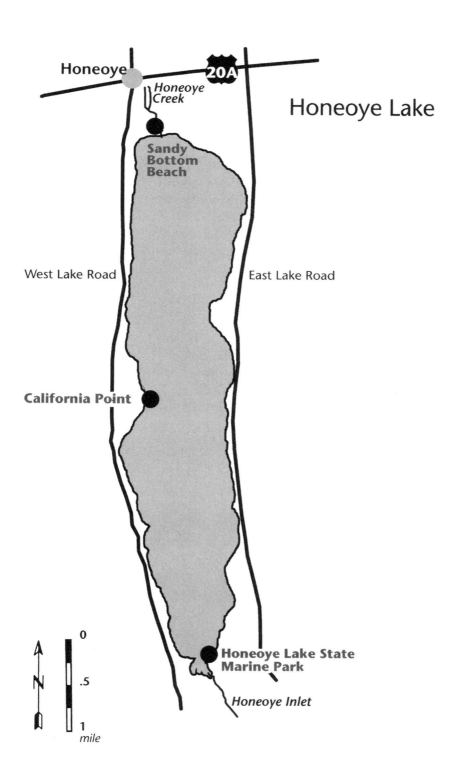

Honeoye

20A

Honeoye Lake

Honeoye
Creek

Sandy
Bottom
Beach

West Lake Road

East Lake Road

California Point

Honeoye Lake State
Marine Park

Honeoye Inlet

N

0

.5

1
mile

electrofishing survey on Honeoye Lake produced a catch rate of 100 bass per hour.

The one caveat that many Honeoye regulars cite when they hear such praise for their pet lake is the average size of its bass. Indeed, Honeoye Lake has a reputation for spitting out an endless stream of 12- to 14-inchers, yet I am suspicious of anyone who has fished it for a while and doesn't admit to catching a slob now and then. To paraphrase the Bard, I think Honeoye's naysayers may be protesting too much.

I put aside my own prejudices about Honeoye's "small" bass for good one July morning when I was sharing a boat with local guide Frank Tennity. This was one of those busman's-holiday deals, with me fishing at no cost and Tennity encouraged to join me in reeling in every bass he could. We started fishing about 100 yards out from the state boat launch and immediately caught a couple of the lake's standard, cookie-cutter bass. However, the third bite was different. When Tennity's Brush Hog jig came to a sudden dead stop in the weeds, he set the hook and his rod bent over.

"This is a better fish," he said. "A lot better."

It turned out to be a 6-pound largemouth, and I fired off 9 or 10 camera shots in a hurry so my mentor could let his prize go and get back to teaching me.

A few minutes later and maybe 50 feet farther down the east shore, Tennity's rod plunged again, so sharply the rig almost slipped from his

Frank Tennity battles a nice Honeoye Lake largemouth.

hands. We could hardly believe our eyes when this fish came aboard. It was 22 inches long and looked even tubbier than the heavyweight Frank had landed a few minutes before.

"Those are the two nicest fish I've caught this season," he said. He does get plenty of 4- to 4½-pound specimens during an average summer, though.

## UNDERWATER JUNGLE MAKES FOR BASS HEAVEN

The productivity of Honeoye Lake can probably be summed up in a single word: *W-E-E-D-S*. Some of the hundreds of lakeshore residents cheer from their docks when the local weed-cutting vessel makes its runs up and down the lake, and there are days when anglers, too, whoop and whistle while the milfoil masher is chugging along. Loose, floating weed mats seem to stir up Honeoye's bass, much as a midsummer downpour triggers a feeding spree in area trout streams. The cocoa-colored flows in streams and rafts of pickerel grass and coon tail both signal chow time. Yet from a bass fisherman's viewpoint, standing weeds are not all that bothersome, once you figure out where the forage species and the game fish are hiding in that soggy jungle.

Tennity uses plastic baits, such as Senkos and Stik-Os, that have subtle wiggling actions and come in a variety of colors to fish edges and bald spots in the sandy- and gravel-bottomed areas around the lake. But when the waves kick up and it becomes hard to eyeball his line as it lands and sinks below the surface, he often switches to heavy, weedguard-fitted jigs that will plunge through the densest weed beds to catch the attention of bass lurking in the wet nooks and crannies. On the other hand, it never hurts to sail a few lures into the shadows beneath unoccupied boat docks or swimming rafts, either.

Tennity's wife, Melody, is every bit the angler her husband is, and she shares management of their guide business. She seems to have a knack for finding big bass, and once made me laugh out loud (and adjust my technique) when she drily observed, "If you want to fish a Senko, you've got to let it sink-o!" I can't argue with that, for the Senko is just one of many baits that produce best when fished at a slow and deliberate pace.

## YOU COULD CATCH THEM BLINDFOLDED

How to catch bass is of more portent on Honeoye Lake than where to catch bass. That's because just about every foot of the 4½-mile-long fishing hole is hospitable to bass. California Point, midway off the west shore, is widely touted and Tennity always gives it a workout, but when

Frank Tennity and a 22-inch Honeoye Lake largemouth bass.

Frank is being frank about Honeoye's hot spots, he is adamant that any of
the dozens of subtle points, drop-offs, and weed edges around the lake can
look like an angling nirvana on a given day.

That's enough about largemouths for now. Honeoye Lake is not a
one-trick pony. It has fair numbers of chain pickerel, and every now and
then Tennity or one of his customers connects with a northern pike in
the 6- to 8-pound range. Most such connections end with a bite-off,
but if you happen to be running a plug of a length or design that deters
toothy critters from getting a good grip, you may be able to slide your
landing net under a big one. Assuming your time is not a problem and
you are prepared to go long hours between bites, you could target pike
in Honeoye Lake, using twin-bladed spinnerbaits, magnum-size stickbaits, or the old standby for northerns: a large shiner suspended under a
slip bobber. Any of the weed lines could produce, but pay extra attention to areas that seem overloaded with cruising perch or golden shiners.
The goldies are preferred by pike, pickerel, and even muskellunge because
their fins are soft-rayed and therefore go down more smoothly than a
sharp-finned sunfish or crappie.

When you are trying for pike but catching sizable largemouths instead,
the next logical step is to go to larger bait, but remember that northerns
aren't nearly as common in Honeoye as they are in nearby Conesus Lake.

Smallmouth bass are not really abundant in Honeoye, either, but they do grow to a respectable size—say, 15 or 16 inches. Your odds of catching one or two bronzebacks will improve if you fish tube jigs or your favorite Rat-L-Trap on or near the flat midsection of the lake, which maxes out at roughly 31 feet on bottom. One of the better spots is the area straight out from the public swimming beach at the north end of the lake.

Next to bass, walleyes are the second most targeted game fish in Honeoye Lake, and the DEC stocks them at the rate of more than eight million fry a year. To monitor the population that results, Austerman and his colleagues catch walleyes in the spring and fin-clip them so they can be identified in subsequent mark-and-recapture studies that can be used to compare growth and survival rates, and evaluate creel limits and minimum lengths, among other things.

## SO WHERE ARE THOSE WALLEYES?

While they are so abundant that the DEC allows anglers to keep three a day of 15 inches or better—compared with the 18-inch rule that applies to the other Finger Lakes—Honeoye Lake walleyes are not at all easy to catch. The degree of difficulty is attributable to several factors, starting with those extensive weed beds. Traditional walleye fishing methods, including trolling with stickbaits and drifting with spinner-and-worm rigs, produce more weed balls than strikes during most of the year. Oh, the old ways are still productive, but you'll need an extra dose of patience to put it all together in this lake—and to keep plucking the weeds off your lure and line.

Another hurdle that anglers must clear is the bountiful diet that Honeoye walleyes enjoy. While the lake, unlike several others in the region, does not harbor a significant population of alewives or smelt, it is home to many species of forage fish as well as the fry and fingerlings of perch, crappies, and sunfish. And don't forget all the little bass swimming in the shallows day and night. I think it is fair to say that Honeoye Lake walleyes are in no danger of losing weight, and that means fishermen must be very good or very lucky if they plan on catching them consistently.

There are two times during the year when Honeoye walleyes are most likely to be on the bite. One is in the second half of May, when the season is barely under way and walleyes are hungrier than usual after a long winter and an intense spawning cycle. This is the perfect oppor-tunity to fall back on that old reliable walleye method, night fishing. Try pulling stickbaits behind a relatively quiet outboard, around and over emergent weed beds. The barer the lake bottom happens to be, the better the trolling is.

If you don't have a boat but do know somebody with a home or camp on Honeoye Lake, get permission to do some after-dark shore fishing. Stickbaits will work as long as you keep your lures free of weeds. Take at least two rods (state regulations specify no more than three per angler) and bait one with a nightcrawler, using a slip sinker and threading the worm on a floating jighead so it will suspend a foot or so off the bottom. I've had some success with the floating jig-worm setup on other lakes and see no reason why it shouldn't be effective on Honeoye Lake, too.

Night fishing hinges on walleye movements, which are often unpredictable. Although some fishermen claim to detect relationships between tides and moon phases, along with other celestial happenings, I am not among them. It does seem to me, however, that walleyes bite better on dark nights than bright, moonlit nights.

## PANFISH ARE POPULAR

Ice fishing can be very good for all species in Honeoye Lake, from bass to walleyes and everything in between, and the topic is addressed in some detail in another chapter.

A few paragraphs back, I cited walleyes as the second most popular game fish living in Honeoye Lake. I stand by that assessment, but the second most popular fish of any kind is a panfish. You could even make a case that the fish I'm thinking of—sunfish in general and pumpkin-seeds and bluegills specifically—attract more anglers during the whole year than largemouths. We'd have to tally all the kids and adults who fish from docks and beaches around the lake and the many Rochester residents who fish for fillets on weekends or on their roundabout way home from work, now and then.

The panfishing on Honeoye Lake during the sunnies' spring spawning period and again through the ice in January and February is simply terrific. On a slow bass-fishing day, Tennity may encourage his customers to grab an ultralight rod and catch a few hand-size sunnies on small jigs. His good friend Will Elliott, who writes a regular column for the *New York Outdoor News* tabloid, spends a few days each May angling for a mess of fillets and usually takes home a cooler full of Friday dinners. Although the impending feasts are made up mostly of sunfish, Elliott's mother lode also includes black crappies, yellow perch, and maybe even a few bullheads.

Worm-and-bobber rigs are extremely effective for sunfish that are making their car-tire-size (and shape) nests in 1 to 6 feet of water, and the same classic combo works well on yellow perch. Expect 9- to 11-inch perch in Honeoye, although you might bump into some nicer ones every so often. Crappies, often called calicoes by local panfish fans, typically run 9 to 12 inches and respond well to jigs with foam bodies and marabou tails. Many tackle shops label these lures "crappie jigs" because they are so often used for that species. Good colors include white, black, and chartreuse. Thread crappie jigs on $\frac{1}{16}$-ounce leadheads and tip them with small perch minnows. A small slip bobber gives the crappie seeker more casting range and easier strike detection.

Don't quit too early if you're on a crappie-catching mission. The water in front of the state launch is one of the better places to get into a school of Honeoye calicoes, and at dusk you will often see their surface-feeding dimples, just out of range, after you've pulled in at the ramp and are getting ready to load the trailer.

Honeoye Lake is in western Ontario County, about half an hour from Canandaigua and Rochester and roughly two hours' drive from Syracuse.

Like most of the Finger Lakes, Honeoye is easily accessible via US Route 20, which skirts the north end of the chain. Just west of Canandaigua, Route 20 drivers should look for the intersection of Routes 20A and 64 in the town of Bloomfield. Go south (a right turn if you're from the Buffalo area, a left if you are a Syracusan) and continue on 20A when it breaks away from Route 64. Route 20A takes you into the friendly hamlet of Honeoye. East Lake Road is a left-hand turn, which quickly leads to the boat launch off Wesley Road. West Lake Road, shown on some maps as Route 36, is also a left, directly across the street from Mark's Pizzeria.

# CHAPTER 9

# Canadice Lake

**LOCATION:** Western Ontario County
**ELEVATION:** 1,096 feet
**SURFACE AREA:** 649 acres
**SHORELINE:** 7.1 miles
**MEAN DEPTH:** 55 feet
**MAXIMUM DEPTH:** 83 feet
**APPROXIMATE THERMOCLINE DEPTH:** 20 feet

You may consider Canadice Lake to be the runt of the Finger Lakes chain, for it spans just 649 surface acres with a normal mean depth of 55 feet, but its cozy atmosphere is a welcome change for fishermen who are weary of more spacious venues. On a reasonably calm day, anglers who have never set eyes on Canadice can launch a small motorboat or even a canoe and see pretty much all there is to see in an hour or two. Then they can concentrate on the fishing without fretting that they're somehow missing the secret spot. Such are the restorative powers of a small lake.

Because of its shared role with next-valley neighbor Hemlock Lake as a century-long supplier of drinking water for the city of Rochester, Canadice has essentially no development on its shoreline. Aside from the small dam and spill channel at its north end, it seems hardly changed from the days when Native Americans and European fur trappers were the only people who hunted and fished in the region. The heavily wooded hills and the puffs of white smoke curling from the chimneys of log cabins and clapboard houses remind me of the Catskills.

The lakeshore was partly developed during the first half of the 20th century. A few camps overlooked its shores, and at least some of the adjacent land remained in private hands until the early 1950s, when Rochester officials completed the city's purchases of the lake and more than 3,000 acres of surrounding lands. Such acquisitions were needed to protect the lake from pollution and assure a high-quality water supply even today.

Fortunately for fishermen, the lake was not closed to public recreation. Instead of barring sportsmen, the city opted to monitor them by requiring visitors to both Canadice and Hemlock Lakes to obtain annual user permits

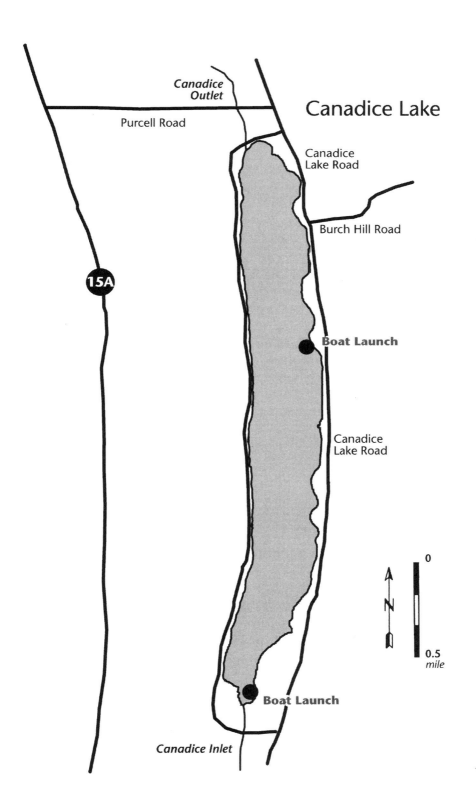

Canadice Outlet

Purcell Road

Canadice Lake

Canadice Lake Road

Burch Hill Road

15A

Boat Launch

Canadice Lake Road

Boat Launch

Canadice Inlet

0

N

0.5
mile

for hunting and fishing. For decades, the permits were issued on a self-serve basis at a kiosk that stood at the north end of Hemlock, off Rix Hill Road. Alternatively, you could obtain the required permit by mail.

During the same period, the city left management of both lakes' fisheries to the old state Conservation Department and its successor, the modern Department of Environmental Conservation, or DEC. According to most reports, the state biologists did a good job, creating new fisheries or enhancing existing populations, and by the 1960s both lakes were renowned for their deep-water trout fishing and good near-shore fishing for bass and panfish.

## A NEW CONSERVATION PARTNERSHIP

In 2010, the DEC, the city and Livingston and Ontario Counties wrapped up a series of agreements that created the 6,684-acre Hemlock-Canadice State Forest. The deal left the state agency in charge of protecting the lands and waters covered by the agreement. A pamphlet explaining the rules for use of the forest is available from the DEC's Region 8 Sub-Office, Attn: Regional Forester, 7291 Coon Road, Bath, NY 14810.

The key rules pertaining to fishing state that it is unlawful in the Hemlock-Canadice State Forest to:

Possess or operate a boat, ice fish, traverse the ice or water or fish from shore on Hemlock Lake north of the lake's northern-most boat launch or between the lake and Boat Launch Road; and on Canadice Lake within 500 feet of the north shore and Canadice Outlet Creek and adjacent property within one mile of the creek's intersection with Route 15A.

The DEC's agreement with the city and two counties also ended the permit requirement, which was not only an annoyance but a legal requirement that confused many traveling anglers and probably deterred some from ever trying their skills on two of the least-fished Finger Lakes. Still intact, however, are the boat-size and motor power restrictions that apply to both Canadice and Hemlock Lakes. In brief, you may not use a boat longer than 17 feet, whether or not it has a mechanical means of propulsion. Nor are you allowed to use a motor with greater than 10 horsepower on either lake.

## EASY ON THE EYES AND THE SOUL

With that regulatory business concluded, let's focus on the fish for a while. Canadice has plenty of them, according to DEC biologist Pete Austerman.

"It has a very unique wilderness setting where you can catch a wide range of species from a small boat," he said, adding that "conditions are usually good for smaller boats to access deep water to fish for trout."

About those trout—Canadice is home to lake trout, browns, and rainbows, in that order of size and abundance. Austerman said that members of DEC sampling crews see 8- to 10-pound lakers regularly, and he recalled the capture of a 16-pounder during a 2003 survey of Canadice's fish population.

When Austerman gave me that titillating nugget of information, I recalled a previous discussion with a brother angler who made a few extra bucks by pouring samples and trading sophisticated observations with wine-tasting tourists at a Finger Lakes winery. When he realized he was talking to a kindred fisherman he brushed other customers aside for a few moments and discussed the lake trout he'd caught earlier in the spring while casting spoons and egg sacs in Canadice and Hemlock Lakes. He preferred night fishing because getting out after dark seemed to put him into more and larger lakers, including one 11-pounder caught the year before. I suggested part of his good fortune might be due to the inclination of baitfish to browse for supper in the gravel-bottomed shallows after dark. Probably the lake trout were not far behind the bite-size prey. Anyway, I had wondered after that encounter if the story was a truthful

Sean Kelly fishing the shoreline at Canadice Lake from a felled tree.

yarn or the wine pourer was just spinning some fish stories for the amusement of the visiting outdoors writer.

Lake trout are the dominant predators in Canadice Lake, in part because they have been able to spawn successfully on gravel and rocks along the east shore points and shoals. The DEC hatchery system supplements the natural reproduction of lake trout in Canadice by annually stocking about 2,100 yearling lakers. Hatchery crews also raise an annual quota of approximately 5,000 yearling brown trout for Canadice. Rainbow trout, however, may or may not remain a major component of the fishery, although 'bows are popular with Canadice anglers. Going into 2013, the DEC was planning to cut rainbow trout stockings for that year, at least. The problem with the rainbows, according to Austerman, is that they aren't browns. Browns seem to be surviving better than the 'bows and are also caught more frequently by anglers.

In both spring and fall, landlubber fishermen who don't have boats can catch all three species of trout by casting bait or lures from the east and west shores of Canadice Lake. Chest waders can be helpful in some areas but are not really critical for success. The trick here and at just about any other trout lake is to be in the right place at the right time. I have learned the hard way, while shore fishing on other Finger Lakes, that simplistic clichés such as "Fish bite best when wind is from the west" and "Big bait, big fish" are basically worthless for analyzing or prognosticating short-term fishing trends.

## WEATHER THAT MATTERS

In most instances, I've found, trout like cloudy skies better than clear. Similarly, a few days of stable weather can be just the thing to give trout a jump start after a long spell of stormy conditions. Finally, with regard to shore fishing, a steady warm-up in the spring or a cool-down in the fall is just what the fish-doctor ordered. Keep track of the daily water temperatures in any of the Finger Lakes you fish. Pay close attention to the days when the surface temperatures are about to pass the 50-degree (Fahrenheit) mark on your thermometer. In the fall, of course, the bite should be hot when readings drop to 50 degrees and then keep chilling. We're rooting for the opposite direction in the spring. We want to see the mercury climbing through the 40s, and we'd better hold tight to our shore-casting rods as the 50-degree barrier is breached.

There are a couple of explanations as to why these temperature changes are often harbingers of good trout fishing. The main reason is that fish are cold-blooded creatures whose comfort levels—and appetites—change as the surrounding water warms or cools. Every species of fish has its own preferred water temperature. Lake trout like 46 to 50 degrees best (but do fairly well between 40 and 55 degrees), while rainbows and browns thrive when readings are in the 55-to-65-degree range but hold their own when thermometers register between 52 and 70 degrees. As a rule, my experience confirms, spring and fall fishing should be good for all three species we're talking about here whenever the water has just hit 50 degrees. How ferocious the bite is or how long it lasts depends on how rapidly temperatures are approaching or departing from my target fish's preferred range.

## YOU CAN GET THERE FROM HERE

All of this matters because Canadice Lake, like Hemlock, is among a very few lake trout waters in New York whose contours make it possible to fish some of their deepest parts from shore. The ledges along the west shore and the points that sprout from the east bank and quickly plunge to 50 or 60 feet below the surface are attractive structures for baitfish—and therefore for lake trout, as well. You will have to pick your spots carefully, make very long casts, and use heavy lures or bait rigs with 1-ounce slip sinkers, but with the right tackle and enough practice, you can get the job done. When you have figured it all out, you will have earned your own access to one of the better places in the Finger Lakes for catching good-size lake trout.

I must admit, however, that boating fishermen have an advantage over shore casters on Canadice, as they do on most lakes, because of their extra mobility. The right boat—one under 17 feet long and powered by a 10-horse motor in this case—will allow the owner to maneuver into casting distance of every fish in the lake, while shore-bound anglers have to settle for whatever parts they can reach. Boat users aren't limited to points, weed beds, and other natural structures, either. On Canadice, effective trolling begins with an understanding of seasonal temperature strata and thermoclines.

Most deep, cold bodies of water have two major temperature shifts a year. In the spring, the sun increases the surface temperature and pushes the colder water downward. Then, in the fall, colder days reduce the surface temperature and force the warmer water toward bottom. Between these dramatic seasonal flip-flops, the water in the lake is said to be stratified, or composed of horizontal layers. The layers can be identified according to their temperatures.

## THE THERMOCLINE, IN ONE EASY LESSON

To understand the thermocline, think of a stratified lake as a big, wet sandwich. The slice of "bread" nearest the surface is the warm, oxygen-rich epilimnion. Deep below is a colder slice known as the hypolimnion. Between the bread slices is the meat in the sandwich, or the thermocline. The thermocline is a zone of rapid temperature change. Readings within it may soar from 40 to 55 degrees within a vertical space of only a few feet. In the thermocline or just above it, trout and salmon can generally find comfortable temperatures, adequate dissolved oxygen levels, and plenty of food. The food consists of alewives or other forage species that are drawn, in turn, to the zooplankton and other tiny organisms that find the thermocline to their liking.

Trout trollers should seek out the Canadice thermocline from about early June to Labor Day. Twenty to 25 feet down is a good place to start the hunt.

The same lures and tactics that take trout in the other cold Finger Lakes will work on Canadice Lake. Anything that's alewife-size will do, including classics such as Sutton spoons and more modern wobblers like Northern Kings. Nickel finishes are good, but don't be afraid of using prism tape or Magic Markers to dress your lures up a little.

See the chapter on Finger Lakes trolling for more information about lures, rigging, and techniques.

While trout are the big draw at Canadice, the lake also has very good fishing for largemouth and smallmouth bass, chain pickerel, and panfish, including yellow perch and rock bass. In fact, if I were to hazard a guess as to which species of fish is the one most frequently hooked, I'd go with the rocky. The west shore of Canadice fairly teems with rock bass, and they simply can't resist a worm or a crayfish. Look for rockies around toppled trees, amid scattered boulders, and along the edges of near-shore weed beds. Keep a cooler with ice in your car and keep a few rockies, as they are much underrated as dinner fare.

Pickerel are very sweet-fleshed, too, but most anglers who hook them at Canadice Lake or anywhere else don't like to bother with those dreaded Y-bones. If you haven't had the pleasure already, do yourself a favor and keep a couple of 20-inchers. Fillet and skin them, just as you'd treat a nice walleye. Then run them once, twice, and thrice through a grinder to render those slender bones soft and harmless. Look up a recipe for "pickerel patties" or "sucker patties" and serve yourself a very tasty supper.

You can catch plenty of pickerel patty fixings in or around any of the weed beds in Canadice. Some are short and skinny "hammer handles," but there are numerous 2-pounders and some 3s and 4s, as well. The best time to catch the bigger ones is during the winter. Ice is usually, although not always, thick enough to support a crowd of tip-up specialists by mid-January.

Bass fishing in Canadice Lake has been underrated for a long time, probably owing to its navigation restrictions. These days, most bass fanatics prefer to explore lakes where they can give the reins to their sleek fishing platforms powered by 150-horsepower motors. Personally, the older I get the more I appreciate a canoe or johnboat pushed around a small lake by an electric trolling motor! A setup like that will do just fine on Canadice Lake. Its bass, which run mostly between 12 and 14 inches but occasionally tickle the 4-pound mark on your De-Liar scale, like the weedy areas of the lake and will take Senkos, small to medium spinner-baits, and assorted crankbaits.

Medium-size sunfish and yellow perch also love the weeds and are fairly common, although not as numerous or abundant as the stocks of panfish in nearby Honeoye Lake.

To find Canadice Lake, take US Routes 20 and 5 west from Canandaigua for about 5 miles to the intersection with Routes 20A and 64. Go left there and take 20A into the hamlet of Honeoye. Continue west on 20A to Barnard Road and make a left turn. Barnard Road becomes Canadice Lake Road, which shadows the east side of the lake. You can't miss the pull-offs or the small launch area near the south end of the lake.

# CHAPTER 10

# Hemlock Lake

**LOCATION:** Eastern Livingston and Western Ontario Counties
**ELEVATION:** 905 feet
**SURFACE AREA:** 1,800 acres
**SHORELINE:** 17.1 miles
**MEAN DEPTH:** 45 feet
**MAXIMUM DEPTH:** 91 feet
**APPROXIMATE THERMOCLINE DEPTH:** 26 feet

Long before I was old enough to drink alcoholic beverages, the Genesee Brewing Company had locked me up as a future beer customer. My capture at a tender age could not be traced to a few surreptitious sips of beer at family reunions, although I did get away with such trickery a couple of times. No, all that was required to secure my loyalty to the Western New York brand of beer was the chance placement of a stack of entry forms for Genesee's annual statewide fishing contest at my neighborhood super-market. The contest brochure included a list of winners, runners-up, and also-rans who instantly entered my personal hall of heroes.

Reading the names of contestants and seeing the places, near and far, where they had struck piscatorial gold, I vowed, then and there, to claim a prize for myself, one day. Considering my age at the time—I was on the cusp of puberty and starting to wonder if I had enough time to give proper attention to both team sports and pretty girls—it was probably a good thing that my foray into competitive fishing took only a year or so to bear fruit.

## A FATEFUL CATCH, YOU BET

As I recall, the folks at "Genny," as all us professional anglers knew her, mailed me a small check and a note of congratulations when I caught what turned out to be the third-place winner in the brown trout division for the month of August 1962.

I read that form letter and admired that check for hours. What an honor!

Looking back, maybe it wasn't that big a deal, but it sure seemed like it at the time. I was only 13 years old when I caught my first whopper

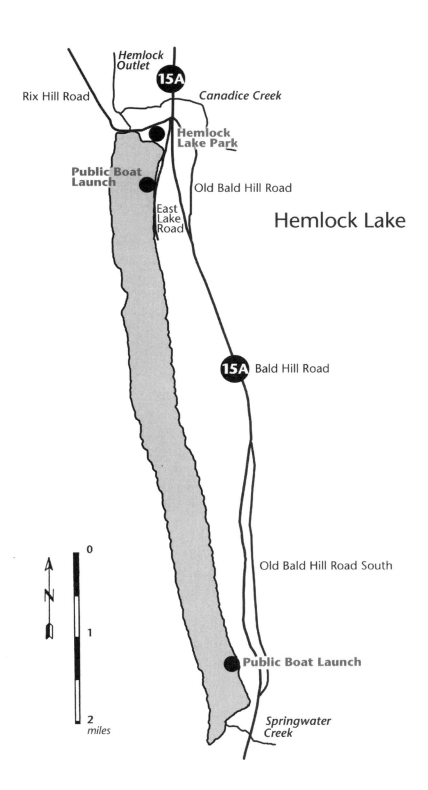

Hemlock
Outlet

**15A**

Rix Hill Road

*Canadice Creek*

Hemlock
Lake Park

Public Boat
Launch

Old Bald Hill Road

East
Lake
Road

# Hemlock Lake

**15A** Bald Hill Road

0

N

1

Old Bald Hill Road South

2
*miles*

Public Boat Launch

*Springwater
Creek*

and sent a snapshot of me and it to the Genesee folks, but I knew there
must have been hundreds of other entrants in the prestigious brown trout
division of the contest. My entrant, a 21¾-inch brown that weighed 4
pounds, 1½ ounces, bit on a nightcrawler under Montague's bridge after
a thunderstorm riled up the currents of Nine Mile Creek. Cousin Matt
Sennett and I spent the next half hour holding the fish over our heads so
the drivers of tractor-trailer rigs would hit their air horns as they sailed
by us. That trout and I made it into the local newspaper the next week.

Many young kids, winners or not, grew up to be avid anglers because
of that contest.

So what does any of this have to do with Hemlock Lake? Plenty,
because the Genny commercials on TV, like the fishing contest brochures,
were constantly touting the fact that this magnificent brew was made
with "pure Hemlock Lake water." Naturally, I and countless others
assumed that Genesee's magic elixir could not have been made without
the pure lake's contribution, and that the brewery must have exclusive
rights to the stuff. In truth, anybody who lived in Rochester could use
Hemlock Lake water to rinse their toothbrushes, because it was the city's
main water supply.

It sold a lot of beer, though.

As I went on to college and grew to enjoy playing in local softball
leagues, I drank more than my share of Genesees, and every bottle or can
made me think about that pure water. I also wondered how the fishing
was in Hemlock Lake, and eventually I found out it was pretty good. It
still is a nice place to fish, and may be even better in the next few years
as DEC biologists proceed with plans to give Hemlock's rainbow trout
fishery a boost.

## MORE THAN A PASSING RESEMBLANCE

Spread over 1,800 surface acres, Hemlock is almost three times as large
as nearby Canadice Lake. Other than the size differential, the two have
much in common. For starters, both are critical components of the
Rochester water supply system, although only one was a key part of a
regional brewer's brilliant marketing campaign. Also, both lakes have
beautiful, undeveloped shorelines, and identical regulations pertaining to
boats (no longer than 17 feet) and boat motors (10 horse, max).

It is hardly surprising that with all these similarities, the lakes also
have exciting, look-alike fisheries for trout, bass, pickerel, and assorted
panfish. Nor does it come as a shock to learn that DEC fisheries personnel
see room for improvement.

Lake trout are at the top of the food chain in Hemlock Lake, as they are in Canadice Lake. DEC Region 8 biologist Pete Austerman and his colleagues think the dominance of lakers and other cold-water predators at least partly explains the recent decline of Hemlock's rainbow trout population.

"Rainbow trout fishing has been poor over the past 15 years," Austerman said in 2012.

In fact, spring spawning runs in Springwater Creek have been inconsistent since the early 1980s, when lakers and rainbows were Hemlock Lake's two primary predators. While lake trout have maintained their dominant position in Hemlock, fishing for other salmonids—including rainbow and brown trout and landlocked salmon—has been a disappointment, lately. Many anglers, discussing the status of the fishery with state biologists, have pined for the old days when fair to good numbers of large rainbow trout pushed their way upstream each March and April to spawn on Springwater Creek's gravel.

## WHITHER GO THE RAINBOWS

In an attempt to learn why Hemlock rainbows seem to be thinning out, DEC survey teams first assayed the creek, which is the lake's only significant spawning stream. The researchers' data indicates that juvenile trout do quite well after hatching from eggs fertilized in the creek, but do not have a high survival rate once they have smolted and swum down to the lake. State biologists strongly suspect little rainbows are being consumed by notably larger predators, including lakers, browns, and other rainbows.

The most scientific way to test the theory is to reduce the number of predators in Hemlock and monitor the impact such reductions have on the lake's rainbow population. DEC biologists and fisheries technicians have just begun such an experiment as this book is being written.

"We are currently trying to reduce the predator levels in Hemlock Lake for a five-year period to see if this helps the rainbow trout population come back," said Austerman. "We will not be stocking brown trout or landlocked salmon during this time period and we will not be permitting walleye stocking, either."

Austerman said anglers may continue to catch large brown trout even after stockings of browns have been eliminated for several years, because some browns from the lake are born wild in Springwater Creek. Landlocks won't be missed by most Hemlock Lake anglers because salmon "are rarely caught," the biologist said. Indeed, many of the fishermen who took part in a DEC-designed creel census during a 2005–06 trout season indicated they were more interested in restoring the traditional spring rainbow run in Springwater Creek than in improving the salmon catch in the lake.

While the DEC anxiously awaits the results of its predation study, there's no reason for anglers to steer clear of Hemlock Lake. Fishing for lake trout, which are stocked in Hemlock at the rate of about 9,000 a year, should be as good as ever, and might even show an improvement. That's because lakers won't have to compete with nearly as many browns or salmon for the alewives, rainbow smelt, and sculpin that are the most abundant prey species in the lake.

## THEY CAN PART THE SEAS, BUT NOT HEMLOCK LAKE

The horsepower limit that applies to Hemlock Lake beckons some anglers but turns off some others. I have no doubt, personally, that the 10-horse maximum causes many bass-fishing fanatics to take their tackle elsewhere. After all, most bass lovers spend serious money to buy and maintain those big beauties with the glittery paint jobs and motors that can part the seas like Moses did. How many fishermen who own such vessels would want to spend Saturdays putt-putting around Hemlock Lake in a small boat when they can just as easily trailer their mini aircraft carrier to Conesus Lake, Keuka Lake, or some other wide-open fishing hole?

On the other hand, the ranks of modern anglers include many who appreciate a few hours of peaceful contemplation even more than a livewell crammed with fish. To such as them, Hemlock Lake (or Canadice) might seem like paradise on earth.

The annual fishing calendar for Hemlock often, although not always, begins with hole-drilling sessions in late January or February. It offers good ice fishing for trout, pickerel, and panfish during some winters but little or no opportunities for hard-water enthusiasts in other years. Its extra surface area and lower elevation explain why ice formation is a chancier proposition at Hemlock than at its three closest neighbors in the Finger Lakes chain. Canadice, Conesus, and Honeoye Lakes all are much more reliable for ice fishing. Otisco, Owasco, and Cayuga all can be counted on for good ice most years, while Skaneateles, Keuka, and Canandaigua may or may not freeze over. Big, broad Seneca Lake, of course, never freezes over except at very localized coves or marinas—but we'll discuss regional ice fishing in more depth in a separate chapter.

Whether it's frozen over the winter or not, Hemlock Lake comes alive in the spring for boat-owning anglers and shore casters alike. Boats can be launched about a mile south of the Rix Hill–Boat Launch intersection, which is at the northeast corner of the lake; and also at the southeast corner, via a short dirt road just north of the Livingston County–Ontario county line.

## DON'T FORGET YOUR HIKING SHOES

Anglers with sturdy legs can get in on some fine shore-casting action by hiking along the access roads that parallel the east and west shorelines of the lake and taking short downhill paths to the water's edge. In April and May, fishermen can get themselves within casting distance of lake, brown, and rainbow trout, along with a full assortment of panfish (perch, pump-kinseeds, rock bass, bluegills, and bullheads), chain pickerel, and both largemouth and smallmouth bass.

I like to park my car near the boat launch at the north end, then walk farther south before stopping to fish at or near several prominent points and coves, but you pick your own spots. In all honesty, the fish-able shore of Hemlock is not subjected to very heavy angling pressure— probably owing to the walking that's required to get to prime locations. While a sturdy gate effectively blocks motorized traffic between the boat launches, there are no barriers that prevent a walking angler in good phys-ical condition from fishing the lake almost end-to-end. For that matter, leg-powered mountain bicycles could get you anywhere you want to go on Hemlock Lake's shore, and quickly, at that.

Sean Kelly fishing for rock bass and other fish at Hemlock Lake.

The fishing in April ranges from trolling for lake trout with Seth Green rigs in mid-lake to dunking gobs of worms for bullhead along the shoreline. Austerman said the bullhead fishing at night is popular, "probably because of all the shore access." One appealing thing about bullhead fishing is the species's tendency to congregate around tributary mouths. While Hemlock Lake has only one major tributary, the aforementioned Springwater Creek, the steep hillsides around the lake are braided by many rivulets of brown water during the spring runoff period. If you can set your rod in a notched stick near one of these seasonal creek mouths on a spring evening, you will probably get a bite before you can pop a soda can or unwrap a sandwich.

## EVEN THE BIG BOYS ARE IN CASTING RANGE

Late April and early May bring other shore-fishing prospects to mind. Lakers will often be in water less than 20 feet deep and actively chasing schools of alewives or smelt. Whether these predators take a left turn occasionally to catch up with a few small rainbows, I do not know, but the DEC will venture its next pronunciation on that controversy soon enough.

Meanwhile, I'd advise my fellow anglers to have a slip-sinker rig close at hand during their springtime forays to Hemlock Lake. Such outfits, with egg-shaped weights allowed to slide freely above a barrel swivel that is in turn placed about 2 feet up from a size 4 bait hook, encourage trout to take a bait and run. Because the fish can't easily detect the sliding weight, it will usually hook itself, and if you've been dozing, daydreaming, or chatting with fellow fishermen, you should have plenty of time to recover and reel the fish to shore. Preferred baits include dead or live alewives, the worm-and-marshmallow combo that is popular on Skaneateles Lake, and compact spoons such as Krocodiles.

Be mindful that Hemlock lakers average about 4 pounds but often are double or even triple that size. Browns and rainbows seem to average around 3 pounds, and top off shy of double figures. They are gorgeous fish, but heavy monofilament lines and leaders aren't required. You'll get more strikes, and therefore reel in more trout, if you opt for a springy, ultralight "noodle" rod and spool its matching spinning reel with 4-pound mono.

Anglers working Hemlock Lake's 91-foot-deep center from boats can score on lakers and the occasional brown or rainbow at this time, too. Seth Green rigs, with their Christmas-tree clusters of five or six flashy lures attached to short leaders that are clipped to a sturdy main line, can be quite effective, albeit cumbersome to deploy and recover without tangles. However, most trollers these days prefer modern downrigger setups, with two cannonball- or shark-shaped weights lowered to a starting depth of 15 or 20 feet and lures trailing as close behind as 50 feet and as far back as 100 yards or beyond.

While the downriggered Northern Kings, AC Shiners, and other flashy and attention-grabbing lures wiggle seductively, today's canny captain is likely to give target trout a couple of other choices, including a surface-skipping lure that is flat-lined with no added weight; and another lure that runs well behind and to the side of the boat, with the aid of a planer board. The last-mentioned trick enables big boats that would otherwise run aground to fish the sandy- or gravel-bottomed shallows that warm up faster than uneven humps or boulder fields. An extra degree or two of warmth often is the only thing standing between an uneventful trolling run and multiple strikes.

By the end of May, many and perhaps most of the trout in Hemlock Lake are likely to have vacated their near-shore environs and dropped into deeper water, too. However, not all of them will hug bottom. Keep an eye on your sonar screen for large crescent marks 30 or 40 feet down.

## SEARCH FOR THE COMFORT ZONE

When the local thermocline has formed, trout tend to feed in or just above the transitional temperature layer, because that's where baitfish will be hanging out. This basic pattern will persist until mid–September or thereabouts, when the lake turns over. A few weeks after that, lake trout will be moving closer to shore and up onto gravel-bottomed areas to begin their spawning rituals.

Bass and pickerel provide plenty of action for shore casters and boaters all season long.

Largemouths may be more abundant, but smallmouth bass are more widespread in Hemlock Lake. While largemouths chow down on anything that moves in the weed beds, they are ambush feeders and prefer to make short swims to capture their prey. Smallmouths are sight feeders, and swim restlessly much of the time, which means you should go after bronzebacks instead of waiting for them to come to you. Another tip—the smallmouth's excellent eyesight gives it an advantage over its prey when it is on the hunt. For that reason, the species is very active at both dawn and dusk. Get up early or plan to stay late on your visits to Hemlock. This simple timing strategy can make a considerable difference in a bass fisher's catch on a given day.

In the spring (when bass are available on a catch-and-release basis only), smallmouths will usually be found in 5 to 20 feet of water, while largemouths should be most active in depths of 8 feet or less, at least until their spawning is complete. By mid-June, largemouths will be spending much of their day in water that's 10 or more feet deep, but they still like to prowl close to shore early in the morning, and any anglers who can get their boats in the water by sunup should devote at least half an hour to using a Zara Spook, a Hula Popper, or some other vintage surface lure in the shallows. Once the sun is climbing, the largemouths will likely retreat to the shady depths of the lake, and wise anglers should work the weed lines and points with Senkos, jig-and-pigs, or deep-diving crankbaits. When autumn rolls around, swimbaits fished on round jigheads and other bottom-zone lures should be able to entice both smallmouths and large-mouths, as bass start migrating to the flat-bottomed areas where they will spend the coming winter.

## LINE BITERS MAKE GOOD PATTIES

Hemlock Lake has extensive weed beds along much of its shoreline, but the vegetation is thickest at the south end and that's where suitably geared-up fishermen can have a blast by targeting chainsides that may run up to 25 or 26 inches long.

Plump shiner minnows fished 2 or 3 feet under a golf-ball-size bobber will draw some pickerel bites more often than not, and on many days all you need do to pinpoint the hiding place of a nice one is reel that bobber in as fast as you can. Pickerel are such single-minded predators that they simply cannot resist taking a swipe at any noisy critter—or bobber—that veers away in apparent terror. The predatory pickerel, which counts northern pike and muskellunge on its *Esox* family tree, doesn't always slam into the bobber but invariably reveals its location with a splashy charge. Chains also go for racket-making lures, such as spinnerbaits and buzzbaits with concave, water-churning blades and suspending stickbaits with ball bearings or beads banging around their insides. In all cases, the shinier the lure you select, the better your chances are of having a line biter latch onto it. And remember, they taste great!

To get to Hemlock Lake, find Canandaigua on your map and follow Routes 5 and 20 west from there to the intersection with Routes 20A and 64. Turn south and take 20A right through downtown Honeoye, then go approximately 3 miles farther to the hamlet of Hemlock. At the dead end bear left onto Route 15A, which becomes East Lake Road.

# CHAPTER 11

# Conesus Lake

**LOCATION:** Central Livingston County
**ELEVATION:** 818 feet
**SURFACE AREA:** 3,420 acres
**SHORELINE:** 18.47 miles
**MEAN DEPTH:** 38 feet
**MAXIMUM DEPTH:** 69 feet
**APPROXIMATE THERMOCLINE DEPTH:** 36 feet

If you're a walleye specialist who has a serious case of spring fever, you should call in sick at work some bright morning in mid-April and take a drive through eastern Livingston County to the south end of Conesus Lake. After parking your vehicle, don a pair of sunglasses with polarized lenses and walk upstream on a well-trod path along Conesus Inlet, the lake's principal tributary. Before you get very far, you'll see the fish of your dreams. In one pool after another, you will gasp at the sight of round-bellied walleyes that are as long as your arms—or perhaps even your legs. Some of these fish, which are on their annual spawning run, would weigh 10 or 12 pounds, if anyone staring at them happened to have the tools or the legal authority to remove these out-of-season monsters from the water and put them on a spring scale. But this is strictly a "look, don't touch" event, so you must be satisfied with your right to exercise an angler's prerogative by stretching the truth about what you've seen this day—just a wee bit, of course.

Astonishing sights and happenings are almost commonplace for anglers devoted to Conesus Lake and its fertile watershed. Besides the inlet pools clogged by stacks of huge walleyes, fishermen who spend the requisite time on Conesus will be rewarded by the ferocious assault of a northern pike on a magnum lure, and the airborne acrobatics of a rotund largemouth that has felt the sharp sting of a size 4/0 worm hook in its upper jaw. Such experiences fascinate anglers, and keep them coming back for more. But Conesus Lake is a bit of an enigma, with a food chain that's subject to population explosions and crashes, and its regulars must resolve to keep on learning if they wish to keep on catching.

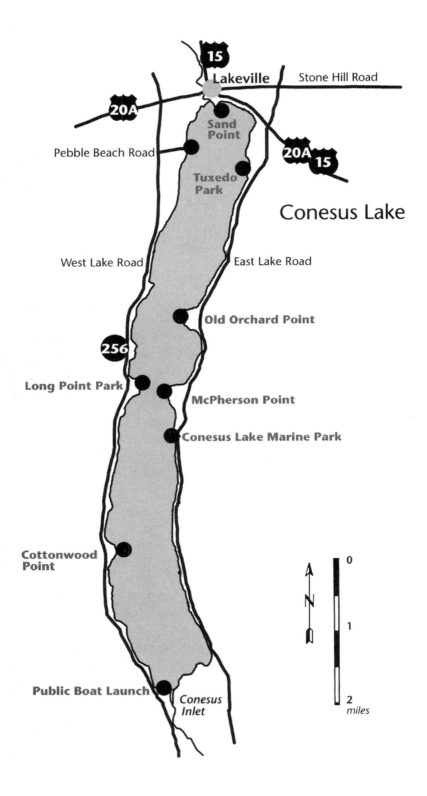

# THE LITTLE LAKE
# OF BIG FISH

Conesus Lake is one of the smaller bodies of water in the Finger Lakes chain, covering 3,420 surface acres and having a maximum depth of 69 feet. The westernmost of the Fingers, it is also a mere half-hour drive from Rochester. That convenient location no doubt had something to do with the early and intense development around its shore. Fishing is extremely popular here, but so are swimming and racing around at high speeds in every kind of watercraft you can picture. No wonder, then, that early morning is widely considered to be the best time of day, by far, to go fishing on Conesus Lake. The mix of predator fish

Paul Lane shows off a largemouth from his home water, Livingston County's Conesus Lake.

in the lake is constantly changing. In the 1960s, yellow perch were so abundant that ice fishermen could easily gather a six-month supply of tasty fillets from favorite hard-water spots, such as MacPherson Point or Old Orchard Point. My late friend and colleague Scott Sampson, the former outdoors scribe for the *Finger Lakes Times*, wrote vividly about the era when several hours was time enough for some Conesus experts to collect hundreds of fat perch. Cleaning so many fish was such a daunting chore that some entrepreneurs paid fellow anglers for their perch, then arranged to sell the combined catch to restaurants. Tempers were apt to go from "simmer" to "red-hot" in a flash when anglers desirous of making a supper of their sport encountered those who were in it mainly for the money.

Such conflicts became a moot point in the mid- to late 1980s, when the perch fishery at Conesus Lake crashed with a thud. The illegal release of alewives into the lake by persons unknown is a prime example of what the DEC calls "bait bucket biology." The concept sounds unsophisticated but harmless to casual anglers, yet anytime an untrained amateur ignores laws against stocking the state's waters without first obtaining the required permit, there are bound to be unintended consequences. In the case of Conesus Lake, when alewives were turned loose they went forth and multiplied, and then multiplied some more. Ultimately, their multiplication was so fruitful and their population so large that they basically ate their way onto the rung of the food ladder that previously was reserved for yellow perch. When they ran out of perch fry, the alewives went after whatever else they could eat, including walleye fry—just as growing perch used to, only on a grander scale.

## BLAME ALEWIFE GLUT ON BAIT BUCKET BIOLOGY

"Restoring the yellow perch fishery is a major management goal [for Conesus Lake]," said DEC Region 8 biologist Matt Sanderson. "Unfortunately, the entire yellow perch food web has been changed by alewives and that limits restoration opportunities."

In other words, we'd all love to see perch make a major comeback in Conesus, but thanks to whoever it was that dumped a few alewives there a quarter century ago, we dare not hold our breath until it happens.

For a couple of years back in the early to mid-1990s, regional fisheries supervisors thought they could tip the predator–prey balance toward the walleyes, pike, perch, and other traditional residents of the lake by basically overwhelming the prolific newcomers. The DEC stocked the lake heavily with walleye fingerlings and also introduced a voracious new eating machine, the tiger muskie. Crossbreeds that result from the natural or hatchery-orchestrated pairing of northern pike and pure-strain muskellunge, "norlunge" or tiger muskies had made a big impression in some lakes (such as Otisco, another of the Fingers), and biologists hoped they would take a bite out of the Conesus Lake alewife population.

All these efforts fell short of the goal of alewife eradication. Through the 1990s and into the 21st century, walleyes of tremendous weight and girth excited fishermen who watched them spawn in Conesus Inlet, but those same fish rarely bit in the lake, once the season was under way, because they were literally stuffed to their gills with alewives. The baitfish got even by outcompeting young-of-the-year perch for their favorite food, the zooplankton that swarmed throughout the lake. Even worse, there were some years when large economy-size alewives were so ubiquitous in the lake that they ate the majority of baby walleyes they came across, whether fry or fingerling. Overall, walleyes seem to be holding their own in Conesus Lake. DEC experts estimated the lake held approximately 20,000 adult walleyes at the start of the 2002 fishing season, or between 5 and 6 per acre. That density compares favorably with Oneida Lake's, but Oneida fishermen, who do not have to worry about alewives, have much higher catch rates than seen on Conesus Lake.

Cornell University's research facility at Shackelton Point on Oneida's south shore is known worldwide for its walleye studies, and some of its resident scientists have been working with DEC biologists to come up with effective tactics for dealing with walleye–alewife stalemates at Conesus Lake and elsewhere. Meanwhile, anglers are doing their own research, trying to identify practical and effective ways to hook walleyes that apparently just don't feel like eating.

In 2003, Sanderson issued a report titled "A Recreational Fishery Survey of Conesus Lake, with Emphasis on the Spring Walleye Fishery." The study was conducted with state and federal funding, and consisted mainly of a creel survey of boating anglers, shore fishermen, and ice fishermen that ran from May 2000 to March 2001. Sanderson estimated that 60,400 angler-hours were spent on the lake during the study period, and 49,100 fish were caught. About 7,100 of those were creeled, but very few walleyes went from lake to food freezer. Sanderson's report indicated that Conesus fishermen caught a grand total of 330 walleyes during the approximately 11-month-long creel survey. All of them were caught in open water. Permit me to repeat that one: According to the report, nobody caught even one walleye through the ice during the study period. Of the estimated 330 caught in open water, 130 were caught in daytime hours and 200 were landed at night.

## CRUNCHING CREEL CENSUS NUMBERS

Experienced walleye fishermen who have spent little or no time on Conesus Lake will probably jump to a couple of conclusions after a quick reading of this summary of catch and effort. First, they are apt to notice right away that night fishing commonly accounts for a good share of the walleyes caught in Conesus. The same, however, could be said of almost any lake with a decent walleye population.

For example, consider Otisco Lake, which is at the far end of our chain, a two-hour drive from Conesus. Any angler who is fairly familiar with Otisco but hasn't done much after-dark casting for walleyes there should know that he has been missing out on some great shore fishing, particularly in May and June. Has he never seen or heard the loud splashing along the Otisco shoreline on dark spring nights? Did he also fail to notice the beams of portable camp lanterns and headlamps flickering from dusk to dawn, starting with the first evening of the walleye season?

Otisco Lake isn't quite as glutted with alewives as it used to be, but, like Conesus, it depends on regular stockings of state-supplied fingerlings to keep its walleye population on the robust side. As with Conesus Lake, Otisco has a fairly thick population of walleyes and even has tributaries large enough to attract some big spawners in April. However, the fry that hatch in those little streams seldom live long enough to "recruit" into adulthood. The explanation is pretty plain to see. The little 'eyes vanish into the hungry mouths of 5- to 8-inch alewives, if something bigger doesn't get them first. And let's not attribute such behavior just to alewives or black crappies or perch or any other small but voracious eaters of their fellow fish. Remember, when they can't tame their growling stomachs by gulping down a few alewives, shad, or whatnot, adult walleyes have no compunctions at all about keeping bad eating habits in the family. Yes, they really do eat their young, and plenty of them.

Another thing about Sanderson's report that rings true is the author's finding that Conesus walleye catches seem to increase after sundown, while hookups with other species slow dramatically—with one exception.

## NORLUNGE WENT MISSING AT NIGHT

Looking at the numbers, the survey reveals that open-water, daytime fishermen in the Conesus Lake survey caught an estimated 27,000 total panfish, 13,000 largemouth bass, 3,200 smallmouth bass, 2,500 northern pike, 790 yellow perch, 340 tiger muskies, and 130 walleyes.

The open-water nighttime catch estimated by Sanderson included 1,500 panfish, 630 largemouths, 200 walleyes, 200 northern pike, 170 smallmouths, 60 yellow perch, and zero tiger muskies. That last one surprises me because it is not at all unusual to catch norlunge after dark in Otisco Lake. Why is the tiger muskie night bite so good at one end of the Finger Lakes and so poor at the opposite pole? Sorry, I'm working on it but I haven't got a clue.

As to the exception to the rule I mentioned a couple of paragraphs back, noting that hookups with all species begin to die down after dark, with one exception, just think *bullhead*. That homely but tasty member of the catfish family is highly sought after by many fishermen in Western New York, and bullheads have a reputation for biting very well after dark. Sanderson said the 2,164 angler-hours his team estimated were put forth by bullhead anglers in April and May accounted for almost one-quarter of the total shore-fishing on Conesus during that two-month period. Most of that fishing was done after dark, when bullheads everywhere can be counted on to feed close to shore.

## ACCESS PROBLEMS LIMIT WALLEYE ACTION

It's likely that a sizable share of the bullhead fishermen plying their skills around Conesus Lake in the spring are full- or part-time residents with houses or camps on or near the shore. They typically don't have any problems finding good spots to catch bullheads. However, I'm not so sanguine about shore locations for walleye fishermen. Public or quasi-public places to hurl stickbaits or jigs into the night are scarce at Conesus and, I'm sad to say, on most other lakes, too.

Because the situation is what it is, traveling anglers should make every effort to find good potential access sites for wading and shore casting when they arrive in town. Better yet, why not spend a couple of days scouting for likely fishing spots around the lakeshore, then make polite inquiries about access at local residences, bakeries, bait shops, gas stations, and so forth? Be sure to let friendly landowners know that you are willing to pay for the privilege of doing some late-hour casting from shore or even private docks, if they happen to be available.

While you're looking for potential private access points, you should be able to do some no-hassle and potentially productive casting from some or all of the vantage points at the DEC properties on the lake. These spots include the previously mentioned Conesus Inlet, off Route 256 at the south end. The wildlife management area there has parking for 40 vehicles, but the only boats allowed are cartoppers small enough to carry in by hand. Look the launch area over before sunset, and if the boat traffic near shore isn't too heavy, give it a try with stickbaits or spoons with a generous touch of alewife silver. The fishing may be worthwhile or it may not, but as a rule you should secure a spot before darkness falls. Bring your chest waders and a personal flotation device, just in case.

Other possible shore-fishing locations include the state Office of Parks, Recreation and Historic Restoration boat launch, on the east shore about 4 miles south of Route 20A. It's a hard-surface ramp with parking for 40 cars and can be quite fishable from shore or from its docks. Another likely shore spot is the DEC launch in the northwest corner of the lake on Pebble Beach Road. It has parking for 120 cars. Finally, check out the 45-car parking and beach area at Sand Point. On the north shore via Route 20A, it's run by the DEC and the town of Livonia.

I am certainly not discouraging boaters from trying to catch a few after-dark walleyes in Conesus Lake, for they generally do better than shore casters, thanks to their mobility and the resulting opportunity to try a variety of lure and bait presentations. There are more ways to catch walleyes than most anglers realize, especially when the fish are in the shallows under a gloomy night sky. When I fish Otisco Lake for walleyes, which is fairly often, I fan cast from shore or perched in a small boat. But while I wait for a head-shaking strike on my Rapala or Thunderstick, I keep an eye and ear on a second rod, which is in a holder and baited with a nightcrawler that sits about a foot off the bottom, threaded on a fluorescent green or orange floating jighead. I don't get many walleyes on that rig, but when the bell attached to the rod tip begins to jingle, it's apt to be a big fish playing the tune. My best to date on the rig was a 27-incher that weighed more than 8 pounds.

## SUMMER IS HOT FOR BASS AND PIKE

Walleye action slows to a crawl on Conesus Lake by mid-June, if not sooner, but die-hards keep after them in the hot months by trolling for suspended fish with the aid of planer boards or even three-way swivel rigs over the tops of weed beds.

For most Conesus anglers, though, summer belongs to bass and northern pike. Both species thrive throughout the lake, and neither is hard to find.

Frank Tennity with a largemouth bass caught in Conesus Lake.

Three- to 5-pound largemouths are run-of-the-mill fish here, which is why area bass clubs like the Avon Anglers hold tournaments on Conesus Lake so frequently. From mid-June into October, hardly a weekend passes without at least one tourney taking place, and some Saturdays there may be several weigh-ins on the slate. I suspect the club-tournament schedule would be even more intense if the lake wasn't already crowded with pleasure boats.

The traffic doesn't get too hectic until midmorning or so, which is why many Conesus Lake tournament contestants look for their lunker prize entry or "kicker" fish as soon as they blast off from their shoreline

launching site. Once they get a 4-
or 5-pounder in the boat, they sigh
with relief and head for a location
that is likely to hold lots of nice
bass, rather than one or two whoppers. Some tournaments, however,
are clinched rather quickly. On a
given day, any of the deep weed
beds that encircle most of the lake
could be playing host to a school
of 4-pounders. If a contestant
lucks into such a pod of fish, he'll
be climbing toward the top of the
leader board for sure.

Tournament fishermen don't
have all the fun on Conesus Lake,
of course. During May and the
first few days of June, when restless
largemouths and smallmouths alike
are attending to their nests and
clouds of just-hatched fry, any cast
delivered to a bare circle of sand or

A closer look at a nice
Conesus largemouth.

a shady dock can provoke a sudden attack from a hefty bass. On the other
hand, if you enjoy sight fishing, you could spend half an hour or more
trying to tease a nice one into inhaling a Senko or a plastic salamander.

## GO A LITTLE DEEPER

A good rule of thumb for Conesus anglers is to concentrate on the near-
shore part of weed beds and other shallow cover until the regular bass
season is open. At that point, you will probably do better if you spend at
least half of your time in somewhat deeper water, perhaps 8 to 15 feet for
largemouths and 15 to 25 feet for smallmouths. All the standard weedless
lures will put Conesus bass on a stringer. Besides Senkos rigged Texas-
style, be sure to give old-fashioned, 8- to 10-inch-long plastic worms a
workout. Jig-and-pig combos perform very well in the weeds, provided
they weigh at least a full ounce to cut quickly through the vegetation with
minimal hang-ups.

To cover lots of water systematically on those frustrating days when
the bass seem to be scattered and not really into chow, nothing works
better than a spinnerbait with nickel-finish blades and a carefully trimmed

skirt. If the fishing is exceptionally slow, work the lure at a speed just fast enough to keep its blades ticking the tops of the weeds. Any color will do, as long as it's white. And I know that's an exaggeration, but I wish I had a dollar for every expert who has said pretty much the same thing. I like white for blades and skirts, personally, because it shows up but doesn't look unnatural, no matter how dark the clouds or how heavy the rain showers happen to be.

Trimming the skirt on a spinnerbait, by the way, makes a big difference if you are getting short strikes with any regularity. Too bad the bass can't tell us these things before we ease them back into the water!

## THE PIKE BITE

One aspect of Conesus Lake that any angler is bound to like is its abundant population of toothy critters. Any member of the *Esox* family merits that fond description, many years after TV fishing personality Al Lindner coined it, but in Conesus the term covers northern pike and tiger muskellunge. They are most worthy of Lindner's handle, for if you expect to land a large pike or muskie on a leader made of anything but steel, you'd better be using a very long lure with multiple trebles. Otherwise you and Mr. Big are probably going to have a very brief relationship. I have netted

some nice pike on 15-pound-test fluorocarbon, but in each case I was trolling a 9- or 10-inch plug or spoon and the fish could not put its teeth on the leader.

Former DEC Region 8 fisheries manager Bill Abraham, who retired about 10 years ago, still enjoys the opportunity to tell people about the size of some Conesus Lake residents. In particular, he raves about the pike, which he says grow to be even larger than a daydreaming angler might suppose.

"We [the DEC] have netted northerns of 30 pounds in Conesus," Abraham declared. "You probably wouldn't believe the size of the pike in there."

Frank Tennity with a Conesus Lake pike.

Abraham went on to say the lake is "loaded" with 10-pounders. Such a pike is large enough to boast about but too small for the taxidermist's attentions. That makes it just right for a beer-batter fish fry. I haven't caught one that big, yet, not in Conesus Lake, anyway, but once Frank Tennity and I had just completed a slow right turn out of the state park's boat launch near MacPherson Point when I popped a fateful question.

## BE ALERT OR BE SORRY

"Do you think we'll get any pike today?" I asked. "Because I could use a couple of pike photos, and the bigger the better."

Tennity was cupping his hand to his right ear to let me know he hadn't heard the question. Before I could repeat myself, I spotted a dark shape in the crystal-clear water, rising up from the bottom and simultaneously closing the distance to my lure. It slammed into the stickbait so quickly I didn't bother to set the hook, which was a critical mistake.

"Speaking of big pike," I said, with my voice about an octave higher than usual. "This is a big one. It has to be 10 pounds, at least. Do you have your net handy here somewhere, Frank?"

My friend was just about to hand the net to me when the fearsome-looking beast at the end of my line shook its head and opened its mouth. The lure, with pike detached, floated to the surface and I muttered one or two of those expletives (deleted) that we fishermen should never use but do, usually in circumstances like those that had just befallen me.

Oh, well. It's not as if I'll never get a second chance. As Matt Sanderson's creel census proved, Conesus Lake has a very healthy population of pike, to go with all those bass, walleyes, et cetera. Since 1991, it has also held some beautiful tiger muskies. The tigers were added to the regional fisheries office's toolbox for the express purpose of increasing the predatory pressure on all those alewives. So far the alewives are holding their own, though they're still under finned assault. But nobody is blaming the hybrid muskies—most fishermen seem to enjoy having them in Conesus.

## TIGER MUSKIES MAKING AN IMPACT

If those anglers should change their mind about the norlunge in the near or distant future, no problem, for the nicest thing about hybrids, from the fisheries manager's perspective, is their sterility. Until the tiger muskies mutate in a way that enables them to procreate, all the DEC has to do to eliminate the species in Conesus or any other lake is simply stop stocking them. Those left behind will die off within a few years.

A close-up of a tiger muskie and the author. Watch for those razor-sharp teeth!

Locating pike or tiger muskies is fairly easy, because both species are in the habit of hunting from ambush. Unlike walleyes, which may roam widely while they're looking for alewives or other baitfish, pike and norlunge will be found consistently in or quite near weed beds, in winter, spring, and summer. In the autumn months, however, those weeds gradually die back, and pike and tiger muskies are forced to move about more than they do earlier in the year. Trollers who use downriggers to pull plugs, stickbaits, or even slow-wobbling spoons at modest speeds (3 knots or less) 100 to 200 feet behind their boats stand a good chance of hooking one of Bill Abraham's monsters under these conditions. The deep-water sides of the largest weed beds in the lake, off Tuxedo Park at the north end and due north of the inlet at the south end, are great places to connect with a trophy-class northern. Cottonwood Point, about 1½ miles north of the inlet via West Lake Road, is another spot with a reputation for holding more than a few big pike. Its quick drop from 10- to 50-foot depths is the likely attraction.

As for the right time, big pike are a lot like heavyweight muskellunge: They bite when they feel like it, and since nobody knows when that will be, it behooves serious trophy anglers to spend as much time on the water as they possibly can.

You have probably guessed by now that tiger muskies are just about as hard to pin down as their parents. I will confess I have not intentionally fished for nor caught any norlunge in Conesus Lake, but I have been fortunate to catch a dozen or so tigers in other regional waters. They are gorgeous to look at, fight like they are being dragged to the electric chair, and occasionally do some very odd but interesting things, such as skimming along at the water's surface with their mouths and caudal fins half out of the water. Some of the aquatic biologists I've asked about such strange behavior have heard of it or even witnessed it themselves, but they don't have a clue, either.

My biggest tiger, at this writing, measured 44 inches and weighed approximately 22 pounds on my bathroom scale. I caught it in my favorite trout stream, and you can read more about it in the chapter on regional trout waters.

To get to Conesus Lake from Rochester, take Route 390 south to Exit 9 and continue south on Route 15 to Lakeville, at the north end of the lake.

# CHAPTER 12

# Trolling for Finger Lakes Trout and Salmon

The Seth Green rig has been fooling deep-water trout for well over a century, and it did nothing to hurt its reputation the last time Wayne Brewer and I gave it a workout. Brewer, who became the commander of the New York Department of Environmental Conservation's Law Enforcement Division during the Pataki administration, had invited me to join him on a Seneca Lake junket with Geneva-area fishing guide Jim Morgan, and I instantly accepted. Morgan is one of the top trollers in the Finger Lakes, and by the time I hung up the phone I could picture trout and salmon leaping into our boat two days hence.

As most experienced fishermen know all too well, daydreams of piscatorial prowess are not necessarily the precursors to real-life triumphs. Jim Morgan is a knowledgeable charter captain and usually has the upper hand in duels with the denizens of Seneca Lake. Yet on this day he couldn't

Captain Jim Morgan readjusts his trolling rigs.

buy a strike. Perhaps it could be blamed on the cold front that was passing through and churning the broad lake into a mass of whitecaps and rollers better suited to surfing than precision trolling. Maybe the fish were over-stuffed from their regular feasting on alewives and other bite-size forage species. The bottom line was, we weren't getting any hookups.

"We're marking fish everywhere, on our sonar," Morgan said. "But they just don't seem to be interested."

He had hoped to get us connected with a few of Seneca's trademark lake trout, and perhaps a couple of fat rainbows or a landlocked Atlantic salmon. But by the time our morning charter was nearly at an end, he was frustrated, and Wayne and I knew the feeling.

"Let's see if we can wake them up," Morgan said. Turning my way, he asked, "Did you ever fish a Seth Green rig?"

Keith Dickinson rigging a Seth Green rig.

## SOME DAYS CALL FOR OLD WAYS

At that time, I had not, but I knew who Seth Green was—an innovative thinker who, according to angling historians, was the founding father of New York's trout-rearing and -stocking system. His old 19th-century hatchery is state-owned and still cranking out fish for DEC-managed trout fisheries, and, oh yes, he also is credited with the development of a popular trolling rig, since named after him.

It would be fun to fish the old-fashioned way for a while, I opined, and within minutes Morgan and his veteran first mate, Keith "Wolfie" Dickinson, were uncoiling stiff lengths of line from one of their onboard tackle drawers and affixing them to two rods, one for me to monitor and the other for Brewer's use. Attached to the rig was a Christmas-tree array of bright, reflective trolling spoons, anchored by a heavy sinker. Morgan said the setup was designed to represent a small school of baitfish, and it sure looked the part. Each lure, in this case five per rod, was attached to a short leader that, in turn, was connected to the main line with a snap swivel. Strategically placed barrel swivels were spread out on the line to keep lures safely separated from one another, and Morgan said we would all minimize entanglements, if fish began to bite, by reeling in one lure at a time and then pausing so the first mate could net fish or disconnect each leader in turn.

It worked like a charm, just as it always has. After a few minutes of trolling with the Seth Green rigs, Wayne and I asked Morgan about some subtle vibrations in the tips of the sturdy rods that he'd chosen for our vintage setup.

"I was wondering if you'd see that," our captain replied. "I think we might have hooked a fish or two. Let's get the rest of these lines in and we'll find out what we've caught."

As it turned out, we had four lake trout, three on Brewer's rig and one on mine. They came in obligingly, as 2- to 3-pound lakers often do, but they salvaged an otherwise-fishless day, and we were delighted that Morgan had maintained a healthy respect for tradition.

In truth, trolling tactics and tackle have come a long way since the late 1800s, and modern experts like Morgan keep up with the changes. Anglers who hire Morgan's Seneca Chief Charters or other guide services in the Finger Lakes region these days will see electric downriggers, planer boards, temperature probes, global positioning systems (GPS), and other high-tech doodads put to work on their behalf. It's a dazzling display, but it all boils down to the same basics that our grandfathers and great-grandfathers relied on—find the precise location and depths where fish are swimming and then show them something that looks good to eat. Our ancestors found their hot spots in the lakes by triangulating, or lining up their boats with cabins, trees, or other recognizable landmarks. Instead of marking "waypoints" on GPS units, the old-timers either wrote down their observations in a notebook or consigned them to memory. Anglers of today start and end their fishing homework just like Grandpa, but they take some very useful shortcuts in between. The electronic gear on the

Wayne Brewer, former commander of NYS Encon Police, and the author with Seneca Lake trout caught "in the home stretch" using Seth Green rigs.

market today does even more for gung-ho amateurs who want to make the most of their limited time on the water than it does for pros like Morgan. In a nutshell, the learning curve for trolling rookies isn't as steep as it used to be.

None of this should be taken to mean that trolling needs to be high-tech or complicated if you're going after Finger Lakes trout or salmon. At any season of the year, but especially in the autumn months, many anglers catch gorgeous rainbows and landlocks in Skaneateles and Seneca Lakes by simply pulling a single- or tandem-hook streamer fly or a small spoon or stickbait along the shoreline. This is fishing at its easiest, and possibly its best, as single anglers using no more than two rods and reels at a time may be kept busy all day, hooking and battling 15- to 20-inch fish—or even larger specimens.

## YOU CAN'T GET TOO CLOSE

Dick Withey Jr. is a superb Skaneateles Lake guide who unfortunately fell in love with Florida saltwater fishing and moved to the Sunshine State in 2011. He used to point his charter boat so close to shoreline hazards that his first mate and clients had to hustle to avoid snagging their trolled lures and flies on docks, buoys, and other hook grabbers. Withey usually reacted to the near misses by using planer boards to take the lures still closer to the bank on cool November afternoons.

"You can't get close enough to shore in the fall," he said. Often, strikes for his clients came in depths of 5 feet or less, and in rapid-fire volleys of action, too, as the lures passed through the dining nooks of trout after trout.

You need not be a professional angler to take Withey's advice to heart. I've seen anglers in canoes, assorted fishing kayaks, and even foot-powered paddle boats score on near-shore trout and salmon. The minimalists who put fish on their stringers in the fall are not all in one-person watercraft, either. Two fishermen who team up in a 12- or 14-foot rowboat with a 10-horse engine can raise Cain with the landlocks and trout residing in several of the Finger Lakes. The advantage of two fishermen in the boat instead of one is the ability to show the fish more colors, sizes, and shapes at once.

My friend Milt Franson of Pompey eagerly awaits the arrival of November, when he expects landlocked salmon fishing to peak on Skaneateles Lake. He uses a variety of tackle, but his sentimental favorite is an ancient bamboo fly rod with a permanent set near the tip. Franson, a superb wildlife artist, catches plenty of fish, but when the salmon aren't biting, he can curl his fingers around that old cork grip and relive days, not so long ago, when *Salmo salar* spent more time in the air than in the water.

Who says you need big flies to catch big fish? Here are five that will work on big brown trout and salmon in Finger Lakes tributaries. Clockwise starting at the bottom: Copper Comet, Glo Bug, Salmon River Flea, Prince nymph, and Sparkle Braid egg cluster.

Like most salmon fishers, Franson has found that landlocks are most aggressive toward trolled flies and lures when they are twisting and turning no more than a foot or 2 below the surface, and at a fairly high speed. A trolling pace of 4 or 5 nautical miles per hour is not too high for landlocks, although it can be a bit much for some streamer patterns. If your fly skips to the top and lies on its side or simply "feels funny" when it's trolled, check to see if a wing feather is wrapped around the hook shank or bend. Adjust your speed accordingly, or else change flies.

## FLIES FOR SALMON, TROUT

As a rule, salmon prefer natural colors, such as white, black-and-white, green-and-white, and similar schemes. They will hit gaudy red-and-orange concoctions of feathers and fur on gloomy days, now and then, but most often they like fairly realistic imitations of local baitfish.

Rainbows are just the opposite, as likely to hit a red, white, and blue bucktail (my version is called The All American) or an orange-and-black, Halloween-ish tandem streamer as an ultra-realistic smelt or alewife imitation. They also seem to favor mid-range trolling speeds of, say, 2.5 to 3.5 knots. While salmon often come up for flies or spoons that are bouncing in a boat wake, rainbows are a bit more cautious and like lures trolled 100 to 150 feet behind the rod.

A traditional Grey Ghost on a size 6 long-shank hook is framed by tandem streamers in red-and-white bucktail (top) and perch (bottom) color patterns. Both are very effective trolling lures in spring and fall, when Finger Lakes trout are feeding in relatively shallow water.

Size counts for at least as much as color where lure and fly selections are concerned. In most of the Finger Lakes, alewives and smelt are the big dogs on the food chain, so they are what local trout and salmon feel comfortable eating. In Skaneateles Lake, however, the main minnow available to resident populations of rainbows, landlocks, and lake trout is the spot-tail shiner, which is perhaps 2 inches long, at most. The game fish in Skaneateles are used to chasing down spot-tails because they are handy and unthreatening. Therefore, anglers are wise to bring along lots of 1½- to 2-inch-long lures such as Needlefish and Mooselook Wobblers when they troll in Skaneateles Lake. Tandem streamers should be on the short side, too.

Fly-rod enthusiasts do not have to be fly-line fanciers when trolling the Finger Lakes. Some successful anglers prefer a New England–style trolling rig, which pairs a 30-foot-long monofilament leader with a floating or sinking fly line, but many others opt for a fly or spinning reel spooled entirely with 6-pound or even 4-pound mono. The latter setup ignores tradition but is certainly easy for a neophyte troller to master. It is also easier on the wallet.

However, deep-water trollers should plan on making a substantial investment of time and money when they sign up for the sport. Oddly enough, trolling is like fly fishing in this respect. Both schools of angling are like bottomless pits: Participants always have something new to learn or vital to obtain.

A first-time troller can debut with a burdensome debt or get off to a cheap start, depending on whether he or she is already the proud owner of a suitable boat. Next to a proper vessel, a motor-powered troller's most essential acquisitions will be rods and reels, downriggers, planer boards, and a useful sonar or electronic fishfinder.

While they're doing the opposite of drifting most of the time, the rods trollers find most compatible with their fishing strategies are often referred to as "drift" rods. They're designed mainly for use in river-run drift boats like those seen regularly on the Salmon River in Pulaski but perform wonderfully in the open water of Seneca Lake, too. Drift rods typically run about 8 or 9 feet long and are partnered with high-end bait-casting reels with skinny arbors and large line capacities. When a big trout or salmon strikes and begins to jump or shake its head, a subtle turn or two of a drag knob on such a rod is all that's necessary to keep the angler in control while the fish is out of control.

## CHOOSING A TROLLING ROD

If I were shopping for a deep-water trolling rod, I'd look for signs of overall durability and quality of manufacturing, including extra coats of varnish and smooth tip and stripping guides. Although quite functional, guides with ceramic inserts are not necessary, since their main purpose is to achieve smoother casts and reduce line abrasion. Deep trollers don't do much casting; instead, they simply open the bail or pay out measured strips of line until the lure or fly is approximately where they desire it to be. Stainless-steel guides are not only sturdy but light, and every ounce of unnecessary weight is a drag on rod—and angler—performance.

The trolling rod of my Finger Lakes dreams would be designed to handle small to medium-size spoons, stickbaits, and crankbaits, and therefore built to fish with light lines, mainly in the 4- to 12-pound-test range. Lastly, it should be made of graphite or a graphite composite.

As for reels, I'd select one with a large line capacity (at least 250 feet of the heaviest line I'll be using) and a drag system that can be tightened or loosened readily. A single large reel handle suits me fine, but some trollers prefer a reel with two handles.

One reel feature that few serious trollers would want to do without, once they have tried it, is a line counter. The counter, fitted to the trolling reel, keeps a running record of how much line a fish has taken since it was hooked. Such devices are valuable during a long scrap with a double-digit lake trout, because they can tell you if angler or fish is winning. Aside from that, they're just plain fun! I have yet to see a Finger Lakes specimen match the 675 feet of line that a Lake Ontario salmon peeled off my rig one day, but I haven't given up hope.

Cork grips are a thing of the past for anything other than a fly rod, but those of the fishing fraternity who wax nostalgic for them should look for the next-best grip material, which is a nonslip foam. The outfitters at Cabela's rod and reel dispensary in Nebraska heard "can I get that in cork?" so often that a couple of years ago they began listing a "Fish Eagle" trolling reel-and-rod combo that features a rod with a cork foregrip ahead of a nonslip foam rear grip. We anglers tend to be nostalgic, if not slow to embrace change. Some Finger Lakes area residents still like to show off the old Victrola record players their dads and grandfathers used to store their copper and leadcore lines, after all. They used to reel these lines by hand, referring to the method as "pulling copper."

For those who, reading this chapter, just wondered what a "record player" was, all I can say in response is never mind. The rest immediately understand why they don't run into too many Finger Lakes fishermen who prefer Seth Green rigs or even leadcore lines over modern-day downriggers. Suffice to say, the goal is to feed lures to deep-swimming trout, salmon, walleyes, or muskellunge, and riggers do it better.

Downrigger trolling requires a specialized reel such as the one pictured here.

Downriggers made their first big splash in the 1960s and have been taking lures to the greeny deep sectors of lakes ever since. Without them, few fishermen of average talent, pluck, and money would have been able to fish offshore for Lake Ontario salmon, and the beautiful Finger Lakes fishery would still be the main attraction for angling tourists in the Empire State. Electronic fishfinders played a big part in the revolution, too; but a sonar screen without a downrigger is like a nuclear bomb without a long-range missile or a speedy bomber plane. In both scenarios, a delivery system is the key component.

## MAKE SURE YOUR GEAR GOES WITH YOUR BOAT

If you're contemplating a maiden voyage with downriggers and accessories, be sure to match the gear to your boat. A 12- or 14-foot runabout or rowboat is a small platform that can easily be overloaded with gear and gizmos. One or two mechanical, hand-cranking downriggers with cables will serve a small boater well in all but the two largest Finger Lakes. Seneca and Cayuga, given their sheer size, are better suited to large economy-size fishing boats—say, in the 16-to-23-foot range. Boats of that bulk can readily take on a couple of downriggers, and their owners usually have no problem affording one of the newer electric models.

The primary advantage downriggers have over the old ways is consistency. By snapping a line and lure to a cannonball- or fish-shaped weight and cable with a depth counter attached, you can rest assured that the lure in use will run at precisely the right level, whether that happens to be 20 feet down over 100 feet of water or scratching bottom in a lake that isn't half that deep.

In other words, downriggers can make good trollers out of guys who formerly didn't know how to bait a hook. They can't do it all by themselves, though.

## WHO WAS SETH GREEN, ANYWAY?

Some folks will answer this question by confidently declaring that Seth Green is the red-headed actor who played a teenage werewolf in the hit TV show, *Buffy the Vampire Slayer*. You know, Willow's boyfriend. That would be true, yet incorrect, for the Seth Green I have in mind was not an actor but a pisciculturalist—a fish farmer.

The Green I'm talking about had a lush full beard, with hair even thicker than a werewolf's, and lived from 1817 to 1888, mostly in and around Rochester. More important, he is credited with building the first successful trout hatchery in the Western Hemisphere, in 1864. It's still standing and still producing trout for the state Department of Environmental Conservation, in the Livingston County village of Caledonia.

In a sense Seth Green is still standing, too, for his basic methods for rearing trout for food or recreational purposes continue to influence pisciculture all over the world. Nor should anyone be surprised that this tall, imposing figure was an avid fisherman, capable of inventing an awkward but deadly tackle item called the Seth Green rig. Unlike other fishing lures, Green's namesake was meant to look not like a single minnow, but like a whole school of them.

Green was not the first American or even the first New Yorker to collect trout eggs, fertilize them, and watch them hatch and grow. That honor befell Stephen Ainsworth, of West Bloomfield, who attempted to make a few dollars by building an artificial trout-rearing system. Ainsworth didn't succeed on the scale he had hoped for, but Green did, after making several trips to Ainsworth's home to observe and soak up some ideas.

Green worked with brook trout, which were native to New York but disappearing from many of their natural haunts by the time he got into fish culture. According to amateur angling historian

Roger Karas, Green experimented with rearing splake, the hybrids produced by crossbreeding brookies and lake trout. He also provided brook trout fry, fingerlings, and yearlings to restock streams and lakes that were losing their fish to pollution, excessive logging, and overfishing.

Although he was not America's first trout culturist, he was the first to raise trout in a hatchery built for that purpose, in 1864. He reared huge numbers of brook trout that fishing clubs, individual anglers, local and state governments, and assorted do-gooders deposited in countless waters. Some streams on Green's post–Civil War stocking list were suitable for trout and many were not, but the man was growing fish, not habitat. Sadly, he and his colleagues effectively inbred various strains of *Salmo fontinalis*, and sometimes passed undesirable traits to previously hearty populations.

If Green's methods were overused, that was not his fault, and he certainly earned his reputation as the founding father of American trout culture. Although he sold his hatchery on Spring Creek (then known as Big Springs) to the state in 1868, Green quickly accepted an appointment to the new state Fish Commission. In that capacity he continued to advise New York's budding hatchery system for many years.

# CHAPTER 13

# Bass Fishing in the Finger Lakes

Since the late 1970s, when professional angling became another career path for high-school guidance counselors to discourage, most of the fishermen who actually managed to make a living in bass tournaments had southern drawls and lots of friends with names like Bubba, Ricky, and Joe Bob.

Northerners—except for Kevin Van Dam of Michigan and a few others bound for the Fishing Hall of Fame—haven't done nearly as well as their colleagues from below the Mason-Dixon line. The compelling question is why, and the most persuasive answer is winters that are too long and fishing seasons that are too short. The combination is extremely discouraging to bass-champ wannabes from hereabouts.

For sure, the lack of big-time tournament contenders isn't due to any shortage of fish. We have bass up to our elbows, at least. Otherwise, why do so many Georgians and Floridians and Tennesseans and other good

Frank Tennity at Conesus Lake with a largemouth bass.

ol' boys keep coming back to our northern lakes and rivers? And what compels competitors on the B.A.S.S. and FLW tournament circuits to test prime fishing holes in the Northeast over and over again? The television exposure and availability of potential fans and sponsors? Maybe that's part of it, but the real story is that any angler who ever used the term *you-all* during a post-tournament fan reception dreams of fishing up this way.

## NEW YORK—WORLD'S BEST FOR BASS

If you don't believe me, ask Frank Tennity, who with his wife, Melody, splits his fishing (and guiding) year between Florida and New York.

A native New Yorker, Tennity has flirted with the notion of going south for good, but so far has always come to his senses. The vigorous retiree who lives on Honeoye Lake from late April through mid-October has gotten used to balmy Florida winters and enjoys guiding snowbirds and such on Lake Okeechobee and other famous bass waters down south. But the grass still looks greener when he faces north.

"New York has the best bass fishing in the world, bar none," Tennity said. "And the Finger Lakes definitely has some of the best in New York."

The Empire State can be proud of its natural resources and how they are managed, according to him.

"Our fisheries are well taken care of," he said. "For the most part, New York bass waters have long seasons and liberal regulations, but not so long or liberal as to harm the fish. Practically speaking, most of our lakes get a lot of fishing pressure but not too much of it."

And while New York's shorter growing seasons (or longer winters) may keep its resident anglers from having any realistic hope of catching homegrown specimens like the 10- to 12-pound largemouths that dodge alligators and big snakes in Okeechobee, we are fortunate to have many lakes that produce countless 3-, 4-, and 5-pounders, year after year.

By guiding in Florida half the year and New York the other half, the Tennitys have "the best of both worlds," Frank declared.

This being New York and not the Sunshine State, I asked him to focus on his home waters—the Finger Lakes—and tell me how to make the most out of my visits to any or all of those fabled bass fisheries.

Tennity firmly believes in beginning at the beginning. Before he shoves off from the boat launch, he has already determined what lures and tactics he's going to try first, and he doesn't need to flip a coin to devise the daily game plan.

"I start by looking at the water and checking it for clarity and temperature," he told me.

Meanwhile, his mind is multi-tasking, for in addition to water-color checks and thermometer readings, Tennity is taking in nearby fish-holding structure, such as sloping points, creek mouths, and emergent weeds. The man is good at it because he does it more days than not throughout the year.

## PRE-SEASON PRACTICE STARTS AT HOME

Between the Tennitys' return from Florida and the mid-June start of New York's regular statewide bass season, it's time to play a daily game of catch and release. Since the Department of Environmental Conservation ratified between-season catch-and-release bass fishing in the Finger Lakes a few years ago, anglers have flocked to try their luck on old favorite spots on sunny days in April, May, and early June.

Guide Craig Nels with a dandy Otisco Lake largemouth.

As soon as he and Melody have reoccupied their cottage, Frank typically makes his first casts of each day near the northwest corner of one of the four Finger Lakes close by—Honeoye, Conesus, Hemlock, or Canadice. On most northeastern lakes and ponds, that's the sector which gets the most sun and warms up the quickest; therefore, it's most apt to hold hungry, aggressive bass in the spring. Weed cover is sparse at this time, and bass that will lurk in ambush a few weeks later are now forced to roam more than usual to find something for dinner. Pre-spawn largemouths frequently feed in the shallows and are susceptible to surface lures such as poppers, buzzbaits, and plastic frogs. However, the Tennitys' go-to baits in the spring—and worth a try in any season—are Senkos, Stik-Os, and other soft plastics with subtle actions and slow sink rates.

"They are very versatile baits," Tennity said. "You can fish them Texas-rigged [hooked once in the nose and again through the midsection with the point buried] or Wacky-style [lightly through the middle so both ends wiggle and the hook point shows]. You can add weight or not, either way works."

One slight but very effective adjustment that Tennity often makes for his clients is the insertion of an inch-long finishing nail or brad in the nose of a Wacky-rigged Senko. This tiny bit of extra weight speeds the fall of the lure through the water column and keeps it in the near-bottom strike zone on a breezy day.

Melody told me that her clients, whether male or female, often are in too much of a hurry to fish Senkos properly, and start retrieving before their lures have come close to hitting bottom.

## YOU HAVE TO LET IT SINK-O

For some, like me, getting the lure down and noticing strikes is much easier when a fine-diameter braided line is on the reel. Such lines can often be observed on the surface as they sink, and any sudden movement means a fish has taken the bait.

Strikes on Senkos can be arm wrenching or barely detectable. Either way, the Tennitys exhort their customers to hit back as hard as they can.

"I tell them to strike hard enough to break the rod," Frank said. "Of course that won't happen, but you need to hit 'em hard to pull the hook through the bait and into a bass's bony mouth."

Senkos and their ilk come in several sizes and dozens of colors from black to bubblegum pink. Watermelon and green pumpkin are two color patterns that produce day in, day out; still, in very muddy water it often pays to replace such unobtrusive shades with something that contrasts with the aquatic surroundings. A black bait with blue flakes is a good choice when the water is stained. At the other end of the spectrum, the aforementioned bubblegum has dirty-water applications, too. By the way, if there is anything in nature that's bubblegum-colored, I have yet to see it, but Frank and I both have caught nice bass on a pink Senko on days when nothing else seemed to work.

I wouldn't want to leave you with the impression that Frank Tennity is a Senko fanatic or specialist, because his tackle boxes are full of lures of every description and he makes use of all types and most models. Should local winds put a boat-rocking chop on the lake he tries on a given day, Senkos and such can be very difficult to track, but some other baits shine. In those circumstances, Frank often chooses from a quartet of stickbaits—Rapalas, Rebels, Rogues, and Reef Runners—to cover a wide patch of water. Call them the Four R's, if you wish, but these old standards are just as effective on bass as they are on after-dark walleyes, and that's saying a mouthful.

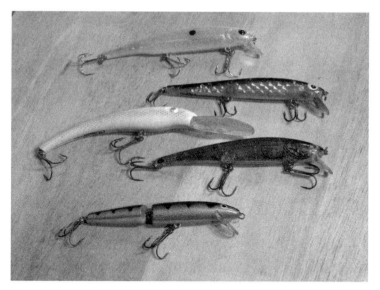

Stickbaits like these, cast from shore or trolled, are effective
lures for walleyes, northern pike, tiger muskies, and bass. Top
to bottom are a rattling, suspending SPX, a black-and-silver
Thunderstick, a Wally Diver (in fire tiger colors of green, orange,
and yellow), a see-through and blue Bomber Long A, and a
floating, jointed Rapala.

## LITTLE THINGS MAKE A BIG DIFFERENCE

Frank likes to add or remove dabs of solder, to change the wobble or
increase the depth at which an individual stickbait will swim. As a rule, the
colder or clearer the water, the slower your stickbait should be retrieved.
A suspending lure generally lends itself to a very slow retrieve. Warming,
off-color water should signal anglers to crank their reel handles faster and
show their baits to more fish.

Like Melody, Frank is convinced the average Finger Lakes bass fisherman is in too much of a hurry to leave one place behind and get to
another.

"A real key to improving your catch is to slow down and take your
time," he said, adding that anglers who race frantically up and down a
lake in search of more "active" fish would enjoy their days more if they
resolved to try a couple of different lures or retrieves at one spot before
moving on.

Every experienced bass angler will attest that weather changes, such
as a large cold front or a hot, bright sun, can have a major effect on the

Kid Corbett with nice Skaneateles Lake smallmouth bass.

Frank Tennity with a 6-pound largemouth bass from Honeoye Lake.

day's sport, but Tennity is not at all convinced about the impact of another factor that many weekend fishermen blame for light stringers. That's boat traffic, which on the Finger Lakes may include canoes, fishing boats of all sorts, racing vessels, Jet Skis, and "party barge" pontoons. The Saturday armada on little Otisco Lake, for example, traces a seemingly endless elliptical parade route on a wet and wild weekend. Tennity's suggestion to bass devotees is to simply pay those boats no heed, other than the courtesies that are required by law.

"That boat noise might bother the fishermen, but I don't think it bothers the fish much at all," Tennity said. "In fact, your own trolling motor probably disturbs close-in bass more than the wake from a larger vessel. Bass hear the racket on the surface all the time, and they get used to it."

Another aspect of bass fishing that many anglers blame for their lack of success on the Finger Lakes is tournament angling, but Tennity, who has competed in many club, state, and regional cast-for-cash events himself, isn't buying it. First, numerous studies by the DEC and its counterparts in other states have consistently shown that fewer than 1 or 2 percent of fish caught, weighed, and released by tournament anglers are turned loose in poor condition. Also, the tournament organizations that used to release bass caught by competitors near the event's weigh-in locations now take pains to redistribute their fish miles distant from where the official awards ceremony takes place.

Honeoye Lake, the Tennitys' home court, has been the site of many bass tournaments, and is reputed to have some of the easiest bass fishing in the state. A skilled angler would have no trouble hooking a limit of largemouths there, and not a few of the lake's regulars are more intent on filling a bucket with fillets than on winning a tournament lunker prize. Fortunately, Honeoye has room enough to accommodate the meat seeker and trophy competitor alike, and I am confident the same can be said for any of the Finger Lakes.

## CHAPTER 14

# Shore Fishing the Finger Lakes

**M**ost of the Finger Lakes quiet down considerably after Labor Day weekend, when "summer people" padlock camp doors, drain water pipes, and move boat hoists to dry ground. Not everyone says such an early good-bye, however. In recent years, it has become increasingly common to see docks left in place long after Halloween. Some of the docks are used to launch trailered boats, but on several of the lakes they serve mainly as casting platforms for ardent shore fishermen. Municipal piers, beaches, and other places where public access is available also bustle with activity after the lakeside foliage turns orange, red, and yellow.

Kid Corbett and a 25-inch rainbow trout caught on a ¹⁄₁₆-ounce jig and 4-pound line while shore fishing at Skaneateles Lake.

The steady angler traffic in the autumn is mainly due to the great shore-fishing opportunities in the region. In fact, while boat-owning anglers can cover more water and therefore hook up with more species on most days of the year, Finger Lakes bank fishermen usually take their share of fish, too. Shore casting can be worthwhile at any time, but as a rule is most productive from early March through mid- or late April and from late September through mid-December. In these cool months, trout, salmon, small-mouth bass, and other sought-after species tend to forage close to shore. The bite can be downright ferocious, and spectacular catches are possible when water surface temperatures are in the 50s or low 60s (Fahrenheit). Partly because of their comparatively easy public access, lakes in the eastern part of the chain—Otisco, Skaneateles, Owasco, Cayuga, and Seneca—give nonboating anglers their best opportunities to catch a variety of species, from delectable panfish and walleyes to hard-fighting bass and pike and shimmering trout and salmon. Based on observed angler effort, the salmonids appear to be the main attractions in the region, especially during the autumn months.

My frequent fishing buddy John "Kid" Corbett has so much "fish sense" that you might think he was born with fins and scales, but unfortunately he didn't get to use his natural talents nearly as often as he'd like, until recently. As head of the Syracuse Police Department's Special Investigations Unit, Lieutenant Corbett rode herd on drug peddlers, prostitutes, illegal gamblers, and gang members, and he planned more midnight raids than fishing trips. Since his retirement in June, 2013, he's looked forward to his fall fishing trips on Skaneateles Lake.

## JUST THE KIND OF BREAK A CRIME STOPPER NEEDS

"It's my favorite time of the year," Corbett explained. "Lots of guys look forward to the first day of trout season in April, or the June opening of bass season, or whatever, but fall fishing is as good as it gets, in my opinion."

He is so tuned in to the fall fishery that he confidently pinpoints the calendar date when the lake trout spawning run begins in earnest on Skaneateles. He may be off a day or two because of extreme weather conditions, but more years than not, he insisted, the magic date is October 26. He always seems to hook a couple of lakers on that date, but seldom connects even a day or two earlier. The bite will always be "on" at creek mouths, shoals, and other laker spawning grounds before Halloween, and it can be expected to peak by mid-November and gradually tail off by the end of that month.

Along with the lake trout, which put up scrappy fights when they latch onto a lure in shallow water, Corbett occasionally ties into land-locked salmon or rainbow trout. Smallmouth bass are a bonus catch for Skaneateles shore fishermen, too, and every now and then Kid finds himself within casting range of a school of plump yellow perch. The bulk of the action is for trout of a pleasing average size, although few ever attain genuine trophy proportions. In Skaneateles, lakers must be at least 15 inches long, and anglers are permitted three such fish a day. Corbett often catches more than a dozen "keeper" lake trout in a morning or afternoon of shore casting, and he releases all but two or three. Although he seldom catches lake trout longer than 21 inches, the more than 50 he landed during the autumn of 2011 included 3 that measured 24, 25, and 26 inches. Those were some of the nicest fish he's logged in his many years of participating in the DEC Region 7 angler-diary program.

While lake trout fishing more than satisfied him in 2011, Corbett found shore casting for rainbows and landlocks to be much slower than usual, with a bottom line showing only half a dozen 'bows and salmon, combined. The disappointing catches couldn't be blamed on any lack of effort or intensity, for Corbett put in many more hours on the water than the average shore fisher. He fishes for autumn trout and salmon mainly at Carpenter's Point on the west shore and Lourdes Camp on the east shore of Skaneateles Lake and typically visits those spots between 10 and 20 times each fall. If he's at the point, rainbows are a secondary target; but big 'bows are almost always the most numerous predators at Lourdes, a summer camp for kids that's owned by the Syracuse Catholic diocese. Lourdes is open for fishing when campers are absent—any time other than July and August, basically. But when snow, sleet, or freezing rain lashes Lourdes' steep access road, wise fishermen give the spot a rest. I've met anglers who kept casting when a freeze was under way and wound up spending a night or two sleeping in their cars. Others, younger and

Mark Gonzalez uses an umbrella to ward off rain and sleet at Lourdes Camp on Skaneateles Lake. Mark is one of the more successful shore fishers around.

more foolish than I, hiked in and out in heavy boots or snowshoes. Some of them caught rainbows, too, but all of them were huffing and puffing when they returned to their cars, parked at the top of the hill. No trout is worth a heart attack!

Even so, as long as the road is dry, you shouldn't be surprised to see fishermen watching rods at the camp's north beach, adjacent to the boat-house or off the point and creek mouth at the southern tip of the property.

Paul McNeilly waits for a bite while shore fishing on the north end of Lourdes Camp.

## LOURDES IS THE SPOT FOR FISHING PILGRIMS

The degree of devotion to Lourdes stems from consistently good fishing for rainbow trout that often measure longer than 20 inches and weigh better than 3 pounds. I have enjoyed years when a personal tally of three dozen autumn rainbows include 10 or more in the 20-inches-plus category. Not bad for a lake whose residents have no significant forage fish to line their bellies with fat!

Landlocks are uncommon but not really rare on both sides of the lake, and the 26-incher Corbett beached a few seasons back would prompt most shore fishermen to hurry to the nearest taxidermy studio.

My personal-best catch along the Lourdes Camp shoreline was 27¼ inches long, but that hook-billed male was not the strongest rainbow I ever caught. No, that honor belonged to a 26-inch bruiser that bit at the western tip of the camp's north shore in October 2009. When one of my rods began bouncing in its holder that afternoon, I set the hook hard and the reel began to scream. Although I couldn't see the fish, its powerful sprint into deeper and deeper water told me it had to be a very large trout. Unfortunately, my line was peeling from the arbor so quickly I thought I was going to be "spooled"—helpless to prevent the fish from stripping every inch of mono from my reel. My line was a wispy 4-pound test, and I dared not pull hard against the powerful trout. In a rare moment of genius, I flipped the bail open just as the fish paused for a few seconds of rest. When the line went slack, the fish seemed to relax a bit and I was able to recover 40 or 50 feet of mono. From that point it was an evenly matched tug-of-war, until the big 'bow surrendered and was drawn up onto the gravel beach about 10 minutes after the battle began.

You're probably wondering what sort of "wonderbait" accounts for all those big rainbows. My go-to rig, and that of most other diehard Skaneateles rainbow chasers as well, is the "marshmallow sandwich," which consists of a garden worm or nightcrawler on the bend and a cock-tail marshmallow on the point of a size 2 or 4 hook. Lieutenant Corbett is one of a few regulars on the Skaneateles fishing scene who deviate from the standard recipe. If he ordered his fall bait rig at a restaurant, he'd ask for a marshmallow sandwich "but double the marshmallow and hold the worm, please." He normally uses two marshmallows and no worm.

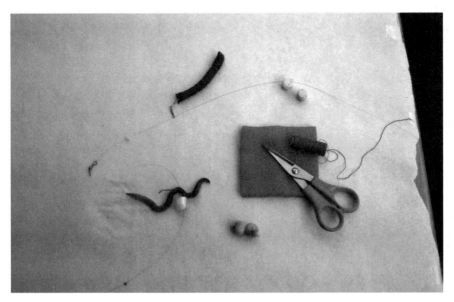

The ingredients to assemble a worm-and-marshmallow rig for Finger Lakes shore fishing.

Of course there's more to fishing marshmallows, with worm or without, than merely baiting up and casting into the nearest water.

The quid pro quo of a successful day of shore casting for Finger Lakes trout and salmon is a location where the targeted fish swim close to shore at least part of the season. If you have a fishy spot, you're on your way to shore-fishing success. Without a suitable location, you can look forward to plenty of casting practice and long waits between bites. Aside from finding a sloping point, creek mouth, sudden drop-off, or other type of structure that is of moderate depth, you will find shore casting to be a rather simple pursuit.

Successful practitioners of the worm-and-marshmallow tactic rig up by putting an egg-shaped slip sinker weighing from ¼ to 1 ounce onto a 4- to 8-pound running line, then knotting a bead swivel to the end of that mono. A 24- to 30-inch-long piece of leader—I prefer 4-pound test—is affixed to the free end of the swivel, and a baitholder hook completes the terminal setup.

The worm needs no dressing up before it hits the water, but I like to wrap my marshmallow in a 2-inch square of Spawnee salmon egg-sac mesh. It's tied off with elastic thread and trimmed neatly. This improvement means my marshmallow will stay on the hook without dissolving for hours, instead of minutes. Whether you are shore casting, trolling, or fly fishing, the more time your bait is in the water, the more fish you will catch.

People who don't do this sort of thing routinely ask why I bother with the marshmallow. After all, worms are the most popular fishing bait of all and work just about anywhere they are legal. It's a good point, but a marshmallow topping has at least three things going for it in the Finger Lakes scenario. One, they must taste good, or trout wouldn't eat so many of them. Two, they are buoyant: When fished on a slip-sinker rig, they float 6 to 12 inches off the bottom. The worm goes along for the ride, bobbing seductively at a depth patrolled by neighborhood predators. Finally, if you use plain white cocktail marshmallows over the pastel-colored ones, as I do, they can be seen far off, as well as at close range.

## SOME SHORE-FISHING ACCESSORIES

This is patient, feast-or-famine fishing. I bring a couple of sand spikes, or tubular rod holders with pointed ends that can be pushed into the soil or gravel to hold my rods upright at a steep angle. If my outing is to last more than an hour or two, another essential is an empty bait bucket or a folding chair sturdy enough to support my weight as I relax between bites.

My rods vary from 5 to 10 feet in length, but they have in common a soft tip that wiggles and then stands at attention when a trout takes the bait.

So that I might trade stories with fellow fishermen now and then and not spend an entire afternoon or evening squinting at my rod tip through polarized lenses, I often attach a small bell to the tip guide. When the bell rings, I hurry to the sand spike, lift the rod, tighten the line, and set the hook with a joyous shout of "got one" to my friends. When the bite is on, bells are ringing and reels screeching up and down the beach.

Not everyone uses the sand spike or a derivative to fish for inshore trout. Kid Corbett is a bit of an innovator—or perhaps just a rebel—in that he frequently sets one of his rods in a horizontal "bait-runner" stand. Unlike sand spike user, who reel their line in just enough after casting to make it bend slightly (and straighten when the bait is picked up), anglers with a bait runner hold the rod parallel to the ground and leave the bail open so that a biting fish can easily pull line off the reel. To detect strikes on such a rig, Corbett takes a loop of line from his reel and puts it under a small rock.

When the loop is gone, Corbett quickly gives his line a visual check, and if it's moving, he lifts the rod from its holder and sets the hook.

He likes to fish marshmallows solo, without worms, because he's found that only trout seem to hit them consistently. And in my memory that's pretty much on the mark. On warmer-than-average days, especially, Skaneateles Lake's rock bass and smaller yellow perch nibble incessantly on my worms yet leave the marshmallow intact.

"If I get bites on my marshmallows, I'm pretty certain they're trout," Corbett said.

However, there is no corollary that says trout don't bite on worms. The indisputable fact is, trout love worms—always have and always will, whether they're washed down with sugar or not.

Everyone who gets serious about Finger Lakes shore fishing will eventually come up with their own little tricks of the trade, and apply them to a variety of species. While Skaneateles Lake is one of my favorites, several others in the chain offer good opportunities for salmonids, and some also feature excellent seasonal fishing—spring and fall—for walleyes. Bass and assorted panfish are also available to shore-bound anglers. Here's a lake-by-lake prospectus:

## Otisco Lake

**STAR ATTRACTION:** Walleyes

**WHEN, WHERE, AND HOW:** From early May through June and again from mid-October until ice-over, walleyes chase alewives and other baitfish after dark along the Otisco Lake shore. Headlamps are recommended for safety, but turn them off while waiting for a strike as light beams may spook the fish. Cast stickbaits such as Rapalas and Thundersticks in black-and-silver, fire tiger, clown, and other color patterns. Night fishermen gain access along Otisco Valley Road, at the dam and at the causeway—a long-retired roadbed at the end of Masters Road on the west shore.

## Skaneateles Lake

**STAR ATTRACTION:** Rainbow trout

**WHEN, WHERE, AND HOW:** As noted above, hefty rainbows are available at numerous locations around Skaneateles Lake, but public access is somewhat limited. The most popular spot is Lourdes Camp, owned by the Syracuse diocese. It's available spring and fall when the kids' camp is not in session, but anglers are urged to pick up after themselves and not build fires. Another favorite location is the retaining wall in the park next to the Episcopal church in the village of Skaneateles, but bring a long-handled net.

## Owasco Lake

**STAR ATTRACTION:** Yellow perch

**WHEN, WHERE, AND HOW:** Shore access is quite limited on Owasco, with one major exception: Emerson Park in Auburn. At the north end of the lake, it has a long pier that attracts a variety of fish, most notably in the late autumn. Perch, pike, walleyes, and lake trout are all possible here. Try minnows and slip bobbers.

## Cayuga Lake

**STAR ATTRACTION:** Lake trout

**WHEN, WHERE, AND HOW:** Taughannock Falls State Park is a west shore hot spot for salmonids located off Route 89 about 8 miles north of Ithaca. The steep drop-off at the mouth of Taughannock Creek provides great shore casting for landlocked salmon and brown, rainbow, and lake trout. Lakers are very abundant and average around 5 or 6 pounds. They—and other trout and salmon—are susceptible to ¾-ounce white jigs, but fishermen do even better by casting a minnow and slip bobber beyond the drop-off.

## Seneca Lake

**STAR ATTRACTION:** Northern pike

**WHEN, WHERE, AND HOW:** Picking the best shore fisheries on Seneca Lake is not easy because public access is somewhat limited even though a wide variety of species can be targeted from its banks. The municipal pier at Watkins Glen and, to a lesser extent, the pier at the north end in Geneva teem with lake trout, northern pike, yellow perch, black crappies, and bluegills at times. Fish with appropriate-size minnows.

## Keuka Lake

**STAR ATTRACTION:** Lake trout

**WHEN, WHERE, AND HOW:** From early November and on into April, bank fishers might connect with lake trout by casting fast-sinking spoons or jigs from Keuka Lake State Park in Branchport.

## Canandaigua Lake

**STAR ATTRACTION:** Yellow perch

**WHEN, WHERE, AND HOW:** The village pier at the north end of Canandaigua Lake is very popular, especially in the spring when big jack perch and other panfish come within casting distance. Use small jigs tipped with mealworms or minnows.

## Honeoye Lake

**STAR ATTRACTION:** Bluegills

**WHEN, WHERE, AND HOW:** Aside from the state boat launch off East Lake Road, and a small town park at its north end, Honeoye Lake has no public shoreline. However, the boat launch area, like the rest of the lake, teems with 7- to 8-inch bluegills, just right for frying. They bite best during the late May to mid-June spawning run, when their rubber-tire-size nests are visible in the shallows.

## Canadice Lake

**STAR ATTRACTION:** Chain pickerel

**WHEN, WHERE, AND HOW:** Almost the entire shore of Canadice is accessible to anyone willing to hike through the surrounding forest, and anybody who can cast a spinnerbait and rapidly retrieve it in weedy areas has a shot at some nice pickerel.

## Hemlock Lake

**STAR ATTRACTION:** Bass

**WHEN, WHERE, AND HOW:** While most think of lakers when Hemlock is mentioned, the conversations among shore anglers inevitably swing toward the plump largemouths and smallmouths that cruise around the weed lines. Almost the entire shore can easily be fished in all seasons.

## Conesus Lake

**STAR ATTRACTION:** Walleyes

**WHEN, WHERE, AND HOW:** The spawning run of walleyes in Conesus Inlet is like a coming attractions trailer shown just before the feature movie begins: Sometimes the preview is better than the reel thing. Still, whopper walleyes can sometimes be caught after dark, for three to four weeks after the season-starter date in early May. Try Long Point Park, midway along the west shore.

# CHAPTER 15

# The Rainbow Run

**A**nglers are notorious for inflating the number and size of the fish they catch, but it would take an imaginative liar, indeed, to exaggerate the length and weight of the giant rainbows that swam upstream to spawn in Finger Lakes tributaries during the 1950s. Anyway, it's no fun to spin a tall tale to an audience that already knows the true story. Back in the era of Elvis, Ike, and Sputnik, fishermen throughout the United States had heard all about New York's spring rainbow run.

Opening day on the tributaries was an event eagerly awaited by fishermen throughout the East. It was not unusual in the 1950s and '60s for a local angler to find himself standing in a favorite pool next to someone who had traveled 1,000 miles or more to take his crack at a whopper rainbow. Some of those hopefuls headed for home at the end of the day with their trout of a lifetime on ice, but the majority of participants didn't catch a thing, for the simple reason that fishermen outnumbered fish more often than not.

It was world-class entertainment while it lasted, but the bubble burst for Finger Lakes fishing-tourism promoters in the late 1970s, when the DEC rejuvenated the steelhead fishery in Lake Ontario and Lake Erie. The 10- or 12-pound beauties that often won prizes in the opening-day contests along Finger Lakes tributaries were considered merely average fish in the Salmon River, Oswego River, and other Great Lakes feeder streams. The year-round seasons in Great Lakes tribs also caused many Finger Lakes regulars to shift their allegiance. Opening day simply lost its significance for many rainbow chasers. Why spend all winter anticipating hookups with large trout, practical anglers reasoned, when you can try for even bigger fish close by, any day of the year?

That's what we trout fishermen call a "no-brainer."

Even so, I have already staked out my favorite spot on Owasco Inlet, a close-to-home Finger Lakes tributary, with the intent of giving it a thorough workout on the coming April Fools' Day, and you can be sure that hundreds, if not thousands of other anglers are making similar plans. Tradition plays a part in such behavior, but don't think for a moment that Finger Lakes trout specialists are willing to get skunked just for old times' sake. Every last one of us is expecting to hook a nice rainbow or two when opening day rolls around. I'm rather old-fashioned, myself, and I get a certain kick out of meeting tributary anglers who have fished the same streams, April after April, with their father and grandfather, and who are now in the process of passing their pet rainbow pools, and their treasure troves of memories, to a new generation.

## A LITTLE SLICE OF HISTORY

DEC records weren't as detailed 80 or 90 years ago as they are now, but it is generally believed that a migratory strain of rainbows was stocked in Cold Brook, a tributary of Keuka Lake, in 1897. Between 1917 and 1927, said Region 8 senior fisheries biologist Brad Hammers, additional stockings spread the steelhead genes to several other lakes and tributaries, including Catharine and Naples Creeks. Naturally, the fish fared better and grew larger in some lakes than others, but by the 1940s rainbows were thriving in a majority of the Finger Lakes and anglers enjoyed good spring fishing in dozens of tributaries. By the late 1950s and '60s, the rainbow runs out of Seneca and Canandaigua Lakes were nationally renowned, but tributaries of Hemlock, Keuka, Cayuga, Owasco, and Skaneateles also produced impressive fish and had many loyal fans.

Rainbows grew to jaw-dropping sizes in Seneca and Canandaigua during the 1950s, due mainly to the proliferation of calorie-laden alewives in those two bodies of water. The alewives in several of the Finger Lakes

The author's son, Sean, staying low and away from the spooky rainbows making their spawning run in Grout Brook.

eventually took over the place in the food chain that had been occupied by rainbow smelt, to the consternation of sportsmen who loved to dip-net tasty smelt in countless small tributaries. But in the late 1950s, alewife-eating trout that weighed 15 or 16 pounds started showing up on the leader boards of opening-day trout tournaments. Not surprisingly, the chance of catching such fish drew hordes of fishermen to the spawning streams. One newspaper reporter estimated the April 1, 1959, crowd along Catharine Creek at more than 10,000 anglers and spectators!

## THE TIMES, THEY ARE A-CHANGING

Head counts of this type are dubious, whether the tally takes place at a fishing event or a political march on Washington, but even allowing for the usual rounding up, it really must have been difficult for anglers to find a parking spot near the creek that day, let alone catch a fish.

Recent trout openers have also drawn crowds to Queen Catharine and her rivals, but the anglers now number in the hundreds or dozens (depending on the stream), not the thousands reported in the old days. There have been other changes in the regional rainbow fishery, both natural and man-made. Some of them were profound. For starters, alewife populations in several lakes in the chain have risen and fallen over the last several decades, and the incredible volume of forage fish that grew 15-pound rainbows no longer exists. The 5- to 8-pound 'bows that are considered worthy of a trip to the local taxidermist's studio nowadays

Mike Brilbeck of Syracuse fly-fishing for rainbows in Cayuga Inlet near Danby.

probably got as big as they did by competing for food with other species of game fish, as well as with their own kind.

Analyzing the data from fishing diaries that many anglers turn in annually to help DEC biologists manage the various Finger Lakes and their tributaries, it's striking that a 20-inch rainbow is a much-admired prize in any of the Finger Lakes watersheds. That's fine with me, for a silver bullet that spans the length of my forearm from elbow to finger-tips can raise havoc when it's on the end of my line and struggling for its freedom in a knee-deep stream. The smaller crowds of fishermen in modern times assure there are going to be more trout for me to play with, and I consider that a definite win–win.

## FISH WORTH FISHING FOR

Catching early-season rainbows in Finger Lakes tributaries is both challenging and rewarding, but who would want it any other way? After catching hundreds of lake-run 'bows over the years, I have come to believe that the fish we remember the most are not necessarily the biggest, but rather the most difficult ones to catch. The hard-to-get rainbows include fish that are hiding in dense cover, spooked by multiple encounters with fishermen, or otherwise protected from easy capture. These trout can be met and conquered by innumerable strategies, but the best thing anglers can do to get their share is to spend more time fishing.

You know the bromide about 10 percent of trout fishermen catching 90 percent of the fish? Well, my observations indicate that about 5 percent of tributary anglers account for 95 percent of the total fishing effort, whether the stream being scrutinized is Catharine Creek, Cayuga Inlet, Grout Brook, or any other feeder that has a significant spawning run. As you get to know a few of the real diehards, you'll realize they fish three, four, maybe five days a week, year after year. I suppose I ought to be slightly embarrassed to say I am one of the gang.

Well, I'm not selfish, but I am a very lucky man. Being an old married guy, I have always asked my wife for her okay whenever I felt the urge to go fishing, and she almost never says no. Chickie's unfailing generosity has convinced me that an understanding and supportive spouse is as critical to a fisherman's long-term success as using the appropriate hooks, line, and sinkers. Whatever it is that I do, I couldn't have done it without her. Now, for the many tributary anglers whose spouse or significant other is not quite as cooperative as mine, I have a few more practical tips to share, in no particular order of importance. Each suggestion will help you catch a few more fish between now and the end of your rainbow-chasing days.

## SETTING THE PACE AND OTHER TIPS

On the first day of trout season, roughly half of all anglers taking part in the fun align themselves shoulder-to-shoulder around a deep pool and stay put for several hours. Most of the others are inclined to hike briskly from one small pool to the next, making only a handful of casts at each stop. Few folks in either category, dunkers or hikers, catch many rainbows.

The most successful anglers, by far, fish at a pace that reflects the mood of the trout. My rule of thumb is easy to remember: If the catching is fast, fish slowly; but if the catching is slow, fish quickly.

It's common sense, really. Why should you leave a spot where you're comfortable and the hits just keep on coming? Conversely, if you haven't scored after an hour or so in your favorite rainbow hole, it may be that the fish have moved on—and you should, too.

Next to knowing how fast to fish (or how slowly), it's important to know how long you can fish. Here I'm not talking about the time of day, for the law determines that. Conservation officers can ticket tributary anglers if they have their line in the water after sunset or before sunrise.

Fishing slowly and stealthily in clear but high water, Mike Brilbeck was rewarded with this nice Naples Creek rainbow.

I'm referring to calendar dates for productive fishing. The trout season on Finger Lakes tributaries runs from April 1 through December 31, but it apparently ends for at least three-quarters of participants around dinner-time on day number one.

Take a good look around on that first morning of the season, because you won't see most of those folks again until next year, same time, same place. Yet the fun has barely started. While first-day action can be hot and heavy, most tributaries continue to hold good-size rainbows, and very few fishermen, several weeks into the season. I landed my personal-best 'bow, a 10-pounder, on April 17, 1981, in a tributary of Owasco Lake. I've caught 20-inchers in May in several feeders and on June 7, 2010, was delighted to land a 21-incher in the upper reaches of Grout Brook, the principal spawning grounds of Skaneateles Lake rainbows. You opening-day wonders don't know what you've been missing!

Few anglers are aware of the late-season possibilities in the Finger Lakes tributaries. If the region has average or above-average rainfall in any given autumn, some rainbows will get a head start on the next spring's spawning run by entering tributaries in December or even as early as mid-November. If you are a deer hunter as well as a fisherman, consider climbing out of your tree stand once in a while to go fishing.

## BAIT AND TACKLE

Most of the opening-day crowd use what the guy or gal next to them is using. The lack of imagination applies to both bait and tackle, and it's a major reason why the elite 5 percent mentioned a few paragraphs ago hook most of the fish. Now and then, they throw a changeup at the trout, with positive results.

Take an inventory of the tackle and methods in general use on your next early-season rainbow pilgrimage. The vast majority of anglers, and most likely you, too, will be using the same thing for bait, namely a spawn sac consisting of a square of orange or yellow mesh wrapped around a dime- or nickel-size cluster of salmon or trout eggs.

Eggs work well but so do nightcrawlers, garden worms, salted minnows, single-hook spinning lures such as the Hildebrandt Flicker, streamer flies, and—especially after a few days of warming weather—artificial nymphs. I've caught spring rainbows up to 25 inches long on nymphs. Most of them were spawned-out fish that seemed to be taking the long way home to the lake so they could pack a few more calories in their tummies. Those that I creeled instead of releasing usually had a smorgasbord of food in their gullets, including but not limited to trout eggs. The artificial fly eaters I've encountered seem to have very adventurous tastes for all sorts of nymphs, with a special fondness for caddis larva imitations.

Those that had been eating eggs were quite willing to ingest a handmade imitation, as well as a real egg sac. Glow bug patterns, nothing more than puffs of yarn crammed together on a hook shank and trimmed into a ball shape, are often effective on Finger Lakes 'bows, but I do better consistently with imitations of egg sacs made of diamond braid or other glittery materials. My favorite is immodestly named "Mike's Better Egg Sac."

## SPARE THE ROD, SPOIL THE TROUT

The second smartest thing I ever did to improve my rainbow-trout-fishing success was switching from the 7½-foot fly rods my friends found "sporty" to extra-long rods that are more practical for dealing with big, wary 'bows. With my 9-foot fly stick I can use shorter lengths of fly line and longer leaders; I can also mend a line easily to correct drag. When I'm fishing with live bait, which to me usually means nightcrawlers, I now go darned near radical, armed with an 11-foot noodle rod. The long stick is fitted with a fly reel loaded with 4-pound monofilament line. That rod always attracts a question or two from other anglers, but it enables me to make a precise cast while staying back on the bank to avoid spooking trout.

Think about how handy such a delivery system can be when its owner is faced with an elbow-to-elbow crowd. You might have to drop and drift your bait through a tiny bit of water or lift and flip your rig across multiple currents to reach active fish while minimizing the possibility of line drag. The long rods are perfectly suited to such conditions, and they are great for float fishing, too. Ironically, some of the anglers who have shifted their loyalties to the Lake Ontario and Lake Erie steelhead rivers have since come home to try Great Lakes tackle-rigging methods on the Finger Lakes tributaries. One of the most portable tackle rigs is the use of a slip bobber to coax strikes out of rainbows suspicious of bottom-bouncing presentations.

So what's the first smartest move I ever made, rainbow-wise? That would have to be dropping down from my former 8-pound mono line to a wispy 4-pound test. The thinner diameter and increased sensitivity of the lighter line has resulted in many more bites and strikes and more than offsets the occasional early break-off. Remember, you don't need an 8-pound line to catch an 8-pound trout, but even if you did, how many fish of that size are you going to tangle with, in the Finger Lakes or almost anywhere else?

I hope you will try some of the advice I've just given you on the following tributaries, which are in most folks' top 10—mine included. I'll start with a Skaneateles Lake feeder creek and then go west, one stream at a time.

## Grout Brook

The principal spawning ground for Skaneateles Lake rainbows traces a fishhook path through the hamlet of Scott in northern Cortland County, and that seems fitting, since Grout Brook is a great place to hook a dandy trout or two. You can get there from the city of Cortland by taking Interstate 81 to the Homer exit, then taking Route 281 to Route 41 and following that road north to Scott. From there you can explore the creek as it winds south and then north to flow into the south end of the lake.

You will see a bridge crossing just west of the intersection of Route 41 and Glen Haven Road. The DEC has obtained public access from the bridge in Scott downstream for about a mile, and you will also find PUBLIC FISHING signs farther downstream on Grout Brook Road as well as at the lower end of Glen Haven Road, near the Scott Town Park. Be sure to ask the owners before you try non-public stretches of the brook, as it is heavily posted already (aside from the access points mentioned here) and we'd rather not see another outbreak of NO TRESPASSING signs.

Grout has a long-held reputation for a late spawning run, which supposedly results from the stream's cold water. However, in my 40–some years on the stream, I have observed rainbows on their redds (the proper term for spawning beds) as early as mid-March, weeks before the season opens on April Fools' Day; and as late as mid-May. Nature tends to spread out spawning runs of trout to assure that at least some share of the eggs deposited and buried in a stream's gravel each year will hatch into fry and then recruit, or survive, long enough to reach adulthood and sexual maturity. It's sort of a fail-safe redundancy. Should a scouring flood or some other catastrophe befall the stream at the peak of the annual rainbow run, the nuptial rites carried out by the trout that arrive early or late on the spawning grounds could be the salvation of the fishery.

Grout Brook is designed mainly for bait fishing, being narrow, clear, and hemmed in by alders, Japanese knotweed, and damnable thickets of multiflora rose in most places. It has high-quality spawning gravel and plenty of deep pools that fish well after a spring shower. Trout average around 18 inches in this stream but occasionally stretch out to 22 or 24 inches and weigh up to 5 or 5½ pounds.

## Owasco Inlet

Because it is a fine brown trout stream as well as a destination for spawning rainbows from Owasco Lake, I discuss Owasco Inlet's attributes in some detail elsewhere. However, a few things need to be said about its rainbow run here and now, before that once-spectacular event fades slowly from memory and finally disappears for good. We can start by admitting the resource needs help.

During the 1980s, Owasco Inlet spawning runs gave anglers a reasonable shot at catching rainbows that weighed 8, 10, or even 12 pounds. Fish like that weren't caught every day, but they were available, and those that eluded the hook did a great job propagating their species. In those days it was common for summertime anglers to catch and release 50 or more juvenile rainbows in a couple of hours prowling the inlet. These were fish that had hatched in the stream the previous year but had yet to make their first trip downstream to the lake. Battling these silver firecrackers, you could only imagine how fat and vigorous they might be after a year or two of nibbling on alewives and smelt in the open water of Owasco Lake.

Times have changed, and not for the better. The inlet's spring run is a fraction of what it once was, and the hook-jawed bruisers that filled inlet tributaries including Hemlock Creek, Mill Creek, and Peg Mill Brook seldom, if ever, cause modern anglers' hearts to pound in their chests. A 20-incher in the inlet is a beauty now; although such fish, paraded on a stringer, hardly rated a second glance just a few years ago.

So what happened? Beaver dams by the dozens.

If Owasco Inlet rainbows are to make any lasting comeback, their champions will first have to resolve the beaver problem.

## Dutch Hollow Brook

Once it was a true gem, so full of bright, spawning rainbows from Owasco Lake that its more zealous followers kept its name and location from all but their closest friends. Lately, however, the run has fizzled, just like that of Owasco Inlet. DEC biologist Jeff Robins and former Region 7 fisheries manager Dan Bishop both lay the blame for Dutch Hollow's decline on behaviors (see above) and also on the state's controversial decision in the late 1990s to stock Owasco Lake with walleyes, which hadn't been present there for 40-some years. Walleyes are a popular and flavorful game fish, but the species appeared to be one predator too many for rainbow trout fry and fingerlings. Lake trout are the other game fish that, according to Robins and Bishop, wax fat on walleyes.

Why not eliminate lake trout instead of walleyes? DEC officials hear that one more than once in a while, and they have a simple, two-part response. First, lakers are native to Owasco Lake but walleyes are not. Second, more than 90 percent of all salmonids caught in the lake are lake trout, and lakers are by far Owasco's most dominant predator. To sum things up, if rainbows and brown trout need a little protection, it is far easier to get rid of a recently introduced fish-eating machine like the walleye than to achieve meaningful cuts in a huge, long-standing lake trout population.

In time, disrupting beaver colonies and disappointing walleye anglers will bring about an increased rainbow trout run in Dutch Hollow Brook and other small streams flowing into Owasco Lake. Until then, anglers can hunt for resident brown trout in the Hollow's upper reaches along Route 38, southeast of Auburn but north of Moravia.

## Salmon Creek

Find a rainbow stream with pools clearer and more picturesque than those in Salmon Creek and I'll buy you a six-pack of your favorite brew, my friend. They just don't come any prettier than Salmon Creek.

The stream I'm talking about spills over a breathtaking waterfall in the Tompkins County hamlet of Ludlowville, which is off Route 34B, about 5 miles north of Ithaca. From the base of the falls, the creek spreads over long stretches of bare bedrock formations that do next to nothing to hide big, spawning rainbows from the sight of sharp-eyed anglers.

After slipping beneath a steel-deck bridge that overlooks a deep pool coveted by opening-day fishermen, Salmon Creek bubbles and bounces over a stretch of perfect-looking spawning gravel that's about 500 feet long. From there, it pounds its way along a route dictated by nature's placement of car-size boulders, runs through a steep canyon with several productive pools, glides under a high bridge, and finally empties into Cayuga Lake at Myers Point.

Give me a day in early April after a downpour has turned Salmon Creek's currents just a tad muddy and I'll show you some pretty good fishing. Remember those car-size rocks I just mentioned? Once I caught a pair of lovely rainbows in that pool, on a size 14 Hendrickson nymph. The first was a male, the second a hen, and each measured exactly 23 inches. You never forget a catch like that.

## Fall Creek

Rainbow trout streams, like certain people, can get by on their good looks—but not forever. Sooner or later the water has to produce or fishermen will leave it to sightseers and hikers. Every once in a while, Fall Creek is so productive that its signature waterfall is hardly noticed by fishermen, whose eyes are focused on battling trout instead of cascading sheets of water and clouds of freezing mists.

Fall Creek meanders for miles between the town of Summerhill in Cayuga County and its namesake cataract in the Tompkins County city of Ithaca, but its upper stretches between Groton City and Freetown offer fair fishing, at best, for stocked browns and a few wild brookies. The rainbows come into the picture, literally, below the falls, which are just across the street (Route 34) from Ithaca High School. The hat-floater pool at the base of the falls is as far as fish can migrate when they enter the creek to spawn. Starting in November or December each year, rainbows averaging about 1½ pounds but occasionally surpassing 5 pounds vacate their homes in Cayuga Lake and swim into the creek. They can go for approximately a mile to the falls, but their route includes at least half a dozen deep pools and runs that are ideal for fly fishing.

In response to the dedicated cadre of fly rodders who frequent the creek, the DEC opted a couple of years ago to open the water between the falls and the railroad crossing downstream for flies only, from January 1 through March 15. The only no-kill water to be found on the Finger Lakes tributaries, Fall Creek gives anglers a fair crack at early-migrating spawners that otherwise would be in and out of the stream well before the April 1 opening of the state regular trout season. Depending on the weather, it gets a fair amount of traffic in early March.

The creek is easy to find. Just watch for the high-school campus as you're heading south into Ithaca on Route 34; bear left when you see it. Drive over the bridge and pick out an off-street parking spot.

## Cayuga Lake Inlet

Flowing by fast-food restaurants and trailer parks, Cayuga Inlet is a Plain Jane compared with Salmon Creek, but it makes up for its shortage of good looks by providing acre upon acre of excellent spawning habitat. The inlet also has excellent cover for hiding big fish, and anglers who work it diligently in April—and some years in November and December, too—are often rewarded with rainbows of 18 to 26 inches in length.

I've fished the inlet often, and taken rainbows up to 25 inches long during the spring run. Many of those fish hit egg sacs drifted over visible redds. Also called spawning beds, redds are oval-shaped depressions that hen trout construct by rolling on their sides and wriggling furiously. After eggs are laid in one patch of gravel, the hen moves slightly forward and repeats the drill. Gravel from the upstream nest covers the previous one, securing the fish's eggs until they hatch or are lost to flooding or some other calamity. Because trout often consume eggs that drift in the currents below completed redds, any deep pool downstream from these nesting areas is apt to hide a very big and very hungry rainbow.

The lower end of the inlet, across Routes 34 and 96 from Buttermilk Falls State Park, is the site of a fish passage device maintained by the DEC to capture trout for use in its hatchery system and, a few weeks later, to collect and kill parasitic sea lampreys during their own spawning run. The fishway, as biologists refer to it, can't be bypassed by migrating trout except during extreme flood conditions. Since trout must navigate through the fishway to reach familiar spawning areas upstream from Ithaca in the town of Danby, technicians can actually count 1- to 10-pound rainbows and estimate the overall number of trout taking part in the spawning in any given year. On average, about 1,000 trout make the trip, some during the autumn but most in March and early April.

Cayuga Inlet has ample public fishing areas between Ithaca south to the headwaters near Danby. It is easy wading, between 10 and 40 feet across, and seldom overly crowded. In addition to the main stream, anglers should explore several productive feeder streams, including Enfield, Newfield, and Van Buskirk Creeks, which flow eastward before spilling into the inlet. Van Buskirk is a tiny stream, averaging less than 10 feet across, but it may hold substantial numbers of 2- to 4-pound rainbows if you hit it a day or two after an April downpour. Access to Van Buskirk is available from state angler parking areas at the junction of Brown Road and Route 96 in the town of Danby.

## Catharine Creek

If you have a deep desire to catch a large, lake-run rainbow trout on a fly, Catharine Creek is the place to fulfill the quest. Her rich variety of pools, runs, and riffles simply beg to be probed with a deep-swimming artificial nymph or perhaps your favorite egg fly. I know of anglers who have taken 8-pound rainbows on flies in the creek, and in recent seasons, too.

On slow days, tell yourself and then tell others that big rainbows will bite if given the chance. Only a lazy angler will deliberately snag these beautiful fish. The rest of us are such skilled anglers, we don't have to cheat, right?

Catharine Creek is the once and future queen of Finger Lakes tributaries because its rainbows come from Seneca Lake, the largest and deepest of the Fingers. They have more room to hide than their cousins in other

Gus Aull III fishes Sleepers Creek, a tributary of Catharine Creek that gets a good rainbow run in April.

lakes, and more to eat, too. The creek itself is a wonderful spawning habitat, with plenty of gravel for egg incubation and hatching. Deep pools, both natural and man-made, abound from the stream's beginning near Pine Valley in Chemung County north to its mouth at Watkins Glen. That's more than 10 miles of prime fishing water, most of it marked by those good old yellow-and-green DEC PUBLIC FISHING AREA signs.

Combined, the above stream conditions make Catharine Creek a likely spot for anyone looking for a trout big enough to display in taxidermy form. If you'd like a preview of coming attractions, telephone the DEC Region 8 office in Avon, (585) 226-2466, in early March and ask when the survey crew plans to do their traditional electrofishing foray. Shortly before the trout season starts, the state researchers will use their backpack generators to send waves of electric current through some of the deep pools between the villages of Montour Falls and Pine Valley. Usually, spectators will get to gawk and gasp at dozens of 'bows, including several in the 8- to 10-pound range.

You can easily explore Catharine Creek on your own in April. It flows roughly parallel to Route 14 for most of its length. If you go, save a few casts for tributaries such as Sleeper Creek, which is just about ½ mile south of the Schuyler–Chemung county line; and Havana Glen, which meets the main creek in Montour Falls.

## Cold Brook

As the principal trout-spawning tributary of Keuka Lake, Cold Brook used to have a heck of a spring rainbow run, but recent returns haven't been impressive at all. The disappointing fishing in the brook has coincided with a long decline in the number of rainbows caught annually in Keuka by participants in the Finger Lakes angler-diary program. DEC experts think the rainbow shortage may be due to a number of changes in the lake and its tributaries.

The changes include the introduction of zebra and quagga mussels to Keuka Lake, the nearly complete collapse of the lake's smelt population, the increased abundance of (rainbow-eating) lake trout, and the periodic clogging of Cold Brook by beavers. Every one of these disruptions in the lake's ecology poses a serious challenge to fisheries managers.

Still, I wouldn't be shocked if rainbow catches rose dramatically soon, thanks to an ongoing DEC experimental program at Cold Brook.

Prior to 2010, the brook had not been stocked with rainbows in 113 years. DEC Region 8 biologist Brad Hammers said the rainbow fishery in Keuka Lake can be traced to the release of 30,000 California-strain 'bows in 1897. As of 2012, the DEC was midway through a five-year stocking experiment that will introduce 4,000 to 5,000 rainbows annually to Cold Brook. My only concern, and it is a mild one, is that the stocked rainbows may in some way interfere with the extant population of wild browns in the stream. In recent years, resident browns have outnumbered and outsized the spawning rainbows in the DEC's electrofishing surveys on Cold Brook. Let us hope that rainbows thrive, but not so much that browns are harmed or diminished.

Meanwhile, if you like to fish small streams that are known to hold a large trout or two, maybe even a 5- or 6-pounder, check your calendar to see if you have a free day in mid- to late April. Cold Brook takes a slightly serpentine course into Hammondsport in Steuben County. Erupting from subterranean springs about 2 miles from the DEC trout hatchery in Bath, it is within shouting range of Route 54 almost all the way to the lake.

Like Catharine Creek (and Naples Creek, covered next), Cold Brook is probed by electrofishing crews in late March. Anglers and others who want to tag along are welcome. Check with the DEC office in Avon to verify the date, time, and meeting place.

## Naples Creek

If I knew ahead of time that I would have only one remaining opportunity in my life to fish for Finger Lakes rainbows, but the day and location would be up to me, I would choose the third day of the coming season, at Naples Creek. How's that for an endorsement?

Naples is one of those fishing holes that's not too big and not too small. No matter what sort of water you enjoy the most—plunge pools, bend pools, deep and dark undercuts, pocket water, riffles, runs, you name it—you will find plenty of it in this short but sweet spawning ground for Canandaigua Lake rainbows.

Big rainbows like this one caught in Naples Creek are prized by anglers who fish New York's Finger Lakes tributaries.

In contrast with most other Finger Lakes tribs, elbow room is not much of a concern at Naples, even on April Fools' Day, for the creek's gravel and cobblestones have carved one enticing pool after another. Upstream and down from the Route 364 bridge, it has pools 30 to 40 feet wide, sufficiently roomy to do some proper fly casting. As you move farther upstream into the village of Naples, some man-made stream-improvement devices come into play. The deepest and probably the hardest-fished hole in the entire Naples Creek watershed is the digger pool constructed under DEC supervision at the top of a bend about 100 yards downstream from the mouth of Grimes Creek.

I generally fish the two digger pools upstream from the Grimes junction, walk across Route 21 (the main street), then fish all the way up to the Eelpot Road intersection. Most of the pools are 8 to 12 feet wide. It's a good mile walk to the bridge, and on your way back you may wish to check out Reservoir Creek, another small tributary that's frequented by some huge fish during the spawning run.

Are you wondering why I picked April 3 for that hypothetical one last rainbow trip? April 1 is simply too crowded with other anglers for my taste. On day two, the fish are still in shock, but by the third day of the season they should be settling down and the crowd will have thinned out considerably.

Access to Naples Creek is easy. From Canandaigua, which is on US Route 20, follow Route 21 south to Naples. That's pretty much it. There are half a dozen official state fisherman parking areas along Route 21, below, in, and above the village. Overflow from those lots is easily accommodated on public streets. Major access points include the creek crossing at Route 245, Ontario Street, two angler parking areas at the mouth of Grimes Creek off Mark Circle, and the Eelpot Road bridge located at the south end of the village, via Route 21.

## Springwater Creek

You don't hear much boasting about the rainbow fishing in Springwater Creek these days. The stream that puts out the welcome mat for romancing Hemlock Lake trout has been hitting lots of sour notes in recent years. Anglers are disappointed and they express their feelings to the Region 8 fisheries office fairly frequently.

Springwater Creek might be one of the major beneficiaries of the management reforms for Western Finger Lakes–region rainbows that took effect on October 1, 2012.

The changes include new or increased rainbow stocking efforts in some of the region's spawning. Also, creel limits have been slashed for the Finger Lakes and their tributaries located within DEC Region 8. The limit for rainbows in those lakes and streams is one 'bow a day, down from the previous five a day in Region 8 Finger Lakes and three a day in their tributaries.

Personally, I see the one-a-day limit as a de facto catch-and-release rule. Most humans, given the chance to have just one of anything, are inclined to hoard that precious whatever until another occasion, because much of its value comes from being so scarce. Such was the impact of a one-steelhead rule enacted for Lake Ontario tributaries.

Although its rainbow run is a far cry from what it was 10 or 20 years ago, rainbows do spawn in Springwater Creek, and some of the fish involved are of a good size, up to 4 or 5 pounds.

Getting to Springwater from Rochester is a matter of taking US Route 20 to Lima. From there, simply follow Route 15A south until you have reached the end of Hemlock Lake and start crossing the small bridges that span the creek and its network of feeders.

If you are in the neighborhood and just happen to have some trout gear in your vehicle, give the stretch between Kellogg Road and the creek mouth a thorough try. The creek, about 10 to 15 feet across in most spots, has a nice gravel bottom and plenty of undercuts to hold migrating rainbows and resident brook trout. The latter aren't abundant in the creek, but several of Springwater's tributaries have natives present, and some of them run downstream when the creek rises and falls following a spring shower. Care to try the tributaries themselves? Then you should be prepared to knock on doors, for posting is rather heavy in this neck of Livingston County.

The brook trout streams to test your angling techniques as well as your diplomatic skills include Pardee Hollow Creek, located at Miller Road in the town of Springwater; Reynold's Gulf Brook, which runs along Reynolds Gulf Road in Springwater; and Limekiln Brook, which crosses Route 15 (not 15A) and then runs alongside it for a short distance, also in the town of Springwater.

*Note:* Hemlock and Canadice Lakes and their tributaries used to be available to the public via special permits from the Rochester Department of Environmental Services. However, since the DEC agreed to take over fish and wildlife management responsibilities for the drinking-water supply lakes, the permit requirement has been abandoned. Visiting anglers should carefully read any DEC signs they encounter to make sure they are keeping up with the agency's regulations.

## MEATBALL SANDWICHES

My longtime friend Mike DeTomaso, who manages the fly-fishing department in the Bass Pro Shops store in Auburn, always recommends "meatball sandwiches" when a customer asks what flies are worth trying on tributary trout.

By meatball sandwiches, he means a sunken fly that bears a rough resemblance to any of the larger bugs living in the region's trout-spawning tributaries, and especially to cranefly larvae. Also called oakleaf grubs, real cranefly larvae are excellent yellow perch baits. Bait sellers find them in the mud and fallen leaves along the margins of small streams. They look somewhat like tomato worms but are much smaller, perhaps 1 to 1½ inches long.

"To a trout that has been seeing little eggs or small nymphs drift by him all day, that cranefly larvae must look like a meatball sandwich," said DeTomaso. "And as we all know, it's hard to resist a good meatball sandwich."

His imitations are tied on weighted, extra-long hooks and consist mainly of olive wool or fur, spiraled around the hook's shank. Easy to craft, they are very effective on big rainbow trout.

# CHAPTER 16

# Panfish Paradise

**Y**ou name your favorite fish; if it can tolerate fresh water, chances are it lives and thrives in one or more of the Finger Lakes. The chain is home to, in no particular order, rainbow, brown, and lake trout, northern pike, pickerel, Atlantic salmon, walleyes, largemouth and smallmouth bass, carp, suckers, catfish, bullheads, bluegills, pumpkinseed sunfish, and rock bass.

Oh, and also tiger muskellunge, yellow perch, white perch, silver bass, black crappies, longnose gar, alewives, rainbow smelt, spot-tail shiners, and probably a few other game fish, panfish, and baitfish I overlooked or haven't come across yet. Except for the compulsion to eat one another now and then, these varied and sundry species get along reasonably well, tending to their own niches in their local ecosystems.

Believe it or not, all of these fish have at least one thing in common, other than calling the Finger Lakes home. And that is, they all taste good to something or somebody. The muskie ate the trout, which ate the alewife, which ate the perch fry.

A mixed bag of two lakers and a 14-inch yellow perch caught from the shores of Skaneateles Lake.

It's a fish-eat-fish world down there, which is why no angler needs to apologize for wolfing down a few batter-dipped fillets now and again.

Fishing for panfish in the Finger Lakes is fantastic and figures to stay that way, as thousands of regional residents pass on family traditions such as Friday-night fish fries and plunking 'crawlers for bullheads next to a warming fire on a chilly night in April. My family, being Catholic, had a custom whereby each child who received his or her First Communion was thereby entitled to go fishing with my father—just Dad and the suddenly holy child. I'm not certain the Almighty had that prize in mind but I do know all the Kelly kids were suitably excited about their big day.

A couple of years after my communion, I broke new ground by going fly fishing for bluegills and crappies at the Otisco Lake dam. Dad and his eldest son did pretty well, as I recall, cranking or yanking (over my shoulder, a few times) about 30 to 40 nice ones from the near-shore weeds. Traditional trout wet flies such as the McGinty and Montreal did the damage, in concert with my grandfather's old bamboo rod.

Before that outing was over, Dad convinced me that we ought to share our catch with a couple of elderly fishermen who were sitting on the rocks a few yards from us but were having poor luck. It was one of many life lessons he taught me in nature's classroom, but I think he was also pleased to have only a dozen bluegills and "calicoes" to clean that evening. Of course, he and I both enjoyed those firm white fillets the following evening.

This rock bass hit a bass lure with a large, size 3/0 hook in it.

## A FAMILY AFFAIR

Panfishing is almost always a rewarding pastime in the Finger Lakes, and not just because several of the right species are available in each body of water in the chain. The rewards extend beyond the mere filling of a freezer, although that can be a satisfying and important achievement for any budget-minded household. I'm thinking here of the pleasure that parents enjoy when they take one or more kids to a bluegill-stuffed bay or a municipal pier that is a perch magnet in the spring. Few moments in life compare to the enthusiastic praise that ensues when a child reels in his or her first "big one." We have dozens of snapshots to commemorate these epiphanies in our family albums, and one of the better things about becoming grandparents is the chance to do over all those family excursions, starring a new cast of characters.

## OLD ISN'T ALL BAD

Another aspect of getting older, as most of us hope, is the chance to—eventually—slow down just a bit and "smell the roses" with our longtime fishing buddies. Just to be clear, many of us mature anglers can still keep up with the younger Joneses on the trout streams and in the bass tournaments, too, but when we go after some fish-fry fixings we aren't in any hurry. That's because age comes with experience, and experience tells us that if the perch spawned out from the pink cottage last April and the one before that as well, they are bound to show up in the same locale this time. If they happen to be running a little late, so what? We'll pass the time trying for bullheads in front of that little creek mouth, or looking through a pair of binoculars at the mallards that are already begging camp owners to toss a few bread crumbs their way.

No great amount of planning is required in advance of a Finger Lakes panfish expedition, as there are dozens of worthy places to explore and very few specialized techniques to master.

During the best times for catching panfish—through the winter ice and for the duration of each species's spawning run—the shore-bound angler who owns little tackle other than a cheap rod and a few hooks, sinkers, and bobbers will fare about as well as the tournament techie who invests thousands of dollars in sonar units, trolling motors, and temperature probes.

The following tips might be helpful to beginners and veteran panfishers alike.

## BONE UP ON BOBBERS

Anglers who disdain bobbers as too basic or simple for "experts" to use should take a gander at the awesome variety of floats offered for sale these days, not only in mom-and-pop bait shops but in the so-called big-box stores, as well. Weighted bobbers, quill floats, slip bobbers, lighted bobbers, and more crowd shelves and confuse shoppers in Bass Pro, Dick's, Gander Mountain, Cabela's, and other big-time tackle emporia. And yes, you can find those old-fashioned red-and-white globes, too.

So many choices, so little time, huh? Let's simplify the selection process by offering a few suggestions.

If you are fishing mainly for bluegills or pumpkinseeds or for anything else in shallow, weedy water, opt for several round, weighted bobbers, about ½ to 1 inch in diameter. The weight (whether incorporated into the bobber at the factory or provided in the form of an inserted peg) makes long casts easier. That's a major advantage because bobbers sometimes make a noisy splashdown, which can frighten sunnies into vacating their inshore spawning beds. With the weighted float, you can cast beyond the fish and quietly and slowly reel your bait to a spot where it will be noticed but won't sound the alarm.

Slip bobbers are a better choice for fish that are suspending or cruising in medium depths, 6 to 12 feet or so. Such a float is designed so that line with a split shot attached will slide through its tube-shaped center core until the sinker hits bottom or a knotted "bobber stop." Thus equipped, you can keep your bait at a precise depth, and experiment until you find the hot spot of the day.

Quill floats are bobbers that, due to their slender shape and minimal weight, can be used in still or moving water with small baits and lures. They do not land with a big splash but they do drift in a straight-up position when balanced by a split shot or two, and make strike detection very easy.

## WINTER, SUMMER—IT'S ALL THE SAME

If you want a surefire catcher of any member of the sunfish family, use the same teardrop jig and insect larva in the spring that you counted on during the winter ice-fishing season. Bluegills and pumpkinseeds will eat them as long as they happen on them.

While many panfishers prefer mousie grubs or waxworm larvae, I favor mealworms, for a couple of reasons. First, they don't go all squishy on me when I poke them with a hook point, which means less of a "gross-out" factor. Second, the mealworm's sturdy construction tells me they last longer on the hook. In fact, I often land three or four sunnies on a single mealworm.

As for jigs, I like a ¹⁄₃₂-ouncer with this application. Green-and-silver and orange-and-silver teardrops work very well.

Paul McNeilly with a nice bluegill from Owasco Lake.

## BRING A BALLOON OR TWO

Did you know that perch usually hang out with their classmates? Well, they do, but in this regard, the term *classmates* means according to their year of birth, and not their year of graduation from anything. It means they school with perch that are as old as they are and therefore approximately the same size.

And that's a roundabout way of saying that if you have caught several 8-inchers in one spot, you probably have to look elsewhere if you want a mess of 10-inchers.

When you find a couple of those nice ones you are looking for, put one of them back. But first inflate a small party balloon and put a 6-foot string on the knotted end. Poke a small hole in the dorsal fin of that desirable-size perch and poke the other end of the string through it. Tie a couple of granny knots in the string so it won't slip back through.

Keep an eye on the balloon; it should enable you to follow the movements of the school of 10-inchers.

## CHUMMING IS A CHEAP TRICK

The next time you see frozen sweet corn on sale in those little cardboard boxes, buy a few and keep them frozen pending the next time you go after bullheads or bluegills at one of your favorite shore-fishing spots. In fact, try to keep them frozen until you arrive at the water's edge.

Once you arrive, grab a golf-ball-size chunk of those ice-melded kernels and heave it as far as you can. That's probably going to be a distance of 30 feet or less, but rest assured, it's far enough. Toss some more corn before you rig up with your normal chosen bait.

The corn draws fish close because its unusual color and smell arouses their curiosity and their senses.

Chumming, as the trick is called, is almost universally effective. It is perfectly legal in most states, and works with many fish attractants besides corn. Boating anglers and shore casters can both do it.

Although chumming in general is permitted in New York, the Environmental Conservation Law prohibits the use of fish eggs for chum.

## STAY LATE FOR CRAPPIES

Black crappies, also known as calicoes or strawberry bass in some angling circles, frequently spend the day suspended partway between the surface and the bottom of a lake, then pop to the top to feed just before sunset.

Look for soft dimples in or just below the surface. If you're having difficulty spotting these "rise forms" because of low light or a slight chop, try to put the sinking sun at your back. If you're on the wrong side of the lake for that, crouch low and use polarized sunglasses to eliminate some of the distracting surface glare.

Once you see the feeding fish and know the direction they are taking, cast well in front of them. For bait, use a white or chartreuse marabou jig, with or without a tiny minnow on the bend. Hang it about 2 feet under a quill bobber and give it a subtle wiggle as the crappies draw closer.

# CHAPTER 17

# Ice Fishing in the Finger Lakes

**W**inters in Central and Western New York can be brutal, benign, or anything between, and the difficulty of putting an accurate forecast over the airwaves is such that any TV meteorologist who nails the overnight numbers three or four evenings in a row quickly acquires a cult-like following among area viewers and listeners. And that's fine with me, for who would want to deny this guy or gal a moment in the sun? This isn't San Diego, after all.

Even so, I can't help but smile when I hear people bragging about "their" personal-favorite weather maven.

If you think this fellow is so wonderful, I say, why don't you dare him, on or about the official first day of winter, to predict when any or all of the Finger Lakes will have a surface solid enough to be fished safely through the ice?

Any weather honchos who take such a wager aren't thinking straight or are their own press agents.

That's among the wildest guesses any daredevil could take, with one notable exception.

You can bet everything you own Seneca Lake will not grow any significant mantle of ice, in this or any other winter of the kind we hearty New Yorkers are accustomed to. The lake is simply too vast and too deep for any ice buildup. Now, please understand that I am not counting the wobbly patches of ice that form occasionally inside harbor breakwalls and such. However, I do feel very confident in declaring that if Seneca should ever sprout a surface hard enough for you or me to walk across from Dresden to Lodi or vice versa, global warming will be yesterday's news, and the doomsayers will be telling us to prepare for the new ice age.

While Seneca is out of the picture, ice-wise, most of the other Finger Lakes are a flip of the coin when their hard-water prospects are considered. During an exceptionally cold winter, any of the remaining 10 (other than Seneca) could have safe ice at some point—not necessarily over its entire surface, but at least covering an area large enough and sufficiently thick to support a reasonable number of tip-up watchers.

Several of the Finger Lakes tend to be partly covered with ice during a typical winter.

Take Cayuga Lake, for example. At 42,956 acres, it is almost as vast as Seneca, on the surface, but it isn't nearly as deep. Much of its north end, from Union Springs north, is less than 6 feet deep, and that feature alone assures that some ice fishing can be had more years than not. But knowing when ice will form and how long it will last? That is pure guesswork.

Skaneateles Lake has a similar prognosis. In my adult life, the south end, which happily has strong populations of yellow perch and chain pickerel, has almost always been safely visited by ice fishermen at least a few times each season. The north end between the village pier and the west-shore country club, about a square mile's worth of water, is surprisingly shallow and therefore can grow 4 or 5 inches of ice in the span of a week or so, but that newly hardened surface can disappear just as quickly when the prevailing winds are blowing from the south. On the other hand, Skaneateles Lake has been completely covered with ice at least twice during my adult life, and one of those times the hardtop lasted into early April. The locals who wanted to spend the first day of the state's general trout season with a little shore fishing were badly disappointed.

Otisco Lake, which is Skaneateles Lake's next-door neighbor and only 5 miles to its east as the crow flies, was completely iced over that same winter. However, Otisco normally freezes from shore to shore for at least a few weeks, more winters than not. The same can be said of Honeoye and Canadice Lakes, while Owasco, Keuka, Canandaigua, and Hemlock typically are safe for ice fishing in some sectors at some point in the winter but can't be counted on for a full freeze-over.

When I was a full-time outdoors writer for The Syracuse Newspapers, one of my duties was the preparation of a weekly fishing forecast, and frankly, I dreaded doing that part of the job from ice-over on. Aware that ice fishermen are notorious risk takers, I always downplayed my dispatches from prime tip-up spots, lest I send some fanatic to thin ice and possibly even death. In those years I do not recall anyone kicking the proverbial bucket on my account, but there were some close calls when eager anglers actually ignored my warnings (and those of local rescue workers) to stay off the ice.

My specific advice to anyone who inquired about ice-fishing prospects on the Finger Lakes or anywhere else always concluded with the same warning: "If in doubt, don't go out." It is just as apropos now as it was then.

Given safe conditions, ice fishing in the region can be an effective means of filling your freezer and an invigorating way to get through a rugged winter. We can only read so many books, right?

My picks for the best ice fishing in the region are about like that local weather reporter's five-day forecast—made with crossed fingers and closed eyes—but here we go, species by species:

- **BLUEGILLS.** Honeoye Lake is the place for platter-size sunnies, hands down; but Owasco, Cayuga, Keuka, and Conesus are all very good when adequate ice is available.

- **CRAPPIES.** Canandaigua Lake is good and Honeoye has its share, too. Most fishermen aren't aware that crappies bite best during low-light conditions, even if the ice is a foot thick.

- **YELLOW PERCH.** Both the north and south ends of Skaneateles Lake can provide exceptional fishing for perch—or none, if the winter is too mild for safe ice. For more consistent prospects, try the north end of Cayuga Lake, especially along the mid-lake channel north of Union Springs.

- **PICKEREL.** The best bite around is at Hemlock Lake's south end, but the north end of Cayuga Lake is good, too.

- **NORTHERN PIKE.** For large pike through the ice, the south end of Owasco Lake is tops, but Conesus Lake is a close second.

- **TIGER MUSKIES.** Otisco Lake grows tigers up to 30 pounds, so it's no contest.

- **WALLEYES.** I'd call this a three-way tie among Otisco, Honeoye, and Conesus Lakes. All have large walleyes and good numbers, too, but the ice fishing for the species is slow.

- **LAKE TROUT.** It's a close call, but I'll give the nod for lake trout to Canadice Lake over Hemlock and Owasco.

## ICE-FISHING SAFETY

Safety is no laughing matter, though I can't help but chuckle when I come across one of those newspaper or magazine articles about safe ice fishing. The ones I'm thinking of list various ice thicknesses, and what type of traffic they can accommodate.

Here's a direct quote from one such article:

"Two inches of ice—one person on foot; three inches—group in single file; seven and a half inches, cars (up to) two tons . . ."

Hold it right there!

If two inches is only safe for you alone, what happens if you step on a thin spot and break through? Who will rescue you? Another lone angler who is also likely to break the ice, or a group of fishermen who will have to walk single-file across what they now realize is a treacherous surface?

My standards are quite a bit stricter than that. Somebody has to be the first one to test the ice, but that somebody isn't going to be me. Before I venture onto a lake, I want to see the tracks of other anglers, several sets of them, heading onto the ice and returning safely, too. Then I take a wading staff or some other solid piece of wood and whack the near-shore ice as firmly as I can. If the ice doesn't crack, I drill a hole. Assuming it's at least 6 inches thick—enough to support several anglers in close proximity—I take three or four steps away from the shore and drill again. I test-drill once more after that. Only then do I feel confident enough to make a day of it on the ice.

By the way, no matter how thick the ice is, you will never see my car parked on it.

# CHAPTER 18

# Trout Streams of the Finger Lakes Region

It is a great pleasure for any angler to fish for trout in the Finger Lakes region, but residents of the area are especially fortunate. By making their homes in or near Rochester, Binghamton, or Syracuse, gainfully employed anglers can usually check out of work in time to catch the evening hatch on a nearby trout stream. The neighborhood has plenty of high-quality streams to explore, ranging from jump-across brooks with knee-deep pools that are best fished with bait to wide waters that can accommodate deft fly casters who wish to hone their hatch-matching skills.

In this section, we will focus mainly on waters other than those that host spawning runs of Finger Lakes rainbows in April. With one major exception, the famous rainbow tributaries do not have particularly good trout fishing during the summer. Indeed, a majority of them are too warm and low in July and August to support anything other than fingerling and yearling rainbows. Only one rainbow spawning stream in the Finger Lakes—Owasco Lake Inlet—makes my personal short list of the region's top-notch trout streams. There are a few other rainbow waters, including Cold Brook, Keuka Outlet, Naples Creek, and Grout Brook, that have decent populations of brown trout, but limited summer fisheries due to low-water conditions.

Happily, plenty of other waters in the area are worthy of a trout seeker's serious interest, and most of them yield good catches throughout the fishing season. The streams I am about to discuss all have dense populations of brown, brook, or rainbow trout. Some support wild trout, stream-bred and brilliantly colored. Several are capable of growing 20-inchers, but as any experienced trout fisher will attest, trout of that size don't get big by being greedy or gullible.

Some anglers would rather catch small trout than big ones, anyway, especially if the "eating-size" fish were bred in the wild and not in a hatchery incubator. Other fishermen don't give a hoot about whether a fish is wild or stocked, but prefer brookies to browns, or vice versa. Many,

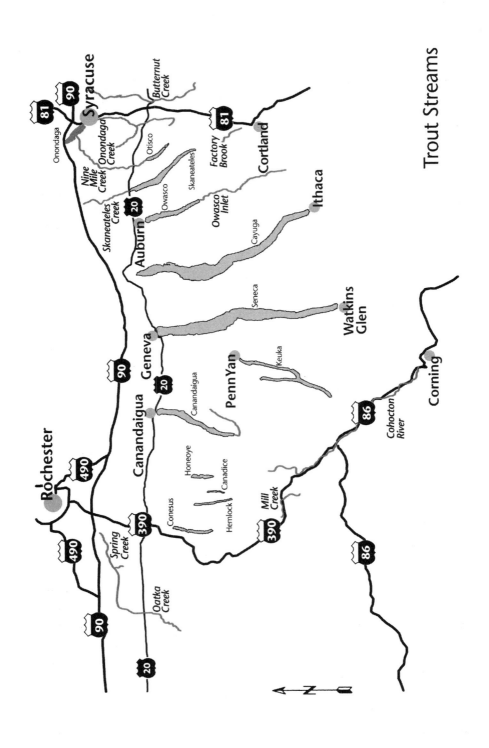

Trout Streams

interested primarily in a soothing, no-hassle day on the water, look hard for public access signs because they are too shy to ask permission from a landowner who may or may not give them the go-ahead to fish awhile.

In the Finger Lakes region, you have these choices and more. The counties that contain or touch upon the lakes in the chain are predominantly rural or suburban in character, and boast hundreds of clear, quick-flowing streams that hold wild trout or hatchery transplants—or both, in many cases. Some of the waters you'll get to know with the help of this book are among the coldest, clearest streams in the state, yet are barely rippled by wading anglers after the first week or two of the trout season.

Writers of fishing books walk a tightrope when they focus on specific streams. Too much hyperbole could trigger an invasion of somebody's favorite honey hole, which is why I try an unfamiliar trout stream at least several times before saying grand things about it in print. On the other hand, muted praise for a lake or stream with widely familiar virtues could erode the writer's credibility. My way of resolving the dilemma is to call 'em as I see 'em, and let the readers decide for themselves whether I can be trusted. Come along while I take a look at 10 of the best trout streams in the Finger Lakes region. Let's begin with a small one in Cortland County, and head west from there.

## Factory Brook

If you're agile, you can clear some segments of Cortland County's best trout stream without getting your boots wet, for Factory Brook is less than 10 feet wide in many places, but getting to fishy-looking pools can be a challenge. The brook is guarded by alders and hidden strands of rusty barbed wire, too. If beavers have been active along the brook, and they often are, you may have to take a long detour to get around one or more dams.

Keep going, regardless. The potential rewards for negotiating this daunting terrain are colorful, bulky brown trout and some of the prettiest native brookies you can imagine. All of Factory Brook's trout are wild, with brilliant markings and orange flesh that is firm and sweet on the palate. If you are patient and stealthy you are bound to hook a couple of good ones, but believe me when I say you will earn every trout you catch.

Factory Brook arises from small springs along West Scott Road in the Cortland County town of Scott. It flows in a southerly direction for about 1½ miles and then slips under state Route 41. From that point it meanders through overgrown pastures and past a housing development called Emerald Estates, where natural undercuts and decades-old log

Paul McNeilly fishing on Factory Brook in Cortland County.

cribbing and other stream-improvement structures serve as hiding places for some large browns. About ½ mile farther on, the brook turns right and goes under Route 41 again. It winds through another thick pasture, fenced to keep livestock out of the water, momentarily disappears into a shadowy culvert at Creal Road, and then wanders through a willow-shaded channel en route to the village of Homer. In the village, the stream veers left, goes under a box-culvert bridge just south of the Route 41–Route 281 intersection, and then winds through a swamp and around a junior-high-school athletic field before flowing into the West Branch of the Tioughnioga River—a decent trout stream in its own right.

Approximately half of the 7½-mile-long Factory Brook is bordered on one or both banks by PUBLIC FISHING signs. These areas include most of the headwaters above the first Route 41 crossing, another mile or so from that bridge to the vicinity of Emerald Estates, and the stretch between the second Route 41 bridge and the north end of Creal Road. Between the Creal Road bridge and the youth baseball and softball fields in Homer, there is intermittent posting, but some landowners have been known to grant access to anglers who politely ask permission. Anglers can also hopscotch from pool to pool within the village of Homer. Just be sure to avoid posted stretches of the creek, including the short section alongside the local water-treatment facility.

I have enjoyed some terrific fishing in Factory Brook, landing brook trout up to 14 inches and browns up to 22 inches long. Most of my time on the stream is spent in the public-fishing areas above Creal Road, in the village of Homer, and in the alder-choked runs and riffles along West Scott Road. The village pools get more angler traffic than the rest of the brook, and their residents, mostly browns, are easily frightened by careless waders.

Browns that call the Tioughnioga River home often migrate a mile or two upstream into Factory Brook to spawn. Consequently, it's not unusual to catch several 12- to 16-inch browns in a single pool just before the season ends in October.

Bait, lure, and fly fishermen all enjoy fishing Factory Brook, since there are no special regulations pertaining to the stream. In the jungle-like headwaters, bait is the only practical choice, but as the brook bounces and shimmies through pastures and bogs farther downstream, careful fly casters can pick their spots and catch some dandy fish during a mayfly hatch. To fly fish Factory Brook, you should carry an assortment of floaters, including size 14 Hendricksons, size 14 and 18 Pale Evening Duns (also known as sulfurs), and a few beetle, ant, and grasshopper imitations for summer action. If you're really confident of your abilities, you ought to get up early on August mornings and look for mating swarms of tiny (size 24 hooks) *Tricorythodes* mayflies.

To pinpoint Factory Brook's location, look for Route 41 in the village of Skaneateles on a regional map and use a highlighting marking pen to plot an easy-to-follow, southward course to Homer.

## Owasco Inlet

One of the few Finger Lakes tributaries that offer good season-long trout fishing as a bonus to the spring rainbow spawning runs, Owasco Inlet is underrated even by local anglers. As you follow it upstream from the Cayuga County village of Moravia, about 3 miles south of its confluence with Owasco Lake, one yellow-and-green-lettered sign after another can be seen on the inlet's banks. More than 13 miles of the inlet is designated PUBLIC FISHING on one or both sides. It's good all the way upstream through Moravia, Locke, and Groton—despite a despite a serious, recurring problem with beaver dams.

The water quality in Owasco Inlet is generally excellent. Top to bottom, the stream is well oxygenated and has enough shade and spring seeps to assure the survival of trout year-round. Mayfly and caddis hatches are prolific, and there are enough deep pools, swift runs, and riffles to suit

The author with a 20-inch brown trout caught in Owasco Inlet in the early season.

the temperament of any angler. You like big trout, you say? I've caught many 20-inch-plus rainbows in the inlet and have slipped my net under resident browns that weighed nearly 4 pounds. Even in midsummer, when the heat can be intense, I have enjoyed hooking wild rainbows of 12 or 13 inches on softly cast dry flies.

You'd naturally assume such a place would be crowded, but between mid-April and the end of the Finger Lakes tributary season on December 31, all those with the desire to fish usually will have hundreds of yards of water to themselves.

Owasco Inlet flows within sight of Route 38 from Peruville down into Groton. This section is pretty well plugged by beaver dams, but if you ask politely, the owners of the small businesses across Route 38 from the high school usually grant permission to fish. Plenty of wild brown trout lurk in the bend pools there. They hit worms, salted minnows, or spinning lures, but watch your step on the slick clay deposits.

In the northern Tompkins County village of Groton, deeper runs and riffles may hold a few spawning rainbows as well as resident browns, but their abundance depends on the status of beaver colonies farther downstream. One small but trout-rich tributary, Peg Mill Brook, joins the inlet about a mile north of Groton.

Between Groton and Locke there is extensive public water, some of the best of which is downstream from a parking area that sits across the road from a farm with a giant plastic steer in the front yard. My friends and I refer to the spot as "the Brown Cow." It's hard to miss, and downstream from the statue the inlet cuts one sinuous bend after another. The Hendrickson mayfly hatch that takes place here from about April 25 to mid-May brings lots of 10- to 12-inch browns to the surface, along with numerous juvenile rainbows, and a good nymph fisherman may hook a large rainbow that has hung around after spawning.

The finest rainbow fishing in Owasco Inlet, however, is found in and below the hamlet of Locke. Hemlock Creek, which passes under Route 38 just south of Locke, is the largest-volume tributary of the inlet. In the good old days before lake trout and reintroduced walleyes sharply depleted Owasco Lake's brown and rainbow populations, Hemlock was the spawning grounds for some truly gigantic fish. My best 'bow there weighed a bit more than 10 pounds, but I've talked with other anglers who have caught even bigger ones in the stream. Few of those fishermen seemed to be aware that Hemlock's deeper pools hold some 2- and 3-pound browns during the summer months. They can be caught on garden worms or minnows at any time but particularly when the creek is running a little high and off-color following a hot-weather rain shower.

Hatch-matching anglers ought to do some exploring on the inlet during the Trico mayfly emergence, which starts about mid-July and lasts until mid-September. The itty-bitty insects are imitated by a few turns of thread, hackle, and dubbing on size 24 dry-fly hooks, and should be fished on a leader with a 6X or 7X tippet. I have a hard time tying the little flies to a leader, but the effort is worth it because you can find dozens of trout rising on the flat pools in and below Moravia on cool summer mornings.

## Butternut Creek

Do you like snakes? That's not a trick question, for most people don't care for them at all, and I'm like most folks where serpents are concerned. They give me the willies, frankly, which is why I talk loudly and bang my wading staff on the ground when I fish certain stretches of Butternut Creek. Water snakes, the big black and brown ones, slither over, under, around, and through loose shale and dense vegetation in these habitats, which are just outside the hamlet of Jamesville in Onondaga County. The only reason I ever visit this spot is that it holds more brown trout than snakes.

Immediately north of Jamesville, the creek tumbles through a shallow but steep gorge and ducks under Jamesville Road opposite the entrance to a large stone quarry, then runs through a golf course before making a long northward run along Route 481 in DeWitt. The water snakes are most common near the quarry, which likely explains why the fishing is better a few pools farther upstream.

Most of the trout in Butternut Creek are of a size that tempts big, hungry serpents—around 8 to 14 inches. However, you can catch some that are too large even for the snakes, if you put in the time.

Butternut Creek is formed by the confluence of several small streams just north of Route 80, near the hamlet of Apulia Station, east of Tully. The creek widens a bit after it plunges through a culvert pipe at Dailey Road; but the alders and other vegetative obstacles are omnipresent most of the way downstream to US Route 20, a distance of about 3½ miles. From the Route 20 crossing to Jamesville, Butternut averages between 10 and 25 feet wide, just roomy enough to fish with flies.

Above the federal highway, the creek is 6 to 10 feet wide for the most part, and its jungle-like surroundings dictate the use of bait or possibly spinning tackle. As you follow the stream's course along Clark Hollow Road, you will see numerous yellow signs with green lettering, declaring Butternut to be a PUBLIC FISHING stream. Two marked angler parking areas are evident along Clark Hollow, too. Yet you will almost certainly have this water to yourself once the early-April rush is over. Hiking upstream is worth the effort, since 10- to 12-inch browns are routine, and you stand a decent chance of catching a wild brook trout, too.

A likely best place to hook a sizable trout in Butternut Creek is in the meandering, heavily shaded mile of water between US Route 20 and Colton Road. This gravel-bottomed section of the creek consists mainly of 2- to 4-foot-deep pools, averaging about 15 feet across. It is hospitable to bait, lure, and fly fishers, and has robust mayfly and caddis hatches from late April through June. The most notable of the spring-season bugs here is the famed Hendrickson mayfly, and tan caddis are abundant, too.

About 5 miles below the Route 20 crossing, Butternut Creek empties into the Jamesville Reservoir, an impoundment that formerly was part of the barge canal system. Immediately below the reservoir dam, a stretch of cool pocket water flows within site of Route 91 into the village of Jamesville.

Butternut is stocked annually with 4,000 or 5,000 trout, including 1,000 or so two-year-old browns from the Onondaga County hatchery. Some of those "stockers" survive their first trout season and then hang on during a rugged winter or two. These rough and ready browns have what it takes to grow to lengths of 16 to 20 inches. My personal best from Butternut, a 19½-inch beauty with a hooked jaw and dime-size spots, bit on a worm in February 2007. I lucked into him while fishing about 300 yards north of the Route 20 bridge. Butternut Creek, along with a couple of other Syracuse-area streams (Limestone Creek and Chittenango Creek), is open to fishing year-round downstream from Route 20, while the rest of the stream opens April 1 and closes after October 15.

## Onondaga Creek

It might seem a stretch, at first, to refer to Onondaga Creek as one of Central New York's top trout waters. Much of the creek is perpetually stained with runoff from clay-colored "mud boils," and parts of it are saltier than a can of red-skinned peanuts. Within Syracuse, the creek conveys raw sewage to Onondaga Lake via an antiquated combined drainage system after heavy rains hit town. At this writing, local officials are struggling to resolve all of the creek's pollution issues.

Not exactly pristine, but the creek has what college basketball TV analysts might call "a good upside."

John "Kid" Corbett and a brown trout that went back in the water near Franklin Square in Syracuse after this photo was shot.

Most of its trout are wild or stocked browns, but the stream is home to a few rainbows and brookies, too. You can catch them if you can find them—and that's no easy trick, for access is problematic. Besides dealing with the usual NO TRESPASSING signs posted by farmers and wary suburban homeowners, anglers wishing to explore Onondaga Creek's treasures will have to pass up pools within the Onondaga Indian Reservation located just south of Syracuse.

### Welcome to Killer Creek

The city itself poses a huge challenge to fishermen. Except for a few gentrified stretches paralleled by one of those trendy urban "creek walks," the city's segment of the creek is literally under lock and key. Padlocked chain-link fences, erected in the mid-20th century, were designed to end a string of child drownings in what newspaper headline writers coined "the Killer Creek." Within the fenced area, which begins in the Onondaga Valley neighborhood in Syracuse and winds up in the downtown business and residential apartment showplace known as Franklin Square, the creek was long ago channelized and almost stripped of its in-stream cover. City officials could give Syracuse's economy a boost by constructing a few angler access trails, pool diggers, and casting platforms, but recent renovation plans have overlooked the creek's fishing potential.

On several occasions, former Syracuse police lieutenant John "Kid" Corbett has guided me on excursions to the downtown trout water, and we have both tied into trout measuring 18 inches long. It is a shame that such productive water is barely fished; not that Corbett and I mind having it to ourselves!

Until the time when Syracuse welcomes anglers to Onondaga Creek, its headwaters and branches are already worth fishing, especially in the spring months or anytime when heavy rains bring on the bite. Sadly, there are very few PUBLIC FISHING STREAM signs along the main stream or its feeders, and newcomers should plan on asking landowners for permission to trespass or else be limited to fishing from rural bridge surfaces, which are generally state-owned and therefore accessible.

### Problems Not Limited to City

The Main Branch of Onondaga Creek flows north in the Tully Valley for about 8 miles before entering the realm of the Onondaga Nation—off limits to non-Indians—in the town of LaFayette. To get a look at the Onondaga, upstream from the reservation, take Interstate 81 to the Tully exit, then head west on Route 80. Take a right onto Tully Farms Road, go down a steep hill, pass the intersection with Solvay Road on your right, and start looking for the angler parking lot just ahead. This parking area and the PUBLIC FISHING signs (and wildflower garden) close to it are one result of years of negotiations and legal discussions between Honeywell Inc. and the state Department of Environmental Conservation related to the decades-old efforts to clean up Onondaga Lake.

For many years, Honeywell property along Tully Farms Road was posted NO TRESPASSING and passing fishermen sighed with envy as they drove over the stream crossing near Solvay Road. Now they can park and fish for wild and stocked browns in pools averaging about 2 feet deep and 10 feet across.

### Plenty of Potential

I once tagged along on a DEC survey of the creek upstream from Route 20 to write a feature story for the *Syracuse Post-Standard*, and the excursion left no doubt in my mind that this was a trout stream with much unrealized potential. The DEC crew collected many more suckers and chubs than trout, as I recall, but several pools held wild browns of 12 to 15 inches, and I could easily imagine a bright future for the creek if proposed environmental cleanups were carried to fruition.

The West Branch of Onondaga Creek had its own, albeit much different, problems, including extensive posting by landowners. Many of those property holders give their assent to polite anglers who request permission to fish, but it is a real shame that there is virtually no public fishing access to the headwaters of the West Branch in the towns of Marcellus, Otisco, and Onondaga. Too many years ago to mention, I shared a family membership at the Tanner Valley Golf Club in Onondaga, off Tanner Valley Road. Every November, golfers watched in amazement as huge brown trout—some of which, I kid you not, weighed 5 or 6 pounds—spawned in plain view of the golf course's first tee.

## Nine Mile Creek

The best trout stream in Western or Central New York? Others might hesitate to make that call, but my pick is Nine Mile Creek in Onondaga County. Having fished Nine Mile for more than 50 years, my honest assessment is that the creek today is better than ever. In fact, I consider it one of the top 10 trout waters in the Empire State.

Nine Mile begins at the outlet dam on the north end of Otisco Lake and meanders through the Onondaga County villages of Marcellus and Camillus before easing into Onondaga Lake just outside the city of

Late-season fly fishing on Nine Mile Creek, the author's choice as the best
trout stream in west-central New York.

Syracuse. While most trout streams have cold headwaters but gradually
warm before emptying into a larger body of water, Nine Mile starts out
warm and winds up cold. It is stocked almost end-to-end with brown
and brook trout reared at the Onondaga County hatchery, but the fishing
quality improves markedly in the vicinity of Marcellus Falls, where a
series of high-volume limestone springs bubble up from the ground and
blend with the creek. From that point downstream through Camillus and
on to its estuary, Nine Mile's water temperature seldom registers higher
than the mid-60s, even on the hottest days of a New York summer.

### A Trout-Friendly Environment

Once, I decided to take my own measure of how important those big
springs are to Nine Mile's continued good health. I launched my inves-
tigation by dipping a stream thermometer in a riffle about 200 yards
upstream from what was then the Martisco Paper Company. When I
pulled the instrument out of the water a minute later, it read a rather
tepid 74 degrees. I took a few steps downstream and checked the temperature of the first spring I could see—just 52 degrees! There were at least
three more springs in the next 100 yards, all pumping out cold water. I
took my final reading immediately downstream from the mill. It was 62
degrees, ideal for trout fishing. Since that day I have taken Nine Mile's

temperature at numerous locations where the creek flows close to Route 174 between Marcellus Falls and Amboy. In midsummer, I have never recorded a reading higher than 68.

Both wild and stocked trout thrive in such temperatures, and Nine Mile Creek would be considered an angler's paradise, were it not for the stream's one serious deficiency. I'm referring, of course, to its extreme popularity among Syracuse-area fishermen. Surveys conducted by the DEC and its research partners at Cornell University have always confirmed my impression that Nine Mile Creek feels the footprints of many more anglers than the average trout stream. The most recent of such studies estimated that the recreational use of the stream amounted to more than 56,000 angler-days per year. In other words, during the six and a half months of the fishing season on the creek (April 1 through October 15), it is visited by an average of 285 anglers every day!

### Crowds Come with the Territory

Nine Mile's annual stocking quota, determined by the DEC but supplied by the Onondaga County hatchery in Elbridge, adds up to an average of more than 25,000 trout, including several thousand two-year browns that average 13 to 14 inches apiece. The creek could get by with far

Nine Mile Creek "flats," one of best stretches of trout water in New York.

fewer fish-farm graduates, for it holds large numbers of wild browns and an expanding population of rainbows, too. But Dan Bishop, the DEC's former Region 7 fisheries manager, maintains that the heavy stockings between mid-April and early June "act as a buffer" and keep the crowds of early-season anglers from decimating Nine Mile's wild browns and 'bows.

No matter, for Nine Mile is what it is, and most Syracuse-area sportsmen and -women seem satisfied with the way the creek is managed. Every now and then, a handful of trout-fishing enthusiasts makes an earnest pitch to set aside part of the creek as a catch-and-release area, but DEC officials so far have been reluctant to put such a popular stream under special regulations. If it's not broke, they figure, why fix it?

### This Stream Can Take a Punch

Then again, the creek already has been broken, and more than once. In the 1940s and '50s, at a time when government at all levels paid relatively little attention to water-pollution issues, it was not unusual to see Nine Mile turning colors, including patriotic reds, whites, and blues, whenever the local woolen mill was changing its assembly-line dyes. In the early 1960s, a mysterious episode of pollution triggered a massive fish kill. Restocking helped the local brown trout fishery to recover, but the creek's once-numerous native brookies never made it all the way back. If you happen to catch a wild brook trout in Nine Mile, please admire it briefly and let it go.

For the foreseeable future, however, Nine Mile Creek is and likely will remain a brown trout stream, augmented here and there by descendants of the wild rainbows that showed up about 2005. I say "about" because I caught my first Nine Mile rainbow on April 29 that year, on a garden worm in very high water. It was 20 inches long, a spawned-out hen that looked exactly like the rainbows I had been catching for decades in Owasco Inlet, Grout Brook, and other springtime spawning grounds. Clearly it was not a stocked fish, and the most compelling explanation anybody has come up with was that rainbows resident to Cayuga, Owasco, or Skaneateles Lake had slid over a dam or two, then taken a wrong turn during their egg-laying time. It would be a fairly easy trip for Skaneateles fish, which could out-migrate via a series of small barriers on Skaneateles Creek to the Seneca River in Jordan. From there, the fish needed only to pass through Onondaga Lake, turn right into Nine Mile Creek, and vault the low dam at Amboy when high runoff flows made such a leap possible.

### *Rainbows Shine, but Browns Rule*

Regardless of where they originated, rainbows are now thriving in Nine Mile Creek, particularly in the first mile or so downstream from Marcellus Falls. Rainbows now average around 11 inches, and quite a few other 20-inch beauties have been caught since I reeled in my first.

Nine Mile Creek produces 20-inch browns every year, although most such fish seem to be caught in the first few days of the new trout season. Stocked trout are available from the outlet at Otisco Lake north, and the fishing with bait, lure, or flies is very good.

The creek's outstanding fly hatches, by far, occur between mid-May and mid-June, when the "sulfurs" emerge. *Ephemerella invaria* and *E. dorothea* are the Latin names for the local sulfurs. The two mayfly species's hatching dates overlap. *E. invaria* kicks things off around May 15, and the last of the dorotheas are done mating by June 25 or so, a day or two before or after orange daylilies sprout along Syracuse-area country roads. Early in the hatching cycle, the bugs pop up on the creek surface beginning at 3 or 4 PM, but the mayflies appear later and later with each passing day until, by around June 5, most of the action occurs at sundown.

Their pale, creamy yellow abdomens and gray wings make the sulfurs easy to identify and imitate. An assortment of size 14 and 16 dry-fly

A beautiful wild brown trout caught on live bait from Nine Mile Creek.

patterns, tied comparadun- or parachute-style, will do quite nicely, but be sure to have a few rusty-bodied flies with spent wings of white or gray Antron to imitate the egg-laying sulfur spinners that carpet the stream surface at dark.

Most of the browns and 'bows you catch during the hatch will be small ones, 8 to 12 inches, but if you like the thought of hooking a monster, take Route 174 past Marcellus Falls, the Martisco railroad underpass, and into Camillus without stopping to fish any of the beautiful water on your right. (It won't be easy!) Go left at the kayak shop, drive past the Route 690 entrance ramp, and turn right just beyond the state DOT garage. Drive over the canal feeder, up the hill, and take your first right, Thompson Road. Follow that about 2 miles to a stop sign, hang another right, and go about ⅛ mile to the creek crossing. The dam just above the bridge once produced a 12-pound brown trout, and there are still some big brownies available upstream or down from that structure.

Enjoy targeting those big boys, but if you happen to be using light line and a Rapala-type stickbait or a weighted spinner, brace yourself for the occasional bite-off. This stretch of the creek, Camillus to Onondaga Lake, always holds a few tiger muskellunge, hatchery hybrids that result from the mating, in the DEC's South Otselic hatchery, of northern pike with purebred muskies.

A slender tiger muskie caught by the author in Nine Mile Creek.

Tigers can grow to scary proportions. I have caught them up to 44 inches long in Nine Mile, and believe me, they are lots of fun in a 25-foot-wide pool of waist-deep water. Where do they come from? The consensus is that most slide over the dam at Otisco Lake, where they are stocked annually, then keep going until they find a place to satisfy their prodigious appetites.

One 33-incher I caught had a 10-inch brown and two baby muskrats in its bulging stomach.

## Skaneateles Creek

In the early 1970s a DEC fish and game cop summed up the recent history of Skaneateles Creek in plain words.

"If your dog fell in it, he would have died," said Syracuse-area conservation officer Bill Hasenjager.

The outlet of one of the purer fishing holes in the Finger Lakes chain, Skaneateles Creek itself was so polluted by industrial effluent and sewage plant discharges that a state stream-survey crew could not turn up a single fish or aquatic insect during a 1971 electrofishing expedition.

By the time Hasenjager took *Syracuse Post-Standard* columnist Bob Peel (also known as "Rod Hunter") on a tour of the creek in 1977, it had made a complete turnaround, thanks to federal and state pollution-control measures that included an upgrade for a local sewage treatment plant and a network of waste-collecting lagoons and dikes at a local chemical factory.

Today, after decades of restocking by the Onondaga County hatchery and significant natural reproduction, Skaneateles Creek is home to thriving populations of brown and rainbow trout. Fish of 10 to 14 inches are common throughout the stream, from the dam at US Route 20 in the village of Skaneateles north to its confluence with the Seneca River in Jordan. In some parts of the 10- to 25-foot-wide stream, skilled anglers have a good chance to tie into trout of 18 inches or longer.

Ironically, the high quality of fishing found in Skaneateles Creek today can be credited to yesteryear's indifference toward chemical pollution. When the DEC discovered PCBs (carcinogenic substances used as insulators in electrical power lines) buried on an industrial property near the creek, a regional fly-fishing club began lobbying for special regulations. If it is unhealthy to eat the fish in Skaneateles Creek, members of the Owaskantisco Anglers reasoned, why not prohibit anglers from creeling the trout? And while you're at it, how about restricting tackle to artificial lures and flies only?

That's just the way it has been ever since 1994, in a 10.2-mile stretch from the creek crossing at Old Seneca Turnpike in Skaneateles to the Jordan Road bridge in the village of Jordan.

Most no-kill areas are crowded with fishermen, but Skaneateles Creek receives only modest angling pressure. Until somebody conducts a social survey on the subject, I can only surmise that many anglers consider the creek too small and too domesticated. By the latter term, I mean that some of the more intriguing pools in the creek flow along the edges of residential lawns and within talking distance of taverns, supermarkets, and other outposts of civilization. Some anglers dislike fishing in streams that are too narrow or too heavily vegetated to permit a reasonable back-cast, and not a few others are uncomfortable wading past family picnics or sunbathers.

For my part, a bit of friendly patter now and then between home-owners and anglers does not ruin the experience, especially when the conversation precedes a heavy mayfly hatch. Starting in early May and lasting until mid-June, Skaneateles Creek erupts daily with hatches of Hendrickson mayflies. The *Ephemerella subvaria* and *E. invaria* overlap each other and are served up along with little blue-winged olive mayflies and assorted tan-, black-, and olive-bodied caddisflies most afternoons and evenings. March brown duns and emergers provide excellent action between the just-mentioned early hatches.

Stock your fly boxes with Hendricksons in a size 14, olives on anything from size 16 to 22 hooks, and March browns on a full size 10. Caddis should be tied mainly on sizes 14 through 18 dry-fly hooks.

Skaneateles Creek has one serious drawback from the fisherman's vantage point. Namely, it warms up to a barely tolerable daytime range of 70 to 74 degrees in the summer. Hooking trout in such tepid water is potentially injurious to their health. If you don't have a thermometer in your gear but feel certain the trout are physically stressed, the smartest thing you can do for the creek's health is to simply reel in and go home until the weather cools.

To find Skaneateles Creek, take US Route 20 to the stream's name-sake village and turn north on Jordan Street. Although you might get permission to drop a line where the water cuts behind houses and apart-ment buildings, the fishing is usually better along the nature trail that begins just below the Old Seneca Turnpike crossing. It's very rocky and full of brush, so be patient. Swing nymphs into likely spots on a leader and a foot or two of line, or flip small Panther Martin spinners. Expect mostly rainbows here and downstream through Skaneateles Falls, where access is intermittent but very worthwhile, especially behind and below the Welch-Allyn medical instruments factory. Water snakes, non-venomous but ill-tempered, are common in this area, so watch where you step.

Nice browns, all wild and brilliantly colored, are increasingly dominant as you proceed downstream to Irish Road and beyond. Since most of the water between Chatfield Road and the crossing at Route 5 in Elbridge is posted, it is likely that some very large browns are waiting for someone who wrangles permission to fish that brushy, "back 40"stretch.

The water between Elbridge and Jordan is the best the creek has to offer, if a little too residential for some anglers' tastes. One reason for its productivity is the fact that old Route 31C, which used to parallel Skaneateles Creek through a scenic gorge, was closed to all traffic after a washout in the 1990s and has never been rebuilt. To fish the gorge, you now must hike upstream from a dead-end barrier about ½ mile from Jordan and, of course, hoof it back to the car afterward. Few make the effort, and even fewer bother to fish the remaining no-kill water through the pleasant village of Jordan, either. Those who don't give the stretch a chance are depriving themselves, and that's all I'm going to say on that subject.

Skaneateles Creek's trout are moody at times. After a fishless afternoon, it often pays to take a dinner break and then return to the water which just humbled you. Between supper and sundown is the time of day when most of the creek's mayfly hatches reach a crescendo. On such happy occasions, trout will be rising everywhere, and a good share of them are apt to be 14 inches or longer.

The largest trout in the creek are usually found in the open water—no catch-and-release rules—in Jordan, between the Skaneateles Street dam and the junction hole where the creek blends into the Seneca River. One lucky angler caught a 30-inch brown in this section a few seasons ago. Most fish of this size are caught on spinning lures or live bait in the early days of the new trout season.

## Mill Creek

Maybe I'm just a glutton for punishment, but I absolutely love small streams that are both hard to find and hard to fish. Such waters are often full of wild trout. Mill Creek in northern Steuben County is a prime example of the genre. If you visit it when conditions are right, you could catch 20 or more trout, and every one of them will be wild, since Mill Creek hasn't been stocked for decades. On the other hand, if you showed up at the creek during a drought year, you'd see plenty of fish through

Spider Rybaak of Bridgeport fishes for trout on Mill Creek.

your polarized sunglass lenses, but you'd likely scatter many more than you hook. Under low-water conditions, Mill Creek browns can be as jumpy as alley cats.

Retired DEC Region 8 fisheries manager Bill Abraham told me that this creek, a few short casts from his home near Wayland, holds more trout per acre than any other in the Western Finger Lakes–Southern Tier area. Statewide, only a handful of streams are thought to have trout densities that compare to Mill Creek's. Wiscoy Creek in Wyoming County may be the closest challenger in terms of population densities because it, too, is no longer stocked yet continues to shelter a great many wild browns.

The typical trout in Mill Creek is about 8 to 10 inches long, but it holds plenty of bigger fish, up to 14 inches or so. There are a few up to 18 inches, but you'll find them in the deepest, narrowest, hardest-to-get-to parts of the stream. You probably know the sort of hiding places I have in mind. Picture alders, burdocks, thistles, and stinging nettles—and all that grabby, prickly stuff must be crossed and dealt with before you are within casting distance of the stream.

Given the nature of the obstacle course along its banks, the best way to fish Mill Creek is to walk right into the stream, facing upstream or down as your surroundings dictate, then let things settle down for 10 minutes before you start working your way from pool to pool. The best time to do this is after a substantial rain has colored the water. Mill Creek seldom muddies to that degree, but if you manage to be there on such an occasion, you are in for a treat.

Finding Mill Creek on a map is itself somewhat of a challenge. Computer programs like Road Atlas USA make trip planning a little easier by displaying and printing the most obscure rural hamlets and hollows, and GPS units can be even more helpful. I still rely on my good old *DeLorme Atlas & Gazetteer* for guidance in most cases. With one or more such tools available, anglers in search of Mill Creek can find it by taking Route 21 south from Naples to Wayland. There continue south and past the Gunlocke factory, which will be on your left. Just before coming to Route 390, the Genesee Parkway, turn right onto Michigan Road. Mill Creek crosses beneath this road, at the hamlet of Patchinville; you can also fish it for short distance upstream if you can fight your way through the dense vegetation.

Upstream from Michigan Road, the creek is narrow enough to jump across—but watch where you leap, as the small pools are inhabited by all-wild brook and brown trout. Below Michigan Road (downstream), browns dominant and brookies are rarely seen.

The downstream stretch here consists mainly of a straightened stream with a surprising number of deep holes and undercuts that can spit out trout one after another when conditions are right. Watch for the PUBLIC FISHING STREAM signs as you proceed. Shortly after the banks return to private ownership, the creek takes a hard left turn toward Perkinsville, which is a mile west via Michigan Road. Another DEC access is on county Route 90 in Perkinsville. There you can either fish back upstream (which would be my preference) via a long abandoned railroad bed, or clamber down a steep hill to a fast-flowing, high-gradient stretch and fish downstream toward Mill Creek's eventual merger with Canaseraga Creek in Dansville. The downstream water looks better, especially at the plunge pool at the Route 90 crossing, but the water above town is generally more productive, as long as you are willing to break some considerable brush along the way.

Spinning gear is a first choice for many Mill Creek anglers due to the tight confines that prevail on most of the banks; also, fly-fishing opportunities are limited at best. If you do fly fish here, don't worry much about hatch matching, for the generally small trout will strike any floater that appears to drift naturally.

Because of its healthy, abundant population of trout, Mill Creek does not need any special regulations for protection, DEC officials have concluded. Instead of shutting down on October 15, Mill Creek can be fished year-round. If you are skilled enough to catch them, you may keep a state-standard limit of five trout per day, two of which may be longer than 12 inches.

## Cohocton River

The Cohocton River is a fickle trout stream, capable of curing what ails you or giving you a migraine. Although it is heavily populated with trout from its beginnings in southern Livingston County to the city of Bath in Steuben County, the Cohocton's better fish tend to be fussy and furtive. Aside from browns fresh off the hatchery truck, the residents of this river are not easily removed from their comfortable surroundings. They may rise readily during a heavy mayfly hatch, but you can be sure they will closely examine your fly before taking it.

The Cohocton's character changes constantly during its nearly 40-mile run. If you ever manage to fish every one of its pools and riffles, you could qualify for a doctorate in trout-stream design. Where it crosses the Livingston–Steuben border near Atlanta, it moves at a slow pace between boggy banks but is cold enough to support fair numbers of wild brook trout. Farther downstream, in the villages of Cohocton and Avoca, the river looks like a brookie stream yet harbors only brown trout, as far as I can tell. Do not take this wistful observation for criticism, though. I never met a brown trout I didn't like, in part because it survives where brookies can't.

The Cohocton's structural diversity makes it equally attractive for bait, lure, and fly fishing. If you can't find a section or two of the river that suits your personal angling style, you simply aren't trying very hard. Nor can anyone raise much of a ruckus about regulations, which provide year-round opportunities for die-hard trout fishers.

As far as habitat and water types are concerned, you can choose from the aforementioned boggy meadows in the headwaters, and from Cohocton downstream to the Veterans Hospital stretch in Bath, long, flat pools that are separated from one another by shimmering riffles. This lower water constricts to a width of about 15 feet at first, then adds the volume of several fishy-looking creeks. At its largest, in Bath and below (where the stream becomes too warm for trout), the Cohocton is approximately 50 feet across, and the river has pools that are 6 feet deep. Some of the flats hide 20-inch brown trout, and if you don't shake in anticipation when you spot such a fish sipping mayfly spinners on a warm evening, well, you must be a better angler than I am.

Avid fly fishers who have not tried the Cohocton before will love the special regulations which govern two river sections: from the north boundary of the Veterans Administration Hospital in Bath to the Route 415 crossing upstream; and from the northern edge of the village of Avoca to the mouth of Neil's Creek. The rules there include one that permits year-round fishing, coupled with a limit of two trout per day, both of which must be at least 12 inches long. Because most trout stocked by the state of New York are in the 8- or 9-inch range when they're first transferred from hatchery to stream, the majority of fish caught in the special-regulations areas must be returned to the water quickly and without intentional harm. That's a good thing, for some of the trout caught in the special-regulations areas hold over from one year to the next. Also, about one-fifth of the 10,000 or so browns stocked in the river annually are two-year-olds that measure 12 to 15 inches when they're introduced to the river's environs. Such trout are quite likely to add a couple of inches as a reward to the anglers who gently release them after a hard fight on a light tippet.

In the special-regulations water, neophytes can work on their backcasts and hatch-matching skills with little fear of hanging their flies in trees or being crowded by other anglers. That's not to say there is no good fly fishing elsewhere. In fact, more of the river is conducive to the long rod than not.

Good hatches can be encountered virtually any day on the river from mid-April until early October, when tiny blue-winged olive mayflies draw trout to the river's surface for one last time before the fall spawning run gets under way. Prime-time hatches include the emergence of the Hendrickson mayfly (*Ephemerella subvaria*) from about the last week in April until the second or third week in May, followed by the March brown during the second half of May and assorted sulfur-colored mayflies in late May and the first half of June. You should also stock your Cohocton fly boxes with Elk-Hair Caddis with tan, olive, and gray bodies; and a couple of attractor-type drys such as the Ausable Wulff, Adams, and Usual. All of the foregoing patterns should be tied on size 12, 14, and 16 hooks, but don't forget to bring some smaller dry flies, especially midges and beetles, that are fashioned on size 18s, 20s, and 22s for low-water usage.

Nymphs that work well elsewhere will take Cohocton trout, too.

Do not be embarrassed if you are a spinning specialist or a bait dunker. The Cohocton has the water you relish and welcomes anyone who is a sportsman rather than a fish hog. Keep a trout or two if you like; just leave enough for the next person who wishes to share the river's bounty. While fly tackle is ideal for the broad pools downstream from Avoca, and spinners, spoons, and such can be worked effectively just about anywhere, a garden hackle or salted minnow shines in the Atlanta-to-Avoca stretch, most notably following a spring or summer downpour.

To reach the Cohocton River from the Rochester area, take Route 390, also known as the Genesee Parkway, south to the village of Cohocton. From there, you can follow Routes 415 and 21 to side roads that cross or closely approach the river between Atlanta and Bath. Approximately half of the river's banks—20 miles or thereabout—are marked with DEC PUBLIC FISHING signs, so access is not a worry.

Wading is generally easy on the Cohocton, but I'd advise anyone who fishes it to wear chest waders with felt or cleat bottoms for maximum maneuverability. Some parts of the river simply can't be covered properly with hip boots.

## Oatka Creek

Like the Cohocton River, Oatka Creek is a favorite recreational spot for Rochester-area anglers. Unfortunately it is much closer to the big city, and a significantly smaller stream, too. Add a couple of access problems, some interesting special regulations, and the lure of big, beautiful browns and one word comes to mind—*crowded*. But that word takes in quite a bit of territory, doesn't it? Compared with the top end of Cairn's Eddy on the Beaverkill River, or the opening day of trout season on Nine Mile Creek or Naples Creek, Oatka doesn't seem crowded at all, more days than not. The one time you might feel pinched is during Oatka's famed Hendrickson hatch in late April, when you may have to choose between good manners and good fishing.

Oatka Creek originates in Wyoming County, flows northward along Route 19 through Warsaw, and crosses the Genesee County border. After passing through LeRoy, it turns east and glides into Monroe County. The last leg of its meandering journey takes it past the state trout hatchery in Caledonia and finally through Scottsville, where it joins the Genesee River.

That sounds like a whole lot of trout water, but it's really not. Oatka Creek can be considered two short trout streams separated by a lengthy barrier of currents that are too warm for trout to tolerate. In the headwaters above and below the hamlet of Rock Glen, which is about 2 miles upstream from Warsaw via Route 19, anglers will find above-average fishing for both wild and stocked brown trout. Thick bank cover (in spots), a mucky bottom, and a discouraging number of NO TRESPASSING signs deter casual fishing, and if you meet anybody while you're trying this water, he or she will almost certainly be a local resident. This part of Oatka Creek is not heavily fished, and part two, from below Rock Glen to LeRoy, is home to northern pike, largemouth smallmouth bass, and panfish.

It is the third segment of the creek that sends a cool shiver up a fly fisher's spine. For the water between the junction with Spring Creek (also known as Spring Brook) just north of the state hatchery at Caledonia and the subsequent meeting with the Genesee below Scottsville is icy cold even in the dog days of summer. A natural network of large springs rejuvenates trout and fishermen alike. The creek here is alive with fish and aquatic insects and beckons irresistibly to anyone with a couple of full fly boxes in his or her possession.

Oatka Creek in its Monroe County stretch is a born-again stream. Like Nine Mile Creek in Onondaga County, Oatka has mostly tepid currents in its upper half but is completely transformed by massive springs into a trout stream of excellent quality. Its trout are among the prettiest you will ever see. A majority are browns, some stocked, some wild. The state stocks the creek with browns only, at the rate of about 10,000 annually, yet a few rainbows and brookies seem to find their way out of the hatchery—via Spring Creek—and into Oatka.

When I think of Oatka Creek, my mind turns to a hot summer afternoon, many years ago, when I stood on a bridge in the town of Wheatland and put clip-on polarized lenses over my sunglasses to peer into the water. I was astonished to see not one but three truly large brown trout finning in the shade alongside the bridge supports. After spotting the fish, I spent a good hour trying to catch them with no luck whatsoever. It was a good lesson in the facts of life, for lunker browns do not come readily to the hook in Oatka Creek or any other stream. No, trout that big, 23 or 24 inches, are landed on purpose by anglers of extraordinary skill, or accidentally by somebody who happens to be luckier than most!

From its meeting with Spring Creek to Scottsville and the Genesee, Oatka Creek is 60 to 75 feet across in most places and averages 2 to 3 feet deep, with plenty of deeper pools in the Oatka and Garbutt town parks. Both of these venues have free public access. The bottom varies from muck to sand, gravel, or cobble rock, with slick sections of bedrock in a few spots. In general, the creek is well shaded, but on clear-sky afternoons you will want to have some sunscreen in your vest. All of this variety makes for some interesting fishing, especially for fly rodders but for bait and spin fishermen as well. The fish are present in a full range of year-classes and sizes, but just because you can see them from a high bridge or some other handy platform doesn't mean you can catch them.

Your best chances of nailing a rod-bending beauty will likely be during the spring mayfly hatches. Hendricksons, the marquee bugs on the creek, are sufficiently large and abundant, themselves, to get the undivided attention of Oatka's bigger trout. At its peak, in early May, the Hendrickson emergence will amount to a near blizzard of insects. Every mayfly life stage, including nymph, dun, and spinner, will attract fish, but it's up to the angler to determine which stage is monopolizing the chow line.

Subsurface or on top, Hendricksons are best imitated with flies tied on size 12 or 14 hooks, the eyes of which even a middle-aged angler with poor depth perception can knot to a tippet in fading light. The species has one other attribute that most fly fishers much admire, and that is the mayfly's punctuality. Hendricksons on Oatka Creek and most other streams emerge starting in early to midafternoon, around 2 to 2:30 PM, exactly when they're supposed to.

Other major aquatic insect hatches in Oatka Creek include the March brown in mid-May, the pale evening duns or "sulfurs" from mid-May through early June, several blue-winged olives in a variety of sizes, and caddisflies with black, tan, or olive abdomens, which hatch sporadically from mid-May through early September, at least.

To find Oatka Creek from the Rochester area, take Route 490 south to West Chili. At the end of the ramp, turn south onto Union Street and drive about 5 miles to a T-intersection. Turn left onto North Road and proceed about 2 miles to Scottsville. Route 383 leads west from there and parallels Oatka almost all the way to LeRoy. You'll see several marked angler parking areas and footpaths as you travel upstream.

Anglers visiting Oatka Creek for the first time should familiarize themselves with the special regulations that pertain to the stream. They are all spelled out in the annual *Freshwater Fishing Guide* that's available to anyone purchasing a state fishing license, but here's a review for folks who might have misplaced their copies.

Starting at Union Street, just west of Scottsville, and continuing for 1.7 miles upstream to Wheatfield Center Road, trout fishing is permitted on a catch-and-release basis, year-round; but only flies or other artificial lures may be used.

From Bowerman Road upstream 1.4 miles to Union Street and from Wheatland Center upstream 2.5 miles to the mouth of Spring Creek, anglers may fish year-round, but from October 16 through March 31 fishing is catch-and-release and artificials-only. During the regular trout season, April 1 through October 15, fishing is permitted with bait, lure, or fly but the creel limit is two trout a day, both of which must be at least a foot long.

The rest of the creek within Monroe County is open all year. Anglers can keep five trout a day. There's no minimum size, but no more than two of the daily five can be longer than 12 inches.

## Spring Creek

If you've been having a tough day on Oatka Creek, why not take a side trip to fish Spring Creek, which flows through New York's oldest trout hatchery and is loaded with browns, brookies, and rainbows?

Admittedly, that's a bit of a come-on. Spring Creek really does cut through the DEC hatchery in Caledonia, just a short distance from its mouth, and Oatka Creek benefits immeasurably from Spring Creek's infusion of cold, clear water. And I do not have my fingers crossed when I tell you that angling is permitted on the hatchery property, year-round. The creek—but not the hatchery's rearing ponds and raceways—is open to fishing from 8 AM to 4 PM daily from April 1 through October 15. During that period, the hatchery stretch invites anglers to keep two trout of 12 inches or better per day, with the proviso that only lures or flies may be used. You can fish the hatchery from October 16 through March 31, too, but that time of the year is for catch-and-release angling, only.

Before you readers start salivating, understand that these are not your average hatchery trout. Most of them are wild, although a very few hatchery escapees wind up in the fishable sections of the stream. Further, Spring Creek trout seldom go hungry. They eat well, as a rule, on scuds (freshwater shrimp), sow bugs, and a variety of mayflies and caddis. The water these fish call home is extremely clear and slow moving, and every little noise or sudden movement will send them scurrying to their favorite hiding places.

All of these factors contribute to the creek's justified reputation as a stream that's fascinating but frustrating to fish.

Finally, you can be sure that most Spring Creek trout have had long, sometimes painful looks at almost every fly pattern you possess. Having made the acquaintance of countless trout fishers, residents of Spring Creek are jaded cynics compared with their relatives in most other streams. If you happen to have a secret pattern that you use as a last resort on your home waters, here's a place where you can give that fly a proper test. If you catch a couple of trout in this mesmerizing stream, give yourself a pat on the back. You have done very well, indeed.

The original hatchery built in Caledonia has been modernized some in recent years but on the outside looks much as it did in the 1860s, when it was operated by the legendary fish culturist Seth Green. We can only imagine what the fishing was like in Green's day, but the trout in Spring Creek are probably as frisky as ever. You won't see many real lunkers, but the creek holds lots of browns and considerably smaller numbers of brookies and rainbows. A 16-incher is a great trout here; most fish are in the 7- to 14-inch range. Almost all of the trout in the creek that top the 12-inch mark on your tape measure will be wild browns with brilliant colors.

To get to Spring Creek from the Syracuse area, anglers should take the thruway west to the Route 390 exit. From there, head south to the Scottsville exit and take Route 251 into the village of Industry. Cross the Genesee River, then go right on River Road and take it to Scottsville, a distance of about 1 mile. Next, go left onto Route 383, go west for about 3 miles, and turn left again, onto Route 36, which takes you into Mumford and Caledonia, in northern Livingston County. In the latter village, the hatchery will be on your right.

Anglers who are used to tumbling freestone trout streams with large boulders and swift currents will be puzzled by Spring Creek, at first. It is, as the name notes, a spring-fed creek that flows at a majestic, gradual pace over a sand-and-gravel bottom that sprouts dense beds of watercress, elodea, and other aquatic plants. Picture a British "chalk stream" like the River Test or perhaps Pennsylvania's famous Letort Spring Run and you will have a reasonable facsimile of Spring Creek. All three streams are gin-clear, have thick weed beds that offer acres and acres of hiding and feeding cover, and host robust populations of aquatic and terrestrial insects and freshwater crustaceans to sustain resident trout in high style.

Like the Test and Letort, Spring Creek is a sort of graduate-level course for fly fishers. If you can catch 'em here, Sinatra might have crooned, you can catch 'em anywhere.

The mile or so of accessible fishing in Spring Creek includes not only the hatchery property but also the short piece of water immediately downstream of it. Locally referred to as "the 900" for its 900-foot total length, this is slightly—and I do mean *slightly*—easier to conquer than the hatchery water. I say that in part because I once had a red-letter day there, catching 13 brown trout on various nymph and dry-fly patterns during an early-June hatch of sulfur mayflies. I have not come close since.

Why is the 900 water just a tad less intimidating than the stretch immediately upstream? At a guess, the 900 is somewhat less popular and therefore less crowded than the hatchery water. It has fewer fans because it has fewer fish—fewer visible fish, anyway—but there are plenty by most anglers' standards. When the sulfurs are popping through the surface at 8 or 9 PM on a June evening, you might do a quick up- and downstream head count and tally 30 or more risers within casting distance. What's wrong with that?

Another difference between the hatchery stretch and the 900 is the prohibition against wading in the former. I know at least a few fly fishers who dislike donning boots and don't mind staying on the bank. The hatchery water is no more than 40 feet wide, after all. Down at the 900, however, you need hip boots at least, and chest waders will take you places where hippers can't go.

# CHAPTER 19

# Other Waters of the Finger Lakes Region

**W**e might all think that the central-western part of our beautiful state couldn't have room for any more fishing holes besides the Finger Lakes, their tributaries, and all of the major trout streams already covered in this volume, but it does. I'm not referring to some running-water ditches that go dry every summer, either. The places I have in mind are scenic lakes that hold mostly warm-water species and several sizable streams that are also home to largemouth bass, panfish, and other non–trout species. For fishermen in this part of the world, the hits just keep coming.

In this section, we'll briefly discuss overlooked waters that merit more attention from resident and traveling anglers alike. I'm going to start with a gem of a lake just minutes from Interstate 81 but at the eastern end of the Finger Lakes region. From there we will work westward across the state map.

## Tully Lake

Straddling the border between Onondaga and Cortland counties, Tully Lake spans 230 surface acres. Created by retreating glaciers much as the Finger Lakes were, this little gem consists essentially of three glacial "kettles," one of them 37 feet deep, which are separated by extensive, weedy shallows.

Although nearly encircled by summer camps and year-round homes, Tully Lake has a public boat launch at its south end and is very popular for summer and winter fishing. The action is chiefly for bluegills, pumpkinseeds, and red-breasted sunfish averaging 7 to 9 inches long, but the lake also holds plenty of chain pickerel and largemouth bass of above-average size. The panfish bite best through the ice and again in May and early June.

The launch area on Friendly Shores Drive is for hand launching only, and the lake has a 10-horsepower motor maximum. Considering these restrictions, Tully Lake seems made to order for canoes, kayaks, and personal pontoon boats.

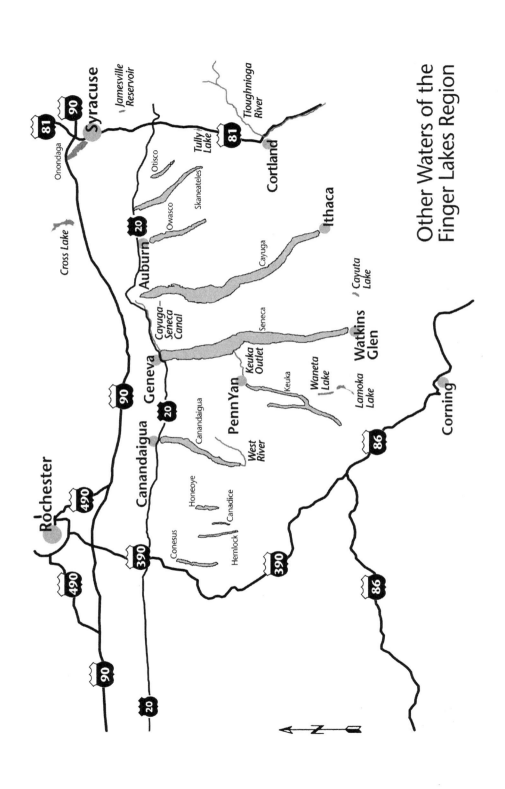

Other Waters of the
Finger Lakes Region

To get to the access site, take Interstate 81 south from Syracuse to the Tully exit. At the exit ramp, cross Route 80 and bear right. Go past a small lake on your right and then go left onto Wetmore Road. Where that road dead-ends, bear left and then right on Saulsberry Drive to Friendly Shores.

## Tioughnioga River

You never know what you might catch in the Tioughnioga River in Cortland County, and I'm not exaggerating one bit when I say that. The "Ti-yo," as many residents call it, is formed by the confluence of the East and West Branches of the Tioughnioga in the city of Cortland, right behind the Ramada Inn and Wendy's off Exit 11. The junction pool has been known to hold brown trout, walleyes, and northern pike, some of them whoppers of 8 to 10 pounds. Most of these fish are not year-round residents of the hole but migrate into it during runoff episodes.

Several hundred yards upstream, in Yaman Park (just off Route 13), big pike prowl all summer. Perhaps the best pools in the river, though, are those at the Blodgett Mills bridge and at Hoxie's Gorge. The former always seems to hold a big walleye, and is often good for pike, too. The pool at the end of the gorge pulses with pike, walleyes, brown trout, and smallmouth bass after an early summer cloudburst.

Trout fishers take note—the West Branch of the Tioughnioga is stocked with browns between the village of Homer and the junction; the East Branch benefits from hatchery visits along Route 13 from Loring Crossing and Truxton.

## Jamesville Reservoir

If not for its mediocre access, Jamesville Reservoir in Onondaga County would be one of the busiest fishing holes in the Syracuse area. As it is, fishing there is pretty much limited to shoreline residents, small-boat owners who can carry their rowboats or canoes across a patch of turf at a county-operated park, and a few people who bank fish the lake at an open area near its outlet dam.

The 333-acre reservoir, an impoundment of Butternut Creek, does hold a rich mix of fish, including some very tubby largemouths, smallmouths, and walleyes. Tiger muskies are stocked occasionally, and every now and then some lucky angler catches a nice brown trout that has swum downstream into the reservoir and gained a couple of pounds.

Jamesville is a nice spot for panfish, too. Bluegills, rock bass, yellow perch, and bullheads are all common and above average size.

To find the reservoir, take Interstate 81 north from Cortland or south from Syracuse to the LaFayette exit. Go east on Route 20 and take a left onto Route 91 at Pompey, which leads directly to the east shore.

## Cross Lake

My grandfather used to fish for northern pike in Cross Lake. How long ago was that? Suffice it to say a Roosevelt was in the White House.

Jeff Robins, the DEC Region 7 biologist who currently keeps an eye on the Cross Lake fishery, said it holds pike "upward of 20 pounds, and 10 to 15 pounds is not an uncommon size there."

The 2,100-acre lake is basically a large backwater in the Seneca River. Forming part of the border between Onondaga and Oswego Counties, it has a maximum depth of 60 feet and plenty of good ambush cover, especially in the weed beds around its two islands—Big Island and Little Island. It also has some steep drop-offs north of the islands and along the east shore.

Pike are not the only predators in Cross Lake. The DEC stocks it with tiger muskies, and it also has a small population of longnose gar. The latter are skinny but hard-fighting fish that are difficult to hook on conventional lures because of their bony jaws. One way to catch them is to cast or troll with frayed lengths of rope, decorated with strands of tinsel and connected to a sturdy leader. The gar's small but sharp teeth become entangled when they strike.

Besides toothy critters, Cross Lake has healthy numbers of bass (both large- and smallmouths) which go up to 5 or 6 pounds, walleyes, white perch, yellow perch, black crappies, and sunfish.

Cross Lake can be reached by driving west from Syracuse on the state thruway to Exit 40 (Weedsport). At the exit ramp, turn right onto Route 31. Take it to Port Byron and go right onto Route 38. From there it's about 3 miles to the Mosquito Point DEC launch site. Cross Lake is approximately a 7-mile boat ride to the east from there. There are no public boat launches on the lake, but if you cross the Bonta bridge and take the next right you will come to Jordan Road. Go left and look for the privately owned Cross Lake Marina, where fishermen can launch for a daily fee. It's in the northwest corner of the lake.

## Cayuga–Seneca Canal

A 23-mile-long excavated channel between Cayuga and Seneca Lakes, the Cayuga–Seneca Canal began providing Finger Lakes–region businesses with a connection to the state barge canal in the 1820s. As the commercial traffic ground to a halt in the 1960s, recreational vessels filled the void. Today the canal is a much-underrated fishing hole, with a local reputation for producing largemouth bass, northern pike, and assorted panfish.

The canal parallels US Routes 5 and 20 from the Montezuma National Wildlife Refuge to the northeast corner of Seneca Lake. Between those two landmarks there are at least a dozen great places to launch a boat or do a little shore fishing.

Among the access points are the DEC boat launch across Route 20 from the Montezuma headquarters building; the Mudlock Canal Park, off Route 90 on River Road 3 miles south of the village of Cayuga; the Cayuga Lake State Park, on Route 89, 3 miles east of Seneca Falls; and Seneca Lake State Park, off Route 20 just west of the Route 96 intersection.

Because of heavy pleasure-boat traffic it is advisable for serious anglers to concentrate their efforts on the weedy edges of the canal. Bridges and docks are also worthy of extra attention. Shore fishermen will sometimes encounter large schools of crappies and bluegills in the villages of Seneca Falls and Waterloo. Look for other anglers and don't be afraid to ask local merchants where they would suggest you park in order to do a little fishing.

## West River

"Good things come to those who wait."

The West River in Yates County always makes me think of that ancient bit of wisdom. I don't know if it always holds true in other settings, but patient waiting definitely nets pleasing results for the West River's devotees. The river has about 3 fishable miles of water between South Hill Road and its mouth at the south end of Canandaigua Lake. Fishermen can, and sometimes do, fish that whole length, which happily flows through state land.

However, the majority of anglers familiar with the West River's geography fish one spot. That's a hand-carry boat launch and channel located adjacent to Route 245 between Middlesex and Naples. Starting in late March and continuing into May, this 60-foot-wide channel attracts runs of black crappies, bullheads, bluegills, and largemouth bass, usually in that order. Anglers with worm-and-bobber rigs are waiting when the fish arrive, and many go home at the end of the day with heavy buckets.

My visits to the West River usually take place at the conclusion of a day of trout fishing in Naples Creek. I have to go past the channel on my way home, and several times its bluegills have salvaged what otherwise would have been a fruitless journey.

## Keuka Outlet

Now, this is what I'd call a sleeper. Folks tend to overlook Keuka Outlet because it has sort of an image problem. It starts with the name, which is correct but not precisely accurate. The stream is not only the outlet of Keuka Lake but also a major tributary of Seneca Lake. As a result, its upper reaches—the outlet—are full of bass, both largemouths and small-mouths, and a very nice population of bullheads. The lower end, below the impassable waterfall at the hamlet of Cascade Mills, has a dependable run of spawning rainbow trout in April and also holds a small run of land-locked salmon in autumn.

The outlet-that-is-also-an-inlet is stocked intermittently with brown trout, and some locals catch holdover browns by fly fishing in and around Cascade Mills.

To find this intriguing stream, take Routes 5 and 20 to Geneva, head south on Route 14 to Dresden, and then follow Route 54 west for about ½ mile to Houghton Road. It will take you along the lower outlet up to Mays Mills. From there you can follow the Keuka Outlet by sight most of the way to Penn Yan.

Access is provided alongside most of the outlet via the Outlet Trail, which is used by walking and bicycling anglers. It was constructed by local communities and volunteers in line with a former canal towpath.

## Cayuta Lake

Yet another out-of-the-way fishing hole with much unrealized potential, Cayuta Lake is in a very rural sector of Schuyler County. DEC biologists and researchers from Cornell University affirm it is chock-full of walleyes, many of which weigh 5 pounds or more. Unfortunately, these fish have a reputation for being extremely difficult to catch. That's because they are "fat and happy" from gorging on alewives.

Since even overstuffed, gluttonous walleyes have to eat sometime, my best advice to frustrated Cayuta anglers is to hang in there and do as much of their fishing as possible during prime times—early and late in the day and in the cool conditions of May and November. If the walleyes don't happen to be biting when you are there, fish for the local largemouth bass and chain pickerel, which are more aggressive feeders than the walleyes and also tend to be on the large side. The lake, which averages 10 feet deep but has a maximum depth of 26 feet, also holds a few tiger muskellunge.

Cayuta Lake covers 518 acres, shore-to-shore. It's about 5 miles east of Watkins Glen, which is a major tourist stop. However, fishing pressure is modest at most.

To get there from Routes 5 and 20, go south on Route 14 from Seneca Falls to Montour Falls. In that village, take Route 224 to Odessa and turn left on Route 228, which leads to Cayutaville Road and the public boat launch on the lake's west shore.

## Lamoka Lake and Waneta Lake

If you are interested in catching some "hawg" largemouth bass, you would be hard-pressed to find a spot any better than Lamoka Lake in Schuyler County—except, perhaps, Waneta Lake, which is right across the road from Lamoka.

In all honesty, Waneta and Lamoka are so similar in key respects, and so close together (linked by a short, navigable channel) that more than one article in outdoors magazines has compared them to conjoined twins.

The two lakes are most alike in their ability to feed and grow some of New York's heaviest largemouths. Retired DEC Region 8 fisheries boss Bill Abraham told me that sampling with nets and electrofishing gear has turned up 8-pounders—fish that might one day challenge our 11-pound, 4-ounce New York state-record bass—in both lakes. While 8-pounders are rarely seen by anglers, let alone caught, in either of these two lakes, 4- and even 5-pound bucketmouths are ho-hummers in the 813-acre Waneta Lake as well as the 588-acre Lamoka Lake. Most such fish live in the thick weeds that wind around the shores of both bodies, and are susceptible to weedless lures including, but not limited to, Texas-rigged plastic worms and salamanders.

Not really common but always lurking somewhere in the connected lakes is the most awesome aquatic predator of all, the muskellunge. Chautauqua-strain muskies have thrived in Waneta Lake for decades, and Lamoka has some duck eaters, too, although not nearly as many as its next-door neighbor.

Are you sitting down? Good, because I thought you would want to know that both Waneta and Lamoka have produced 40-pound muskies in the past.

To find your way to these fertile lakes, take Route 14A from Geneva to Coles Corners, which is just south of the Yates –Schuyler county border. Turn right on Route 226, go about 5 miles to Route 23 at Tyrone, and turn right again. Route 23 leads to the DEC launch area at the channel between the two lakes, at Weston.

# CHAPTER 20

# Conserving the Finger Lakes

**D**oes anyone out there, other than me, remember when an angler's biggest worry was whether the alarm clock would ring when it was supposed to on the opening day of trout, bass, or walleye season?

Whatever happened to those simple times? Nowadays, we don't bother to set the alarm clock because we can't sleep anyway—that television report on climate change was damned frightening—and there doesn't seem to be any such thing as a secret fishing hole.

I wish it weren't so, but I hesitate to turn on the car radio when I'm en route to a favorite lake or stream, and that's especially so if my destination is somewhere in the Finger Lakes region. The ominous headlines in area newspapers and the quasi-bulletin "News at 11" snippets that breathless reporters fire at us all day make me wonder if my family and I should pick up and go.

There's global warming, threatening to bake or suffocate my beloved brook trout; and hydrofracking, a process for mining natural gas that, to hear some folks tell it, is going to blow the roof off my house, in addition to polluting groundwater everywhere. The rhetoric from fracking opponents is so hot and alarming that our governor, like quite a few others around the Northeast, seems paralyzed by the whole thing.

And then I get a thumping headache, thanks to a fishing buddy who mentions all the round gobies he's been catching in Lake Ontario, and how those homely little pests have been picking worms off his hooks in Oswego harbor. He muses how it's only a matter of time before gobies find their way into Seneca Lake or some other honey hole of ours, despite our best efforts to the contrary.

That prompts me to give another example of our inability to turn back the barbarians at our gates: zebra mussels. Nobody but a few radical environmentalists saw them coming in the 1980s, and now they're like gray

Zebra mussels from Canadice Lake.

squirrels and political yard signs, which is to say, ubiquitous. (*Ubiquitous* is one of my favorite words, which is why I used it instead of "everywhere." But it's what a former editor of mine dismissed as a 10-cent word, as in "We don't use 10-cent words when a 5-cent word will serve the purpose.") Well, it's hard to come with any word that adequately describes just how far zebra mussels, and their larger and even more adaptable cousins, the quagga mussels, have penetrated American lakes and major rivers. In the course of writing this book, I revisited all of the 11 Finger Lakes; each of them had uncountable mussel shells clustered along its shoreline. Not only are creatures that prolific ubiquitous; they have become part of the landscape, and may remain so forever.

Other invasive species are troubling to fishermen and more so to aquatic biologists and fisheries managers:

- Eurasian milfoil is a plant that spreads rapidly once introduced to a new lake or river, and quickly suppresses desirable aquatic vegetation. Municipalities and lake-protection associations have battled milfoil with mowing machines, skin-diving volunteers, and chemical treatment, mostly to no avail. Even the more pristine of the Finger Lakes, such as Skaneateles Lake, are battling milfoil. Yet some fish, such as yellow perch, seem to thrive in the stuff.

- Water chestnuts are one of the more alarming invasive plants. They spread easily when well-meaning lakeshore residents uproot them but fail to gather them up. Their sharp-edged, buoyant seedpods drift away from shore when a boat motor's propellers become snarled in a mat of chestnuts. Constant vigilance is necessary to keep new infestations from getting out of hand.

- Japanese knotweed is one of the more underrated invaders. Sometimes known as Japanese bamboo, it's a weak-stemmed plant that sprouts along trout streams and, when knocked down, is capable of tripping and injuring a clumsy angler. Its worst sin is crowding out beneficial plants that limit shallow-water erosion and provide shade and shelter for trout as well as hatching mayflies.

- For their size, which is nearly microscopic, water fleas can be a huge nuisance to trolling anglers in Cayuga Lake and several other Finger Lakes. Because they move about in vast swarms, they pile up on fishing lines, until the clumps they form are too thick and sticky to pass through line guides.

There are many other animals and plants worth worrying about—and I do my share—but some of the most serious concerns are about giant-scale disasters and thoughtless human behavior. As individuals or in concert with our brother and sister anglers, we can't do much to fend off droughts, hurricanes, and other run-of-the-mill calamities, never mind worldwide climate change. In contrast, whether we act alone or as members of conservation organizations, we can help quell agricultural runoff in our rural watersheds and put a stop to most types of industrial effluents that threaten to wind up in our beloved lakes and streams.

Perhaps one of our most pressing problems, as angler-conservationists, is to distinguish problems we can solve, now, from those we can't—yet.

The other challenge facing conservationists in the Finger Lakes and elsewhere is to lead by example. If we are to be effective protectors of the region's magnificent natural resources, we will have to educate ourselves about the nature of our enemies, whether they are of natural or political origins. We must also share our knowledge, once honestly acquired, with friends, families, and co-workers, if they are willing to hear us out. Finally—and here is the hard part—we must take seriously our right and privilege to *vote*, in local, state, and national elections.

# Summary of Special Fishing Regulations for the Finger Lakes

State-standard regulations apply unless otherwise stated in the DEC's annual *Freshwater Fishing Guide*, which is available at no cost to anyone who purchases a New York fishing license from an authorized vendor.

The following is a summary of special regulations by lake and species as of October 1, 2012.

## All Finger Lakes

**NORTHERN PIKE:** Northern pike season starts the first Saturday in May and extends through the following March 15. The minimum creel length for pike is 22 inches and the daily limit is five. Ice fishing for pike is allowed.

**WALLEYE:** Walleye have the same open season as northern pike, the first Saturday in May through the following March 15. The minimum creel length is 18 inches except in Honeoye Lake, where it is 15 inches. The limit is three a day, and ice fishing is allowed.

## All Finger Lakes Except Cayuga, Otisco, Owasco, and Skaneateles

**BLACK BASS (LARGEMOUTH AND SMALLMOUTH):** The regular season for bass is the third Saturday in June through November 30. In the regular season, the minimum creel length is 12 inches and the daily limit is five. Between bass seasons, fishing for bass is allowed on a catch-and-release, artificial-lures-only basis.

**BROWN, RAINBOW, AND LAKE TROUT AS WELL AS LANDLOCKED SALMON:** Fishing is permitted all year. The minimum creel length is 15 inches and the daily limit is five, including no more than one rainbow trout or three landlocks.

## Honeoye Lake and Skaneateles Lake

The possession of alewives is prohibited.

## Owasco, Cayuga, Otisco, and Skaneateles Lakes

**BROWN, RAINBOW, AND LAKE TROUT, AS WELL AS LANDLOCKED SALMON:**
Fishing is allowed all year. The minimum creel length is 15 inches, except
for a 12-inch minimum for brown trout in Otisco Lake and a 18-inch
minimum for landlocks in Cayuga Lake. The daily limit is five in combination, including no more than three lake trout or three salmon.

**TIGER MUSKELLUNGE:** Statewide regulations apply except in Otisco Lake,
where the minimum length is 36 inches.

# Summary of Special Regulations for Finger Lakes Tributaries

State-standard regulations apply unless otherwise stated in the DEC's annual *Freshwater Fishing Guide*, which is available at no cost to anyone who purchases a New York fishing license from an authorized vendor.

The following is a summary of tributary regulations, by lake and species, as of October 1, 2012.

## All Tributaries to Canadice, Canandaigua, Hemlock, Keuka, and Seneca Lakes, Upstream to the First Barrier Impassable by Fish

**BROWN, RAINBOW, AND LAKE TROUT, AS WELL AS LANDLOCKED SALMON:** Fishing is permitted April 1 through December 31. The minimum creel length is 15 inches and the daily limit is three in combination, including no more than one rainbow.

**ALL OTHER SPECIES:** Open seasons, daily limits, and minimum lengths that apply to the Finger Lakes also apply to their tributaries.

## All Tributaries to Owasco, Otisco, and Skaneateles Lakes, Upstream to the First Barrier Impassable to Fish Except Tributaries Listed Below

**BROWN, RAINBOW, AND LAKE TROUT, AS WELL AS LANDLOCKED SALMON:** Fishing is permitted April 1 through December 31. The minimum creel length is 9 inches for browns and rainbows and 15 inches for salmon and lakers. The daily limit is three in combination.

## All Tributaries to Cayuga Lake, Upstream to the First Barrier Impassable to Fish Except Tributaries Listed Below

**BROWN, RAINBOW, AND LAKE TROUT, AS WELL AS LANDLOCKED SALMON:** Fishing is permitted April 1 through December 31. The minimum creel length is 15 inches, except 18 inches for salmon.

## Fall Creek (Cayuga Lake Tributary), from the Downstream Edge of the Railroad Bridge Under Route 13 Upstream to Ithaca Falls

**BROWN, RAINBOW, AND LAKE TROUT, AS WELL AS LANDLOCKED SALMON:** From April 1 through December 31, fishing is permitted, with a daily limit of three trout or salmon in combination and minimum creel lengths of 15 inches for trout but 18 inches for salmon. Fishing is also allowed from January 1 through March 15, on a catch-and-release, artificial-lures-only basis. Angling is prohibited March 16 through March 31.

## Spafford Creek (Otisco Lake Tributary) Upstream to the First Barrier Impassable to Fish

**TROUT:** Fishing is allowed April 1 through October 15. There is no minimum creel length but the daily limit is five trout, of which no more than two may be longer than 12 inches.

# More Tributary Dos and Don'ts

In addition to creel limits and other basic regulations, DEC administrators have put in place some rules of the water that are designed to manage fishermen more than fish. The following codes of behavior were initially adopted to curb the practice of snagging (also known as foul hooking or lifting) and promote sportsmanship and ethical means of fishing in the Finger Lakes tributaries.

- Trout aren't cattle, therefore it is prohibited to herd, drive, kick, or stone them from places of concealment.

- Fishing is prohibited from January 1 through March 31 in most tributaries below impassable barriers in order to protect trout that attempt to spawn before the season opens on April 1. Exceptions, most of them made to accommodate the few anglers interested in fishing for white suckers, are listed in the state *Fishing Regulations Guide.*

- Only one hook point is permitted in most of the tributaries, and that hook must not have a gap of more than ½ inch between shank and point. Possession of lures with tandem or treble hooks is not allowed, period, and diligent conservation officers will ticket persons who carry such devices in their creel, pocket, or fishing vest, even if said persons disclaim any intention of using them.

- Fishing after sunset or before sunrise is prohibited from April 1 through May 15 and October 1 through December 31 in the Finger Lakes tributaries.

# Public Boat Launches on the Finger Lakes

### Otisco Lake (Onondaga County)

**LOCATION:** Town of Spafford, west side of the lake. **DIRECTIONS:** Take Otisco Valley Road to Saw Mill Road, turn right onto West Valley Road, go 2 miles to causeway. **LAUNCH TYPE:** Hand carry. **PARKING:** 10 cars. Skaneateles Lake (Onondaga County)

**LOCATION:** Town of Skaneateles, Route 41A. **DIRECTIONS:** From US Route 20 in village of Skaneateles, turn onto West Lake Road and go south 2.5 miles. **LAUNCH TYPE:** Concrete ramp. **PARKING:** 35 cars and trailers.

### Owasco Lake (Cayuga County)

**LOCATION:** Emerson Park, Auburn. **DIRECTIONS:** From US Route 20 in Auburn, take Route 38A south to the park, at the north end of the lake. **LAUNCH TYPE:** Concrete ramp. **PARKING:** Approximately 20 boats and trailers.

### Cayuga Lake (Cayuga County)

**LOCATION:** Long Point State Park. **DIRECTIONS:** East shore of the lake, off Route 90, 1 mile southwest of village of Aurora. **LAUNCH TYPE:** Hard-surface ramp. **PARKING:** 35 cars and trailers.

**LOCATION:** Mudlock Canal Park. **DIRECTIONS:** From village of Cayuga, take Route 90 and go north 3 miles to River Road. **LAUNCH TYPE:** Concrete. **PARKING:** 16 cars and trailers.

### Cayuga Lake (Seneca County)

**LOCATION:** Dean's Cove State Marine Park. **DIRECTIONS:** On Route 89, 24 miles north of Ithaca. **LAUNCH TYPE:** Concrete ramp. **PARKING:** 48 cars and trailers.

**LOCATION:** Cayuga Lake State Park. **DIRECTIONS:** On Route 89, 3 miles east of village of Seneca Falls. **LAUNCH TYPE:** Concrete ramp. **PARKING:** 50 cars and trailers.

## Cayuga Lake (Tompkins County)

**LOCATION:** Taughannock Falls State Park. **DIRECTIONS:** Eight miles north of Ithaca on Route 89. **LAUNCH TYPE:** Concrete ramp. **PARKING:** 16 cars and trailers.

**LOCATION:** Allen H. Treman Marine Park. **DIRECTIONS:** One mile north of Ithaca on Route 89. **LAUNCH TYPE:** Concrete ramp. **PARKING:** 141 cars and trailers.

## Seneca Lake (Seneca County)

**LOCATION:** Seneca Lake State Park. **DIRECTIONS:** Routes 5 and 20 and Route 96 in city of Geneva. **LAUNCH TYPE:** Hard-surface ramp. **PARKING:** 30 cars and trailers.

**LOCATION:** Lodi Point State Park. **DIRECTIONS:** Off Route 136, 5 miles west of village of Lodi. **LAUNCH TYPE:** Hard-surface ramp. **PARKING:** 68 cars and trailers.

**LOCATION:** Sampson State Park. **DIRECTIONS:** On Route 96A in Romulus, 12 miles south of Routes 5 and 20 in Geneva. **LAUNCH TYPE:** Concrete ramp. **PARKING:** 64 cars and trailers.

## Seneca Lake (Schuyler County)

**LOCATION:** Smith Memorial Park. **DIRECTIONS:** Off Route 414 on Peach Orchard Point Road in Hector. **LAUNCH TYPE:** Concrete ramp. **PARKING:** Five boats and trailers.★

**LOCATION:** Watkins Glen. **DIRECTIONS:** On Route 414, adjacent to mouth of Catharine Creek, 1 mile east of Route 14. **LAUNCH TYPE:** Concrete ramp. **PARKING:** 60 cars and trailers.

## Seneca Lake (Yates County)

**LOCATION:** Severne Point. **DIRECTIONS:** On Severne Point Road, west shore of the lake, on Route 14, 8 miles south of Dresden. **LAUNCH TYPE:** Concrete ramp. **PARKING:** 30 cars and trailers.

## Keuka Lake (Yates County)

**LOCATION:** Keuka Lake State Park. **DIRECTIONS:** Off Route 54A, 6 miles southwest of village of Penn Yan. **LAUNCH TYPE:** Concrete ramp. **PARKING:** 50 cars and trailers.

**LOCATION:** Village of Penn Yan. **DIRECTIONS:** Off Route 14A. **LAUNCH TYPE:** Concrete ramps. **PARKING:** Six cars.

## Canandaigua Lake (Ontario County)
**LOCATION:** Canandaigua Lake State Marine Park. **DIRECTIONS:** In city of Canandaigua, off Routes 5 and 20. **LAUNCH TYPE:** Hard-surface ramp. **PARKING:** 110 cars and trailers.

**LOCATION:** Naples. **DIRECTIONS:** On Route 21, 3 miles north of Naples. **LAUNCH TYPE:** Concrete ramp. **PARKING:** 86 cars and trailers.

**LOCATION:** West Lake Road. **DIRECTIONS:** 6.5 miles south of Canandaigua on West Lake Road. **LAUNCH TYPE:** Concrete ramp. **PARKING:** 25 cars and trailers.★★

## Canandaigua Lake (Yates County)
**LOCATION:** Hi Tor Wildlife Management Area. **DIRECTIONS:** DEC West River fishing access site, on Route 245 about midway between Naples and Middlesex. **LAUNCH TYPE:** Hand launch. **PARKING:** Six cars.★★★

## Honeoye Lake (Ontario County)
**LOCATION:** Honeoye Boat Launch. **DIRECTIONS:** Route 264, 4 miles south of hamlet of Honeoye. **LAUNCH.TYPE:** Hard-surface ramp. **PARKING:** 30 cars and trailers.

**LOCATION:** Sandy Bottom Boat Launch. **DIRECTIONS:** On Route 36, 0.4 mile south of Route 20A in Honeoye.

## Canadice Lake (Ontario County)
**LOCATION:** Canadice Lake Road. **DIRECTIONS:** Seven-tenths of a mile south of intersection with Burch Hill Road. **LAUNCH TYPE:** Hard-surface ramp. **PARKING:** Parallel parking for cars and trailers on shoulder of the road.★★★★

## Hemlock Lake (Ontario County)
**LOCATION:** Southeast shore launch. **DIRECTIONS:** Take Route 20A west from hamlet of Honeoye to intersection at Route 15A. Follow gravel access road to southeast corner of the lake. **LAUNCH TYPE:** Hard-surface ramp. **PARKING:** Parallel on road shoulder.

## Hemlock Lake (Livingston County)
**LOCATION:** Northeast shore launch. **DIRECTIONS:** Take Route 20A west from Honeoye to Route 15A intersection. Take gravel access road and follow shore to gate and turnaround parking area. **LAUNCH TYPE:** Hard-surface ramp. **PARKING:** 12 cars.

## Conesus Lake (Livingston County)

**LOCATION:** Conesus Inlet. **DIRECTIONS:** At south end of Conesus, off Route 256. **LAUNCH TYPE:** Hand launch. **PARKING:** 40 cars.

**LOCATION:** Livonia. **DIRECTIONS:** From Route 390, take Exit 8. Go 3 miles east on Route 20A, then 4 miles south on East Lake Road. **LAUNCH TYPE:** Concrete ramp. **PARKING:** 45 cars and trailers plus 25 more cars.

**LOCATION:** Pebble Beach. **DIRECTIONS:** On Pebble Beach Road, go ¼ mile south of Route 20A in Lakeville. **LAUNCH TYPE:** Hand launch. **PARKING:** 120 cars.

---

*Peachtree Point is accessible by a very steep road, recommended for small boats only.

**West Lake Road launch is for winter months only, to offset closures of state park ramps.

***The short channel here, fit for canoes and johnboats with electric motors, dead-ends at the West River, which can be used to get to the lower east shore of Canandaigua Lake.

****On Canadice and Hemlock Lakes, motor-powered boats must be less than 17 feet long and motors must be 10-horsepower or less. Non-mechanical boats no longer than 24 feet are permitted.

# Finger Lakes Fishing Guides

### Otisco Lake
• Upstate Guide Service: Mike Crawford, (315) 283-8871,
  http://www.upstateguideservice.com

### Skaneateles Lake
• Finger Lakes Angling Zone: John Gaulke, (607) 319-0450,
  http://www.fingerlakesanglingzone.com
• Upstate Guide Service: Mike Crawford, (315) 283-8871,
  http://www.upstateguideservice.com

### Owasco Lake
• Finger Lakes Angling Zone: John Gaulke, (607) 319-0450,
  http://www.fingerlakesanglingzone.com
• Reel Hooked Up Charters: Sean Brown, (607) 742-6287,
  http://www.reelhookedup.com
• Upstate Guide Service: Mike Crawford, (315) 283-8871,
  http://www.upstateguideservice.com

### Cayuga Lake
• Billy V. Sportfishing: Bill Ruth, (607) 592-9012,
  http://www.billyvsportfishing.com
• Black Dog Adventures: Corey Redditt, (607) 592-0556,
  http://www.blackdogadventuresfishing.com
• Blue Moon Sportfishing: Scott Fletcher, (315) 283-8878,
  http://bluemoon.lakeontariounited.com
• Eagle Rock Charters: Glenn Quick, (315) 899-5925,
  http://www.eaglerockcharters.com
• Finger Lakes Angling Zone: John Gaulke, (607) 319-0450,
  http://www.fingerlakesanglingzone.com

- First Class Bass Charters: Terry Jones, (716) 875-4946, http://www.1stclass-bass.com
- NY Bassinaction: Kirk McMullen, (412) 760-1694, http://www.nybassinaction.com
- Reel Hooked Up Charters: Sean Brown, (607) 742-6287, http://www.reelhookedup.com
- Seneca Chief Charters: Jim Morgan, (607) 582-6089, http://senecachiefguide.com
- Short Hook Charters: James Stewart, (607) 426-1915, http://shorthookcharter.com

## Seneca Lake

- Black Dog Adventures: Corey Redditt, (607) 592-0556, http://www.blackdogadventuresfishing.com
- Captain Don's Charters: Don DeSio, (315) 585-6704, http://www.captaindonsfishingcharters.com
- Captain Joe's: Joe Rao, (315) 440-4191, http://www.fishsenecalake.com
- C-Dog Charters: Chad Carlini, (585) 704-6903
- Finger Lakes Angling Zone: John Gaulke, (607) 319-0450, http://www.fingerlakesanglingzone.com
- Fishing the Finger Lakes: Jonathan Evans, (607) 857-6269, http://www.fishingthefingerlakes.com
- Reel Hooked Up Charters: Sean Brown, (607) 742-6287, http://www.reelhookedup.com
- Seneca Chief Charters: Jim Morgan, (607) 582-6089, http://senecachiefguide.com
- Short Hook Charters: James Stewart, (607) 426-1915, http://shorthookcharter.com
- Tennity's Guide Service: Frank and Melody Tennity, (585) 229-4843, http://www.mudlines.com

## Keuka Lake

- Bobber's Fishing Excursions: Thomas Beers, (607) 569-2791, http://www.bobbersfishnex.com/
- Finger Lakes Angling Zone: John Gaulke, (607) 319-0450, http://www.fingerlakesanglingzone.com
- Fishing the Finger Lakes: Jonathan Evans, (607) 857-6269, http://www.fishingthefingerlakes.com

- Reel Hooked Up Charters: Sean Brown, (607) 742-6287, http://www.reelhookedup.com
- Short Hook Charters: James Stewart, (607) 426-1915, http://shorthookcharter.com
- Tennity's Guide Service: Frank and Melody Tennity, (585) 229-4843, http://www.mudlines.com

## Canandaigua Lake

- Fishing the Finger Lakes: Jonathan Evans, (607) 857-6269, http://www.fishingthefingerlakes.com
- Happy Hooker Charters: Bill Reeser, (607) 522-5564, http://canandaigualakecharters.com
- Hookjaw Charters: Nick DeMuth, (607) 857-8314, http://www.hookjawcharters.com
- NY Bassinaction: Kirk McMullen, (412) 760-1694, http://www.nybassinaction.com
- Reel Hooked Up Charters: Sean Brown, (607) 742-6287, http://www.reelhookedup.com
- Short Hook Charters: James Stewart, (607) 426-1915, http://shorthookcharter.com
- Tennity's Guide Service: Frank and Melody Tennity, (585) 229-4843, http://www.mudlines.com

## Honeoye Lake

- NY Bassinaction: Kirk McMullen, (412) 760-1694, http://www.nybassinaction.com
- Tennity's Guide Service: Frank and Melody Tennity, (585) 229-4843, http://www.mudlines.com

## Canadice Lake

- Tennity's Guide Service: Frank and Melody Tennity, (585) 229-4843, http://www.mudlines.com

## Hemlock Lake

- Tennity's Guide Service: Frank and Melody Tennity, (585) 229-4843, http://www.mudlines.com

## Conesus Lake

- Crazy Yankee Sportfishing Richard Hajecki, (585) 704-7996, http://www.crazyyankeesportfishing.com/

- First Class Bass Charters: Terry Jones, (716) 875–4946, http://www.1stclass-bass.com
- NY Bassinaction: Kirk McMullen, (412) 760–1694, http://www.nybassinaction.com
- Tennity's Guide Service: Frank and Melody Tennity, (585) 229–4843, http://www.mudlines.com

# INDEX

References in **boldface** indicate photographs